Social Constructionism

'In recent years the trickle of social constructionist writing and research has become a flood. The once eccentric idea of paying attention to the social and linguistic processes by which psychological phenomena were brought into being is close to becoming a new orthodoxy in many places. The "maverick gurus" have become "grand old persons".

'Vivien Burr has followed up her earlier book introducing social constructionism with a masterly summing up of the state of the art, bringing together the main threads into a coherent tapestry. The book emphasises the rich field of applications of the approach, from its beginnings in the critical reworking of social psychology to its current influence in psychopathology and psychiatry. There are loose ends and unfinished developments which find their place too, with a rousing critical chapter to complete the picture. This book will be of value not only to encourage further development but also as the basis for the kind of introductory courses which the field increasingly needs.'

Rom Harré, Georgetown University, Washington, and Linacre College, Oxford

Social Constructionism (second edition) will be a useful and informative resource for undergraduate and postgraduate students of psychology, as well as students from related areas such as health, social work and education.

Vivien Burr is Principal Lecturer in Psychology at the University of Hudders

Social Constructionism

Second Edition

Vivien Burr

Routledge
Taylor & Francis Group

LONDON AND NEW YORK

First edition published 1995
by Routledge
First edition reprinted 1996, 1997, 1998 (twice), 1999, 2000 and 2001
by Routledge

Second edition published 2003
by Routledge
27 Church Road, Hove, East Sussex BN3 2FA

Simultaneously published in the USA and Canada
by Routledge
270 Madison Avenue, New York NY 10016

Reprinted 2004, 2005, 2007 and 2008

Routledge is an imprint of the Taylor & Francis Group, an Informa business

Typeset in Times by Mayhew Typesetting, Rhayader, Powys
Printed and bound in Great Britain by TJ International Ltd,
Padstow, Cornwall
Paperback cover design by Richard Massing
Paperback cover illustration by John Foxx/Alamy

This publication has been produced with paper manufactured to strict
environmental standards and with pulp derived from sustainable forests.

British Library Cataloguing in Publication Data
A catalogue record for this book is available from the British Library

Library of Congress Cataloging-in-Publication Data
Burr, Vivien.
    Social constructionism / Vivien Burr.— 2nd ed.
        p. cm.
Originally published as: An introduction to social constructionism.
London ; New York : Routledge, 1995.
Includes bibliographical references and index.
    ISBN 0-415-31761-4 (alk. paper) — ISBN 0-415-31760-6 (pbk. : alk.
paper)
    1. Social psychology. 2. Cultural relativism. 3. Subjectivity. 4.
Discourse analysis. 5. Social interaction. 6. Social problems. I.
Title.
    HM251.B83 2003
    302—dc21

                                                        2003004358

ISBN 978-0-415-31760-3 (pbk)

To Amelia, my partner in crime

Contents

Preface

Since the publication of *An Introduction to Social Constructionism* in 1995 I have been delighted by and grateful for the many messages of appreciation I have received from readers. In preparing this book I have tried to remain faithful to the intentions of the original while aiming to reflect the growing complexity and richness of social constructionism. As in the earlier publication, I have generally adopted the position of the advocate, so that my overall strategy has been to persuade the reader of the advantages of a social constructionist approach. However, this is not an uncritical advocacy and I have also discussed the weaknesses and inadequacies of social constructionism and indicated the areas where I believe it needs to be developed. I hope that, whether social constructionist territory is already familiar to you or you are a new and curious explorer, you will enjoy this book.

Acknowledgements

In addition to the usual suspects (especially Geoff Adams, Trevor and Darren) I would like to thank the staff at Psychology Press, whose cheerful and prompt assistance made a difference.

Chapter 1

What is social constructionism?

Over the last twenty years or so, students of the social sciences in Britain and North America have witnessed the gradual emergence of a number of alternative approaches to the study of human beings as social animals. These approaches have appeared under a variety of rubrics, such as 'critical psychology', 'discursive psychology', 'discourse analysis', 'deconstruction' and 'poststructuralism'. What many of these approaches have in common, however, is what is now often referred to as 'social constructionism'. Social constructionism can be thought of as a theoretical orientation which to a greater or lesser degree underpins all of these newer approaches, which are currently offering radical and critical alternatives in psychology and social psychology, as well as in other disciplines in the social sciences and humanities. Social constructionism, as it has been taken up by psychology and social psychology, is the focus of this book, and my aim is to introduce the reader to some of its major features, while also elaborating upon the implications it holds for how we are to understand human beings, and for the discipline of psychology itself.

In this introductory chapter, my first task will be to say what kinds of writing and research I include within the term 'social constructionism' and why. This will not necessarily be where others would draw the boundary, but it will serve as an initial orientation for the reader, giving some indication of what it means to take a social constructionist approach. I will say something about the contributors to the field, and why I have included them as social constructionists. It is quite possible that I will be guilty of labelling as 'social constructionist' writers who would not wish to be labelled as such, and vice versa. I apologise in advance to those who feel uncomfortable with my description of them, but must adopt the rationale which appears to me to make sense of the area. I will then go on to outline something of the history of the social constructionist movement, especially as it has been taken up by social psychology. As we shall see, social constructionism as an approach to the social sciences draws its influences from a number of disciplines, including philosophy, sociology and linguistics, making it multidisciplinary in nature. Finally, I shall raise the major issues that will be addressed by this book, indicating the chapters where they will be dealt with.

Is there a definition of social constructionism?

First of all, I would like to point out that social constructionism is a term that is used almost exclusively by psychologists. As Craib (1997) points out, many of its basic assumptions are actually fundamental to one of its disciplinary cousins, sociology, and it is a measure of the unhelpful separation of the disciplines of sociology and psychology since the early 20th century that psychologists are only just 'discovering' social constructionist ideas. There is no single description, which would be adequate for all the different kinds of writers whom I shall refer to as social constructionist. This is because, although different writers may share some characteristics with others, there isn't really anything that they all have in common. What links them all together is a kind of 'family resemblance'. Members of the same family differ in the family characteristics that they share. There is no one characteristic borne by all members of a family, but there are enough recurrent features shared amongst different family members to identify the people as basically belonging to the same family group. This is the model I shall adopt for social constructionism. There is no one feature, which could be said to identify a social constructionist position. Instead, we might loosely think of as social constructionist any approach which has at its foundation one or more of the following key assumptions (from Gergen, 1985). You might think of these as something like 'things you would absolutely have to believe in order to be a social constructionist'.

A critical stance toward taken-for-granted knowledge

Social constructionism insists that we take a critical stance toward our taken-for-granted ways of understanding the world, including

ourselves. It invites us to be critical of the idea that our observations of the world unproblematically yield its nature to us, to
challenge the view that conventional knowledge is based upon
objective, unbiased observation of the world. It is therefore in
opposition to what is referred to as positivism and empiricism in
traditional science – the assumptions that the nature of the world
can be revealed by observation, and that what exists is what we
perceive to exist. Social constructionism cautions us to be ever
suspicious of our assumptions about how the world appears to be.
This means that the categories with which we as human beings
apprehend the world do not necessarily refer to real divisions. For
example, just because we think of some music as 'classical' and
some as 'pop' does not mean we should assume that there is
anything in the nature of the music itself that means it has to be
divided up in that particular way. A more radical example is that of
gender and sex. Our observations of the world suggest to us that
there are two categories of human being, men and women. Social
constructionism bids us to seriously question whether the categories 'man' and 'woman' are simply a reflection of naturally
occurring distinct types of human being. This may seem a bizarre
idea at first, and of course differences in reproductive organs are
present in many species. But we become aware of the greyness of
such categories when we look at practices such as gender re-
assignment surgery and the surrounding debate about how to
classify people as unambiguously male or female. We can thus
begin to consider that these seemingly natural categories may be
inevitably bound up with gender, the normative prescriptions of
masculinity and femininity in a culture, so that that whole categories of personhood, that is all the things it means to be a man or a
woman, have been built upon them. Social constructionism would
suggest that we might equally well, and just as absurdly, have
divided people up into tall and short, or those with ear lobes and
those without. Social constructionism's critical stance is particularly adopted toward mainstream psychology and social psychology, generating radically different accounts of many psychological
and social phenomena.

Historical and cultural specificity

The ways in which we commonly understand the world, the
categories and concepts we use, are historically and culturally

specific. Whether one understands the world in terms of men and women, pop music and classical music, urban life and rural life, past and future etc. depends upon where and when in the world one lives. For example, the notion of childhood has undergone tremendous change over the centuries. What it has been thought 'natural' for children to do has changed, as well as what parents were expected to do for their children (e.g. Aries, 1962). It is only in relatively recent historical times that children have ceased to be simply small adults in all but their legal rights. And we only have to look as far back as the writings of Dickens to remind ourselves that the idea of children as innocents in need of adult protection is a very recent one indeed. We can see changes even within the timespan of the last fifty years or so, with radical consequences for how parents are advised to bring up their children.

This means that all ways of understanding are historically and culturally relative. Not only are they specific to particular cultures and periods of history, they are seen as products of that culture and history, and are dependent upon the particular social and economic arrangements prevailing in that culture at that time. The particular forms of knowledge that abound in any culture are therefore artefacts of it, and we should not assume that *our* ways of understanding are necessarily any better, in terms of being any nearer the truth, than other ways.

Knowledge is sustained by social processes

If our knowledge of the world, our common ways of understanding it, is not derived from the nature of the world as it really is, where does it come from? The social constructionist answer is that people construct it between them. It is through the daily interactions between people in the course of social life that our versions of knowledge become fabricated. Therefore social interaction of all kinds, and particularly language, is of great interest to social constructionists. The goings-on between people in the course of their everyday lives are seen as the practices during which our shared versions of knowledge are constructed. For example what we understand as dyslexia is a phenomenon that has come into being through the exchanges between those who have difficulties with reading and writing and others who may teach them or offer them diagnostic tests. Therefore what we regard as truth, which of course varies historically and cross-culturally, may be thought of as our current accepted ways of understanding the world. These are a product not of objective observation of the world, but of the social processes and interactions in which people are constantly engaged with each other.

Knowledge and social action go together

These negotiated understandings could take a wide variety of different forms, and we can therefore talk of numerous possible social constructions of the world. But each different construction also brings with it, or invites, a different kind of action from human beings. For example, before the Temperance movement, drunks were seen as entirely responsible for their behaviour, and therefore blameworthy. A typical response was therefore imprisonment. However, there has been a move away from seeing drunkenness as a crime towards thinking of it as a sickness, a kind of addiction. The alcoholic is not seen as totally responsible for their behaviour, since they are the victims of a kind of drug addiction. The social action appropriate to understanding drunkenness in this way is to offer medical and psychological treatment, not imprisonment. Descriptions or constructions of the world therefore sustain some patterns of social action and exclude others. Our constructions of the world are therefore bound up with power relations because they have implications for what it is permissible for different people to do, and for how they may treat others.

How is social constructionism different from traditional psychology?

If we look closely at the four broad social constructionist tenets outlined above, we can see that they contain a number of features which are in quite stark contrast to most traditional psychology and social psychology, and are therefore worth spelling out.

Anti-essentialism

Since the social world, including ourselves as people, is the product of social processes, it follows that there cannot be any given, determined nature to the world or people. There are no essences inside things or people that make them what they are. Although some kinds of traditional psychology, such as behaviourism, would agree with this, others such as trait theory and psychoanalysis are based on the idea of some pre-given 'content' to the person. It is important to stress the radical nature of the proposal being put forward here. People sometimes misunderstand the social constructionist argument for cultural and historical specificity, and see it as just another way of taking the nurture side in the 'nature/ nurture' debate. But social constructionism is not just saying that one's cultural surroundings have an impact upon one's psychology, or even that our nature is a product of environmental, including social, rather than biological factors. Both of these views are essentialist, in that they see the person as having some definable and discoverable nature, whether given by biology or by the environment, and as such cannot be called social constructionist. Social constructionism opposes the essentialism of much traditional psychology. Often this is because essentialism traps people inside personalities and identities that are limiting for them and are sometimes pathologised by psychology, which then becomes an even more oppressive practice. For example, if someone is described as a manic-depressive and this is seen as an abiding feature of their personality, they not only face a future in which change appears unlikely but may also become subject to invasive psychiatric procedures.

Questioning realism

Social constructionism denies that our knowledge is a direct perception of reality. In fact it might be said that as a culture or society we construct our own versions of reality between us. Since we have to accept the historical and cultural relativism of all forms of knowledge, it follows that the notion of 'truth' becomes problematic. Within social constructionism there can be no such thing as an objective fact. All knowledge is derived from looking at the world from some perspective or other, and is in the service of some interests rather than others. For example, I may say that my dining-room table is made of excellent wood. Someone else may say that is of contemporary design, and yet another may comment that it is too small to be practical. None of these statements is *the* truth about the table, and each description is driven by a different concern, such as quality, style and practicality. The search for truth, the truth about people, about human nature, about society, has been at the foundation of social science from the start. Social constructionism therefore heralds a radically different model of what it could mean to do social science. The social constructionist critique of the realist philosophy of much traditional psychology focuses upon psychology's denial that its own grasp on the word must itself be partial. It is partial both in the sense of being only one way of seeing the world among many potential ways and in the sense of reflecting vested interests. Although social constructionism is generally suspicious of realist claims, some social constructionists embrace a form of realism known as critical realism (see below).

Historical and cultural specificity of knowledge

If all forms of knowledge are historically and culturally specific, this must include the knowledge generated by the social sciences. The theories and explanations of psychology thus become time- and culture-bound and cannot be taken as once-and-for-all descriptions of human nature. Stearns (1995) notes that there are numerous emotional states recognised and clearly experienced by people in non-western cultures that just do not translate into western terms. For example, for the Japanese, *amae* refers to a 'feeling of sweet dependence on another person' (p. 42). The disciplines of psychology and social psychology can therefore no longer be aimed at discovering the true nature of people and social life. They must instead turn their attention to a historical study of the emergence of current forms of psychological and social life, and to the social practices by which they are created. Social constructionism criticises traditional psychology for adopting an implicit or explicit imperialism and colonialism in which western ways of seeing the world are automatically assumed to be the right ways, which it then attempts to impose on others.

Language as a pre-condition for thought

Our ways of understanding the world do not come from objective reality but from other people, both past and present. We are born into a world where the conceptual frameworks and categories used by the people in our culture already exist. We do not each conveniently happen to find existing categories of thought appropriate for the expression of our experiences. For example, if I say that I prefer to wear clothes that are fashionable rather than out-dated, it is the concept of fashion that provides the basis for my experienced preference. Concepts and categories are acquired by each person as they develop the use of language and are thus reproduced every day by everyone who shares a culture and a language. This means that the way a person thinks, the very categories and concepts that provide a framework of meaning for them, are provided by the language that they use. Language therefore is a necessary precondition for thought as we know it. The relationship between thought and language has been the focus of a long-standing debate in psychology, with a number of different conceptualisations of this relationship being offered. A significant difference for our purposes exists between the positions adopted by Piaget and by Whorf (1941). Piaget believed that the child must develop concepts to some degree before verbal tags could be given to them, but Whorf argued that a person's native language determines the way they think and perceive the world. Most of traditional psychology at least holds the tacit assumption that language is a more or less straightforward expression of thought, rather than a pre-condition of it.

Language as a form of social action

By placing centre-stage the everyday interactions between people and seeing these as actively producing the forms of knowledge we take for granted and their associated social phenomena, it follows that language too has to be more than simply a way of expressing ourselves. When people talk to each other, the world gets constructed. Our use of language can therefore be thought of as a form of action, and some social constructionists take this 'performative' role of language as their focus of interest. As pointed out above, traditional psychology has typically regarded language as the passive vehicle for our thoughts and emotions. Social constructionism challenges this, because language has practical consequences for people that should be acknowledged. For example, when a judge says, 'I sentence you to four years' imprisonment', or when a priest says, 'I pronounce you man and wife', certain practical consequences, restrictions and obligations ensue.

A focus on interaction and social practices

Traditional psychology looks for explanations of social phenomena inside the person, for example by hypothesising the existence of attitudes, motivations, cognitions and so on. These entities are held to be responsible for what individual people do and say, as well as for wider social phenomena such as prejudice and delinquency. Sociology has traditionally countered this with the view that it is social structures, such as the economy, or the major institutions such as marriage and the family, that give rise to the social phenomena that we see. Social constructionism regards as the proper focus of our enquiry the social practices engaged in by people, and their interactions with each other. For example, a child with a learning difficulty is pathologised by traditional psychology by locating the difficulty within the psychology of the child. The social constructionist would challenge this by looking at how the learning difficulty is a construction that emerges through the interactions between the child, its teachers and others. Similarly, a person with a physical disability can only be seen as such when we take into account the fact that this person must inhabit a world in which social practices, for example driving long distances to the workplace and playing sports at the weekend, and material facilities, for example the standard height of kitchen units, are geared to the capabilities of the majority. Social constructionism therefore relocates problems away from the pathologised, essentialist sphere of traditional psychology.

A focus on processes

While most traditional psychology and sociology has put forward explanations in terms of entities, such as personality traits, economic structures, models of memory and so on, the explanations offered by social constructionists are more often in terms of the dynamics of social interaction. The emphasis is thus more on processes than structures. The aim of social enquiry is removed from questions about the nature of people or society towards a consideration of how certain phenomena or forms of knowledge are achieved by people in interaction. Knowledge is therefore seen not as something that a person has or doesn't have, but as something that people do together.

Where did social constructionism come from?

Social constructionism as it is now infiltrating British and North American psychology and social psychology cannot be traced back to a single source. It has emerged from the combined influences of a number of North American, British and continental writers dating back more than thirty years. These in turn are rooted in philosophical developments that began two to three hundred years ago. I shall describe here what may be considered an outline of its history and major influences, bearing in mind that this history itself is only one of many possible constructions of the events!

The Enlightenment, modernism and postmodernism

The cultural and intellectual backcloth against which social constructionism has taken shape, and which to some extent gives it its particular flavour, is what is usually referred to as postmodernism (see Hollinger, 1994 for a discussion of postmodernism in the social sciences). Postmodernism as an intellectual movement has its centre of gravity not in the social sciences but in art and architecture, literature and cultural studies. It represents a questioning of and rejection of the fundamental assumptions of modernism, the intellectual movement which preceded it and exists alongside it, generating much argument and debate. In many ways it embodies the assumptions underlying intellectual and artistic life that have been around since the time of the Enlightenment, which dates from about the mid-eighteenth century.

The Enlightenment project was to search for truth, to understand the true nature of reality, through the application of reason and rationality. This is in sharp contrast to the mediaeval period, in which the church was the sole arbiter of truth, and in which it was not the responsibility of individual human beings to discover the truth about life or to make decisions about the nature of morality. Science, as the antidote to the dogma of the mediaeval period, was born in the Enlightenment period. The philosopher Emmanuel Kant was an advocate of 'Enlightenment', and saw the motto of this project as *sapere aude!* – have courage to use your own understanding. He argued that all matters should be subject to publicity and debate. The individual person, rather than God and the church, became the focus for issues of truth and morality. It was now up to individuals to make judgements, based on objective, scientific evidence, about what reality was like and therefore what were appropriate moral rules for humans to live by.

The Modern movement in the artistic world took up its own search for truth. This generated much debate and argument about, for example, the value of different ways of painting (was the Impressionist way better than the pre-Raphaelite way, or the Expressionist way?) This search for truth was often based upon the idea that there were rules or structures underlying the surface features of the world, and there was a belief in a 'right' way of doing things, which could be discovered. The classical architecture of the Romans and Greeks was based upon the use of particular mathematical proportions, like the 'golden section', which were thought to lie at the heart of beautiful forms and Modern architecture too embodied the assumption that a good design in some way expressed the underlying function of the building.

In sociology, the search for rules and structure was exemplified by Marx, who explained social phenomena in terms of the underlying economic structure, and psychologists such as Freud and Piaget each postulated the existence of underlying psychic structures to account for psychological phenomena. In each case the hidden structure or rule is seen as the deeper reality underlying the surface features of the world, so that the truth about the world could be revealed by analysing these underlying structures. Theories in the social sciences and humanities which postulate such structures are known as 'structuralist'. The later rejection of the notion of rules and structures underlying forms in the real world is thus known as 'poststructuralism', and the terms 'postmodernism' and 'postructuralism' are sometimes used interchangeably. The common feature to all of these theories is that they constitute what are often called 'metanarratives' or grand theories. They offered a way of understanding the entire social world in terms of one all-embracing principle; for example, for Marx it was class relations. And therefore recommendations for social change were based upon this principle, in this case revolution by the working class.

But the Enlightenment also had its critics in the counter-Enlightenment movement. The philosopher Nietzsche claimed that it had in fact turned science, reason and progress into its own dogmas. He took the more nihilistic view that history and human life are not progressing, that there is no grand purpose, grand narrative or meaning to be discerned from history. We see the beginnings of postmodernism here. Postmodernism is a rejection of both the idea that there can be an ultimate truth and of structuralism, the idea that the world as we see it is the result of hidden structures. In architecture, it is exemplified by the design of buildings, which appear to disregard the accepted wisdoms of good design. In art and literature it is seen in the denial that some artistic or literary forms are necessarily better than others, so that Pop art claimed a status for itself and the objects it represented equal to that of, say, the works of Leonardo da Vinci or Michelangelo. In literary criticism, it also led to the idea that there could be no 'true' reading of a poem or novel, that each person's interpretation was necessarily as good as the next, and the meanings that the original author might have intended were therefore irrelevant.

Postmodernism rejects the idea that the world can be understood in terms of grand theories or metanarratives, and emphasises instead the co-existence of a multiplicity and variety of situation-dependent ways of life. This is sometimes referred to as pluralism. It argues that we in the west are now living in a postmodern world, a world that can no longer be understood by appeal to one over-arching system of knowledge, for example a religion. Developments in technology, in media and mass communications means that we are now living in a condition where there are available to us many different kinds of knowledge. There are a variety of natural and social scientific disciplines, many religions, alternative medicines, a choice of lifestyles and so on, each of them operating as a relatively self-contained system of knowledge which we can dip in and out of as we please. Postmodernism thus rejects the notion that social change is a matter of discovering and changing the underlying structures of social life through the application of a grand theory or metanarrative. In fact, the very word 'discover' presupposes an existing, stable reality that can be revealed by observation and analysis, an idea quite opposed to social constructionism.

Sociological influences

Despite their differences, Kant, Nietzsche and Marx held in common the view that knowledge is at least in part a product of human thought rather than grounded in an external reality. A number of sociologists took up this theme in the early twentieth century in the form of the sociology of knowledge. This was concerned with how sociocultural forces construct knowledge and with the kind of knowledge they construct, and was initially focused on concepts such as ideology and false consciousness.

But a major and more recent contribution having its roots in the sociology of knowledge is Berger and Luckmann's (1966) book *The Social Construction of Reality*. This book draws on the sub-discipline of symbolic interactionism, which began with the work of Mead (1934) at the University of Chicago. Fundamental to symbolic interactionism is the view that as people we construct our own and each other's identities through our everyday encounters with each other in social interaction. In line with this way of thinking, the sociological sub-discipline of ethnomethodology, which grew up in North America in the 1950s and 1960s, tried to understand the processes by which ordinary people construct social life and make sense of it to themselves and each other.

Berger and Luckmann's anti-essentialist account of social life argues that human beings together create and then sustain all social phenomena through social practices. They see three fundamental processes as responsible for this: externalisation, objectivation and internalisation. Berger and Luckmann show how the world can be socially constructed by the social practices of people but at the same time experienced by them as if the nature of their world is pre-given and fixed (see Chapter 9 for more details of Berger and Luckmann's theory). We could say that social constructionism itself has now achieved the status of an object. In writing this book and ostensibly describing it I am contributing to its objectivation in the world. And in the future, students who read this and other books about social constructionism will tend to think of it as an area of knowledge that has been discovered rather than as an effect of social processes. In writing this book, then, I am contributing to what might be called 'the social construction of social construc-tionism'.

The turn to language and the 'crisis' in social psychology

In psychology, the emergence of social constructionism is usually dated from Gergen's (1973) paper 'Social psychology as history' in which he argues that all knowledge, including psychological knowledge, is historically and culturally specific, and that we therefore must extend our enquiries beyond the individual into social, political and economic realms for a proper understanding of the evolution of present-day psychology and social life. In addition, he argues that there is no point in looking for once-and-for-all descriptions of people or society, since the only abiding feature of social life is that it is continually changing. Social psychology thus becomes a form of historical undertaking, since all we can ever do is to try to understand and account for how the world appears to be at the present time. In this paper can be seen the beginnings of Gergen's later work on social psychology, history and narrative.

Gergen's paper was written at the time of what is often referred to as 'the crisis in social psychology' (e.g. see Armistead, 1974). Social psychology as a discipline can be said to have emerged from the attempts by psychologists to provide the US and British governments during the Second World War with knowledge that could be used for propaganda and the manipulation of people. It grew out of questions like 'How can we keep up the morale of troops?' and 'How can we encourage people to eat unpopular foods?' It also grew up at a time when its parent discipline of psychology was carving out a name for itself by adopting the positivist methods of the natural sciences. Social psychology as a discipline therefore emerged as an empiricist, laboratory-based science that had habitually served, and was paid for by, those in positions of power, both in government and in industry.

Social psychologists in the 1960s and early 1970s were becoming increasingly worried by the way that the discipline implicitly promoted the values of dominant groups. The 'voice' of ordinary people was seen as absent from its research practices, which, in their concentration on de-contextualised laboratory behaviour, ignored the real-world contexts which give human action its meaning. A number of books were published, each in their own way trying to redress the balance, by proposing alternatives to positivist science and focusing upon the accounts of ordinary people and by challenging the oppressive and ideological uses of psychology (e.g. Brown, 1973; Armistead, 1974).

While Gergen was writing in America, in the UK Harré and Secord (1972) were arguing for a new vision of the science of psychology, based upon the view that people are 'conscious social actors, capable of controlling their performances and commenting intelligently upon them' (preface). They therefore opposed the positivist, experimentalist tradition in social psychology and saw people as skilled social practitioners who are able to monitor and comment upon their own activity. The importance of language as something other than a way of describing things – as a social resource for constructing different accounts of the world and events – is implicit in these works as it is in that of Berger and Luckmann.

These concerns are clearly apparent today in the work of social psychologists in social constructionism. Its multidisciplinary background means that it has drawn its ideas from a number of sources, and where it has drawn on work in the humanities and literary criticism, its influences are often those of French intellectuals such as Michel Foucault and Jacques Derrida. Its cultural backdrop is postmodernism, but it has its own intellectual roots in earlier sociological writing and in the concerns of the crisis in social psychology. Social constructionism is therefore a movement which has arisen from and is influenced by a variety of disciplines and intellectual traditions.

What kinds of psychology can be called social constructionist?

One of the biggest difficulties in presenting an account of varieties of social constructionism is the wide range of terms that are used by writers and researchers to describe their theoretical and methodological positions. By and large, this reflects the fact that there are a great many commonalities and differences in the field, so that it would be a misrepresentation to suggest that there exist coherent and identifiable types of social constructionism. Nevertheless, for the purposes of this chapter some broad-brush characterisations are necessary. In the following account I have chosen terms which some may feel are misleading, but I have tried to explain, where appropriate, the reasons for my choice.

Critical psychology/critical social psychology

As Danziger (1997) points out, the most obvious feature of the relationship between social constructionism and mainstream psychology is that social constructionism functions as critique. This critique encompasses the questions that psychology chooses to ask about human beings and the methods it adopts to investigate these as well as the answers it has traditionally provided, and is therefore in part a continuation of the 'crisis' debates in social psychology. Some writers and researchers have focused upon this critical approach, and there is now a considerable literature that has come to be termed critical psychology (Fox and Prilleltensky, 1997; Sloan, 2000; Stainton Rogers et al., 1995) and critical social psychology (Gough and McFadden, 2001; Ibáñez and Iñiguez,

1997). Critical psychology looks at how the individual is located within society in relation to difference, inequality and power and has provided alternative readings of a range of psychological phenomena, such as mental illness, intelligence, personality theory, aggression and sexuality.

However, although some critical psychologists build their critique upon social constructionist principles, others have arrived at critical psychology through other theoretical routes and may draw more upon ideology, Marxism or various forms of feminism. So that although much critical psychology can be said to be social constructionist in spirit, some critical psychologists would not necessarily refer to themselves as social constructionists. Critical social psychologists may also adopt a political stance, but for some the political agenda is less explicit and they are critical in the sense of raising awareness of the assumptions underlying the theory and practice of social psychology. Since there is no reason to make a distinction between the terms here, I shall refer to all such work as critical psychology.

Discursive psychology

The focus on social interaction and language as a form of social action that are characteristic features of social constructionism have been placed centre-stage by a number of theorists and researchers. This work has more recently come to be termed 'discursive psychology' (Edwards and Potter, 1992; Harré and Stearns, 1995). Discursive psychology has been self-adopted as the preferred term to describe the work of a number of researchers whose work is now widely known, and I have therefore chosen to use this generic title here. Discursive psychology also shares the radically anti-essentialist view of the person of social constructionism, and in particular it denies that language is a representation of, or route to, internal mental states or cognitions such as attitudes, beliefs, emotions and memories (e.g. Harré and Gillett, 1994; Harré, 1995a). Discursive psychology does not necessarily try to deny the existence of such cognitions; discursive psychologists, rather than debating the existence or nature of things, 'bracket' this issue. Potter says:

> . . . I am certainly not trying to answer ontological questions about what sort of things exist. The focus is upon the way people construct descriptions as factual, and how others

undermine those constructions. This does not require an answer to the philosophical question of what factuality is.

(Potter, 1996a: 6)

The particular concern of discursive psychology is to study how people use language in their everyday interactions, their 'discourse' with each other, and how they are adept at putting their linguistic skills to use in building specific accounts of events, accounts which may have powerful implications for the interactants themselves. It is therefore primarily concerned with the performative functions of language as outlined above.

Discursive psychologists have applied this understanding of the constructive, performative use of language to a number of psychological phenomena, thereby challenging the mainstream understanding of these. Examples include memory (Edwards and Potter, 1995), emotion (Edwards, 1997), attribution (Edwards and Potter, 1993) and learning disability (Mehan, 1996/2001). The action orientation of discursive psychology therefore transforms traditional psychology's concern with the nature of phenomena such as memory and emotion into a concern with how these are *performed* by people. Thus memory, emotion and other psychological phenomena become things we do rather than things we have. Some psychologists taking a discursive approach have gone beyond analysing the accounting practices of interactants to an examination of how these may be intimately related to the power of ideologies in contemporary society, for example sexism (Edley and Wetherell, 1995) and nationalism (Billig, 1995).

Deconstructionism and Foucauldian discourse analysis

Discursive psychology, which emphasises the constructive work that people do in building accounts of events, can be contrasted with deconstructionism. This draws on the work of poststructuralist French philosophers such as Michel Foucault and Jacques Derrida, and the term 'deconstruction' was introduced by Derrida. Deconstructionism emphasises the constructive power of language as a system of signs rather than the constructive work of the individual person. It is concerned with how the human subject becomes constructed through the structures of language and through ideology. The central concept here is the 'text':

A text is any printed, visual, oral or auditory production that
is available for reading, viewing or hearing (for example, an
article, a film, a painting, a song). Readers create texts as they
interpret and interact with them. The meaning of a text is
always indeterminate, open-ended and interactional. Deconstruction is the critical analysis of texts.

(Denzin, 1995: 52)

In terms of the features of social constructionism outlined above,
its focus is upon the historical and cultural specificity of knowledge
and the relationship between such knowledge and the possibilities
for social action and power. The varieties of approaches that share
this broad concern really don't appear under a generic title in the
literature that you may encounter. Although deconstruction as a
method of analysis is often associated with the historical development of discursive psychology (see Potter, 1996a), its research
application today often appears under the rubric of 'Foucauldian
discourse analysis' and is often associated with a concern to
identify the ideological and power effects of discourse.

Foucault argued that the way people talk about and think about,
for example, sexuality and mental illness – in other words the way
these things are widely represented in society – brings with it
implications for the way we treat people. Our representations entail
particular kinds of power relations. For example, as a society we
think of people who hear voices as mentally ill and refer them to
psychiatrists and psychologists who then have power over many
aspects of their lives. Foucault referred to such representations as
'discourses', since he saw them as constituted by and operating
through language and other symbolic systems. Our ways of talking
about and representing the world through written texts, pictures
and images all constitute the discourses through which we experience the world. Deconstructionism is therefore an axiomatic
example of social constructionism, since it is the structures of our
socially shared language that are seen as producing phenomena at
both the social and personal levels. The way that discourses
construct our experience can be examined by 'deconstructing' these
texts, taking them apart and showing how they work to present us
with a particular vision of the world, and thus enabling us to
challenge it. Examples of the critical use of deconstruction include
Parker et al. (1995), Parker and the Bolton Discourse Network
(1999) and Wodak (1996).

Constructivisms

Readers may become confused by the fact that the term 'constructivism' is sometimes used to refer to theoretical approaches that seem to share fundamental assumptions with social constructionism. This is becoming less of a problem, as writers and researchers have clarified some of their similarities and differences. I shall use the term social constructionism, rather than constructivism, throughout this book.

Constructivism is sometimes used to refer to Piagetian theory and to a particular kind of perceptual theory, but in the current context readers may encounter it in the form of perspectives that, in one form or another, see the person as actively engaged in the creation of their own phenomenal world. The contrast being made by such approaches is usually with the view that things and events have an essential nature or meaning that then impacts upon the person in some predictable manner, and that perception is ideally a matter of internalising a truthful representation of the world. Much of traditional psychology fits this description, including behaviourism, psychoanalytic theory and evolutionary psychology. Constructivist psychologies, by contrast, argue that each person perceives the world differently and actively creates their own meanings from events. The 'real' world is therefore a different place for each of us. This is the stance of 'radical constructivism' (von Glasersfeld, 1981), which assumes a Kantian distinction between an individualised phenomenal world and an unknowable real world.

A similar position is espoused by Kelly (1955) in his personal construct psychology (PCP). Kelly argues that each of us develops a system of dimensions of meaning, which he calls 'constructs'. We perceive the world in terms of these constructs and our actions, although never predictable, can be understood in the light of our construal of the world. Everyone construes the world differently, so in this sense we each inhabit different worlds, although it is possible for us to gain some appreciation of others' constructions, and Kelly termed this 'sociality'. The power of Kelly's constructivist position is that we have the capacity to change our own constructions of the world and thereby to create new possibilities for our own action. Likewise, narrative psychology (Gergen and Gergen, 1984, 1986; Sarbin, 1986; Crossley, 2000) argues that we tell each other and ourselves stories that powerfully shape our possibilities.

The essential difference between such constructivisms and social constructionism are twofold: in the extent to which the individual is seen as an agent who is in control of this construction process, and in the extent to which our constructions are the product of social forces, either structural or interactional. However, given the obvious points of agreement between constructivism and social constructionism, some writers have tried to bring them together in a synthesis. (e.g. Botella, 1995; Burr and Butt, 2000).

Differences and debates in social constructionism

I present here a very brief outline of some of the major differences and debates in the field, and these will be further elaborated in later chapters.

Critique

As Danziger (1997) points out, one thing that seems to unite different forms of social constructionism is their role in forming a radical critique of mainstream psychology. But he cautions that in this sense social constructionism therefore paradoxically 'needs' the mainstream. There is therefore something of a tension in the field around the extent to which social constructionist theory and research is able to generate its own theoretical and research pro-grammes, as opposed to maintaining a kind of guerrilla warfare upon mainstream psychology from the margins of the discipline. For some (e.g. Parker, 1999; Parker et al., 1995) the primary aim is to use social constructionism to subvert the more damaging or oppressive aspects of mainstream psychology. Social constructionist theory and research has been taken up in a variety of ways by those wishing to challenge oppressive and discriminatory practices, for example in the areas of gender and sexuality, disability and race.

Research focus

As indicated above, there exist at present two broad, major forms of social constructionist theory and research, the first focusing upon the micro structures of language use in interaction and the second focusing upon the role of more macro linguistic and social structures in framing our social and psychological life. Danziger

(1997) characterises the difference in focus as 'light' and 'dark' social constructionism, emphasising the more 'hopeful' message implicit in the idea that people construct themselves and each other during interaction (rather than being outcomes of 'dark' social forces). These terms may be seen as preferable to, for example, 'strong' and 'weak' constructionism, which may imply that one form is more fragile. However, it has been argued that 'dark' and 'light' also carry negative connotations (Burman, 1999). At the risk of introducing further confusion into the literature, I am going to adopt the terms 'micro' and 'macro' social constructionism to refer to these two broad approaches. The most prominent representatives of micro and macro social constructionism may be said to be discursive psychology and Foucauldian discourse analysis respectively. Confusingly, both kinds of research may be referred to as 'discourse analysis'.

Micro social constructionism

This sees social construction taking place within everyday discourse between people in interaction. It includes those who refer to themselves as discourse psychologists. For micro social constructionism, multiple versions of the world are potentially available through this discursive, constructive work, and there is no sense in which one can be said to be more real or true than others; the text of this discourse is the only reality we have access to – we cannot make claims about a real world that exists beyond our descriptions of it. All truth claims are thus undermined, giving rise to a keen scepticism in line with the first of the definitive characteristics of social constructionism outlined above. If power is referred to, it is seen as an effect of discourse, an effect of being able to 'warrant voice' (Gergen, 1989) in interaction. Micro social constructionism includes, in the USA, the work of Kenneth Gergen and of John Shotter. Gergen focuses upon the constructive force of interaction, stressing the relational embeddedness of individual thought and action (Gergen, 1994, 1999). Shotter takes the conversation as his model, emphasising the dynamic, interpersonal processes of construction, which he calls 'joint action' (Shotter, 1993a, 1993b), a term borrowed from the symbolic interactionist Blumer. In the UK, those sharing this emphasis on discourse in interaction include Jonathan Potter, Derek Edwards, Malcolm Ashmore, Margaret Wetherell, Rom Harré and Michael Billig, although Billig's work goes somewhat beyond a concern with micro processes, as it incorporates the concept of ideology. Some of these writers currently work together at the University of Loughborough.

Macro social constructionism

Macro social constructionism acknowledges the constructive power of language but sees this as derived from, or at least related to, material or social structures, social relations and institutionalised practices. The concept of power is therefore at the heart of this form of social constructionism, which includes the deconstructionist approach outlined above. Macro social constructionism is particularly influenced by the work of Foucault (1972, 1976, 1979). It informs the critical realism of Parker (1992, 1999) and Willig (1997, 1999a) in the UK, and has been successfully adopted in the USA by Rose (1989, 1990) to show how notions such as 'science' and 'the individual' have been socially constructed. Macro social constructionism has also been attractive to some writers interested in feminist analyses of power, for example Hollway (1984, 1989), Kitzinger (1987, 1989), Burman (e.g. Burman, 1990) and Ussher (2000). Since their focus is on issues of power, macro social constructionists are especially interested in analysing various forms of social inequality, such as gender, race and ethnicity, disability and mental health, with a view to challenging these through research and practice.

Macro and micro versions of social constructionism should not be seen as mutually exclusive. There is no reason in principle why they should not be brought together in a synthesis of micro and macro approaches. Danziger feels that this is where most further reflection is needed in social constructionism, and some writers have attempted such syntheses (e.g. Burkitt, 1999; Burr and Butt, 2000; Davies and Harré, 1990). Wetherell (1998) also calls for a synthesis of the two 'versions' of discourse analysis, arguing that we need to take account of both the situated nature of accounts as well as the institutional practices and social structures within which they are constructed.

The realism/relativism debate

This is not so much a debate as a locking of horns between some social constructionists. Realism asserts that an external world exists independently of our representations of it. Representations include perceptions, thoughts, language and material images such as pictures. Realism claims that our representations are underpinned by this reality, although they are not necessarily simply accurate reflections of it, and that we can at least in principle gain knowledge about this reality. Relativism, by contrast, argues that, even if such a reality exists, it is inaccessible to us. The only things we have access to are our various representations of the world, and these therefore cannot be judged against 'reality' for their truthfulness or accuracy. Relativists therefore cannot prefer one account to another on the basis of its veridicality.

Although the tenets of social constructionism appear to lead automatically to a relativist position, some, usually critical, social constructionists have resisted this and have maintained some concept of a reality existing outside of discourse and texts (e.g. Cromby and Nightingale, 1999; Willig, 1999a). One reason for this has been the problematic nature of morality and political action that ensues from a relativist position. If all accounts of the world are equally valid, then we appear deprived of defensible grounds for our moral choices and political allegiances. Other reasons include the inadequacy of discursive accounts of the material body and embodied subjectivity (e.g. Harré, 1995b; Burr, 1999; Nightingale, 1999). Those taking up a relativist stance as well as those adopting a more critical realist viewpoint have both made defensible arguments regarding the moral and political implications of these positions, and these will be examined in more detail in Chapter 5.

Agency and determinism

More or less mapping on to the distinction between micro and macro versions of social constructionism is the issue of personal agency. The emphasis upon the constructive work of individuals in interaction that is the focus of the micro approach implicitly affords us personal agency. Accounts must be constructed to suit occasions and are crafted in such a way as to further the speaker's current agenda. Macro social constructionism tends toward the 'death of the subject' where the person can be conceptualised only as the outcome of discursive and societal structures. The implication of this latter view is that individual persons, either alone or collectively, have no capacity to bring about change. However, it is also true that neither form of constructionism allows the vision of personal agency seen in mainstream psychology, since both would deny that structures such as beliefs, values or attitudes exist as part of our intra-psychic make-up, forming the basis for our action.

Research methods

All the forms of social constructionism outlined above take the constructive force of language as a principal assumption, and it is therefore the analysis of language and other symbolic forms that is at the heart of social constructionist research methods. It would be a mistake to suggest that there are particular research methods that are intrinsically social constructionist; social constructionist research simply makes different assumptions about its aims and about the nature and status of the data collected. However, the insistence of social constructionism upon the importance of the social meaning of accounts and discourses often leads logically to the use of qualitative methods as the research tools of choice. In practice this has often been the analysis of interview transcripts and written texts of other kinds. But the specific requirements of a social constructionist approach to such work has led to the development of a range of methods of analysis referred to as discourse analysis. Confusingly, exactly what is meant by discourse analysis depends upon the particular theoretical and research orientation of the writer. I will elaborate on some of these differences in Chapter 8.

Plan of the book

In Chapter 2 I will use the examples of personality, health and illness, and sexuality to flesh out some of the main features of social constructionism and to make a case for social constructionism as an alternative way of understanding the world. Although social constructionism may initially seem counter-intuitive, by appealing to everyday experiences I will explain why we should find it persuasive.

Chapter 3 deals with the claim that it is language that provides the framework for the kinds of thought that are possible for us, and with the performative role of language. I will explore the view that our descriptions and accounts of events have consequences in the world and that language is therefore a site of struggle. I will look at the view of language within deconstruction before going on to take a closer look at discursive psychology's understanding of discourse.

In Chapter 4, I look at the Foucauldian concept of discourse and the relationship between discourse, knowledge and power. Discourses make it possible for us to see the world in a certain way, producing our 'knowledge' of the world, which has power implications because it brings with it particular possibilities for acting in the world. I will look at Foucault's notion of 'disciplinary power', in which we are thought to be effectively controlled through our own self-monitoring processes, and its implications for traditional psychology.

The problematic nature of 'truth' and 'reality' is explored in Chapter 5. The claim that 'nothing exists outside the text' often provokes the reaction that social constructionism is clearly fanciful. Such questions go right to the heart of current debates in social constructionism about the status of the real and the material world and in this chapter I outline the nature of the issues that have fuelled the realism–relativism debate and indicate the extent to which I think the disagreements are capable of resolution. The heat in the debate between realism and relativism has largely been generated by concern over morality and politics. I explore the strengths and weaknesses of both sides of the debate with respect to these, as well as looking briefly at the possibilities for theoretical progress lying in some accounts that have tried to re-write the terms of the debate.

In the following two chapters, I address the problem of the psychological subject. Social constructionism takes us so far from psychology's traditional understanding of what constitutes a person that we must begin to rebuild ourselves according to a different model, and the first step in doing this is to work out the implications that the various forms of social constructionism have for us as persons. I discuss the psychological subject as it appears in both micro and macro forms of social constructionism, including issues of identity, agency and change, and explore some of the conceptual tools that social constructionists have developed for the task of re-writing the psychological subject.

Chapter 8 looks at some of the research approaches developed and adopted in social constructionist research. After examining theoretical and methodological issues, such as objectivity, value-freedom and reflexivity, I go on to describe some of the methods that have been used. Using brief examples of real research studies, I look at the aims and something of the method of analysis of four approaches: conversation analysis, discursive psychology, interpretative repertoires and Foucauldian discourse analysis. Although throughout the book I will point out some of the limitations of and difficulties with different forms of social constructionism, it is in the final chapter that I take a more critical stance and explore in depth my own arguments with social constructionism. This focuses upon the nature of subjectivity, the psychology of the person and the need for a concept of self, as well as the need to transcend the various dualisms that have haunted both mainstream psychology and social constructionism.

A word about words

Perhaps more so than other areas of social science, social constructionism abounds with words and phrases that may be unfamiliar, and their meaning may be hard to grasp at first. In reading more advanced social constructionist material, students are often confused by the terms they meet and some of what is written is, I would argue, unnecessarily difficult and obscure. To make matters worse, the same terms are often used by different writers to mean different things, so that it is sometimes impossible to come up with a definitive account of what a term means. This is partly because, as work in this field has accumulated and progressed, lines of theory and research have splintered and the thinking of individual theorists and researchers has also changed over time. Gergen (1985) wrote about 'social constructionism', but Potter and Wetherell (1987) took up the spirit of these ideas as 'discourse analysis' and Billig (1987) as ideology and rhetoric. Edwards and Potter (1992) later wrote about what they referred to as 'discursive psychology' and Wetherell and Edley (e.g. 1999) about 'critical discursive psychology'.

In this book I have done my best to explain the meaning of terms that I think may be new to readers coming from traditional social science, particularly psychological, backgrounds. As mentioned above, I will use the terms macro and micro social constructionism to refer to the two broad approaches to theory and research that I have outlined, but will also use specific terms such as 'discursive psychology' and 'Foucauldian discourse analysis' where these are more appropriate in particular contexts. To aid readers in their struggle for understanding, I have provided a brief glossary of common terms at the back of the book.

Chapter 2

The case for social constructionism

Many students initially find it difficult to accept social constructionist arguments because they appear to run so counter to our everyday understanding of our experience, as well as to traditional psychological explanations. This chapter is therefore about convincing you that social constructionist ideas have something to offer. My aims are to challenge common-sense understandings of the person, to lay the way for an alternative, social constructionist, view and to draw attention to a number of central features of a social constructionist view of the person. Although this book will often be critical of some aspects of social constructionism, at this point it is important to see why it might be useful.

To an extent I am using the terms 'traditional psychology' and 'common sense' interchangeably here. This is not because I believe that psychology is just common sense presented in complicated jargon. Nevertheless, psychology has often based its theories upon the taken-for-granted assumptions of the societies and culture in which it arose and these, translated into popular psychology, have in turn infiltrated the everyday thinking of us all. It is these assumptions that I want to expose in this chapter. So I shall make a case in support of social constructionism by discussing the ways in which traditional psychology and these taken-for-granted assumptions may be seen as inadequate and by indicating how social constructionism may sometimes offer a better 'fit' with our experience and observations of the world.

This means that social constructionism does not just offer a new analysis of topics such as 'personality' or 'attitudes', which can simply be slotted into our existing framework of understanding. The framework itself has to change, and with it our understanding of every aspect of social and psychological life. Social constructionism is often counter-intuitive; it is precisely that which we take for granted which is rendered problematic by this approach. But at the same time it allows us to highlight and address some of the areas where common-sense assumptions and traditional psychology do not give us satisfactory explanations. What it is like to be a person – and to be a particular person – involves a wide range of factors such as our personality and emotions, our gender and sexuality, and whether we are healthy, ill or have a disability. So in making my case for social constructionism I have divided this chapter into three sections, each of which functions as a kind of case study. Each of these illustrates and makes a case for social constructionism and demonstrates its differences from traditional psychology in terms of the features that I outlined in Chapter 1.

Personality

The common-sense view of personality

We think of our personality as more or less unified and stable. Although we possess a number of traits, we feel that these are brought together in a coherent way to form a whole, and that our personality is fairly stable. Although we may change somewhat over time, say from a child to adulthood, or as a result of a major life event, we think of our personality as mostly unchanging. Much, though not all, of contemporary mainstream psychology, and the common-sense understanding that it has encouraged, takes for granted the idea that people have personality characteristics and that these are what make us feel and behave differently from each other. For example, we tend to think of our emotions as private events that are bound up with the kind of people we are. A person with a 'depressive' personality might be expected to often feel 'sadness'. We imagine a 'caring' person to have loving feelings. We think of anger as something we feel inside us, and which is manifested in the things we say and do. These feelings or emotions are thought of as the internal, private experience of the individual, and are intimately connected to the type of person they are. This way of thinking is referred to as 'essentialism'.

Essentialism is a way of understanding the world that sees things, including human beings, as having their own particular essence or nature, something which can be said to belong to them and which explains how they behave or what can be done with them. Tables and desks are hard (a property) and therefore don't bend when you put a pile of books on them. In the same way, we think of the nature of the shy person being such that it is unsuited to the conditions of a noisy social gathering. This essentialist view of personality bids us think of ourselves as having a particular nature both as individuals and as a species, a 'human nature', and this nature determines what people can and can't do. For example, if we believe that the nature of the human species is essentially aggressive and self-interested, the best we can do is to ensure that society provides ways of restraining people and physically preventing them from behaving naturally. Most people today settle for a model of personality which suggests that these biological 'givens' are to some extent modifiable by environmental influences, such as the kind of childhood experiences you have. But the fact that we find personality change so difficult when we attempt it (perhaps you are a timid person trying to become more confident, or a worrier who is trying to be less anxious) seems to give credence to the idea that, even if personality isn't entirely determined biologically, one way or another, once your personality is formed your programming has been fixed for the future.

The social constructionist case

First of all, how can you be sure that you have a personality at all? If I were to ask you for evidence that, say, you have brown eyes, or that you live in a second floor apartment, the matter would be settled very quickly. You could let me look at your eyes, and you could show me your apartment. But can you show me your personality? Where is it? Even if a surgeon were to open you up and look, they wouldn't find it. There is no objective evidence that you can appeal to which would demonstrate the existence of your personality. What this shows is that whatever this 'personality' creature is, its existence is inferred. This means that in order to account for the things you find yourself and other people doing, the ways you behave, you have come up with the idea that people have a thing called a personality that is responsible for this behaviour.

What this amounts to is a kind of circular reasoning. For example, if we witness someone physically attacking another person, unless we have good reason to think otherwise (perhaps that they were acting in self-defence, or that it was an accident) we are likely to infer that the attacker is an aggressive person. This is a description of their personality. However, if someone were to ask us why we think the attacker did it, we are likely to say something like 'If you're an aggressive person, that's the kind of thing you're likely to do'. This is circular reasoning. We have observed the behaviour (the attack) and inferred from it that the attacker has an aggressive personality. But when asked to say what made them do it, we account for the behaviour in terms of the 'aggressiveness' that this behaviour itself was used to infer. We call someone aggressive because of their behaviour and then say it was their aggressiveness that made them do it, but we have had no way of establishing the real existence of this 'aggressive personality' outside of the personality–behaviour circle that we have created.

One of the fundamental assumptions of the common-sense view of personality is that personality is stable across situations and over time. However this does not stand up to scrutiny when we examine our own day-to-day experience. Do you talk to your closest friend in the same way as your bank manager? Do you feel confident and outgoing with people you know and like? What about when you go for a job interview? These examples may look trivial, but the overall message is an important one. We behave, think and feel differently depending on who we are with, what we are doing and why. There already exist a number of psychological and social psychological theories which, while they fall short of being social constructionist in the sense used by this book, offer explanations of the person that reside in the social situation rather than within the person. For example, social learning theorists talk about the 'situation specificity' of behaviour. They suggest that our behaviour is dependent not upon personality characteristics but upon the nature of the situations in which we find ourselves. Behaviour is therefore 'specific' to a particular situation and, social learning theorists would say, is acquired through the particular set of reinforcers present in those situations. According to this view we should expect a person to be different in different situations, whereas for the traditional personality view these differences are problematic. Just as we take for granted the idea that our personality is stable, so do we also tend not to question the notion that each person has a unified, coherent personality, a self which is made up of elements that are consistent with each other. Psychologists themselves have found it necessary to come up with hypothetical structures and processes precisely because our experience of ourselves and of each other is just the opposite of coherent. We talk of being 'in conflict', we say that our thoughts lead us in one direction and our feelings in another, we say that our heart rules our head, or that we have acted out of character.

Secondly, we can question the idea that our personality is inside us. Think of some of the personality-type words that are used to describe people, for example: friendly, caring, shy, self-conscious, charming, bad-tempered, thoughtless. Most 'personality' words would completely lose their meaning if the person described were living alone on a desert island. Without the presence of other people, i.e. a social environment, can a person be said to be friendly, shy or caring? The point is that we use these words as if they referred to entities existing within the person they describe, but once the person is removed from their relations with others the words become meaningless. They refer to our behaviour toward other people. The friendliness, shyness or caring exists not inside people, but in the relation between them. Of course you could reply that, even on the desert island, a person can still carry with them the predisposition to be friendly, shy etc. We can neither prove nor disprove the existence of personality traits, and similarly we cannot demonstrate the truth of a social constructionist view simply by an appeal to the evidence. In the end our task may be to decide which view offers us the best way of understanding ourselves and others and thus of guiding our research and action.

Thirdly, if personalities really are essential features of all human beings then we should expect to find personality as we know it in all human beings, no matter what part of the world they inhabit. But it is clear that all peoples do not subscribe to our western view. In some cultures, people account for their actions by reference to invisible spirits and demons and would find our idea that behaviour originates in personality a very strange one. Many people today, as well as in the past, see their actions as the result of divine guidance and in some circumstances, people who claim that they are directed by invisible spirits are labelled 'insane'. Also, the personal uniqueness and private nature of things like emotions is not an assumption made by all cultures, as Lutz (1982, 1990) has pointed out. For the Ifaluk (Samoan and Pintupi Aborigine), emotion words are statements not about a person's internal states but about their relationship to events and other people. The Ifaluk talk of *song*, which in translation comes out as something like 'justifiable anger'. This justifiable anger is not a privately owned feeling, but a moral and public account of some transgression of accepted social practices and values.

Of course we could claim that these cultural differences are due to differences in education and understanding. We could suggest that non-western cultures and those of previous historical periods do not have the benefit of our knowledge. What we would be doing then is making a claim about the truthfulness of our own view as opposed to the falsity of theirs. We would be saying 'we know that in fact people have personalities, and that the way a person behaves is heavily influenced by their personality. People in other cultures haven't realised this yet, and they therefore hold a false view of reality.' This is to state the case rather strongly, but it makes the point that, unless we have complete confidence in the 'truth' of our own view, we have to accept that personality may be a theory which is peculiar to certain societies at a certain point in time.

Some writers, such as the psychoanalyst Fromm (though not a social constructionist), have suggested that 'human nature' is a product of the particular societal and economic structure that we are born into (e.g. Fromm, 1942, 1955). For example, in a capitalist society, competition is fundamental; society is structured around individuals and organisations that compete with each other for jobs, markets etc. The assumption is that the person with the most skill, intelligence, ability, charm etc. will succeed where others will fail. So that where competition is a fundamental feature of social and economic life, what you will get is 'competitive' people and a model of the person which is framed in terms of individual differences. In other words, we think of ourselves as individuals differing from each other along a number of personality dimensions because we live in a society founded on competition. Competitiveness and greed can then be understood as products of the culture and economic structure in which we live rather than as features of an essential human nature.

As well as cultural differences in how people think about and describe their experiences our language is constantly changing and we accept that the meanings of words mutate over time. But the way in which some meanings have changed, and often quite recently at that, is of interest. The verb 'to love' is a good example. To children learning the intricacies of grammar, verbs are described as 'doing' words – they are words that tell you what people are doing, like 'working' or 'crying'. But the way in which today we employ the verb 'to love' has different connotations. When we say we love someone, what we are often referring to are our feelings for them, not our actions. And yet this has not always been the case. When I was a child, my grandmother sometimes used to say, 'Come here and give me a love' or 'Let me love you for a minute'. To 'love' someone here means to physically embrace them, and perhaps to comfort them. Perhaps this meaning is still used occasionally, but in the vast majority of cases when we talk about loving someone, we are talking about private events, our feelings, things which are taken to exist inside us and which influence how we treat people. Love has therefore become something which is seen as motivating our behaviour rather than as a word which describes our behaviour. The social constructionist argument is that loving feelings don't give rise to a language which then describes them, but rather that the use of such language itself encourages us to identify and experience our feelings as loving. Ironically, when love is relegated to this internal domain it can become so unrelated to conduct that it can be used to excuse the most appalling behaviour ('I hit her when I get angry – but I love her really . . .').

This trend toward using words to describe internal events, like feelings, rather than actions can be called 'psychologisation'. In other words, we are tending more and more to describe human life in terms of psychological qualities such as feelings and personality traits rather than in terms of what we are doing with or to other people. 'Caring' is another good example. To care for someone, in today's language, means not only to look after them and tend to their needs, but also to have caring feelings toward them. To be a caring person today is taken to be a description of the kind of person you are rather than of the type of activities you are engaged in. This move towards accounting for ourselves in terms of internal essences is of course entirely consistent with the above idea that the way people think about themselves and represent their experience to themselves and others is dependent not upon some pre-existing essential human nature but upon the particular social and economic arrangements prevailing in their culture at that time.

Summary

The social constructionist view of personality is that it is a concept that we use in our everyday lives in order to try to make sense of the things that other people and we do. Personality can be seen as a theory for explaining human behaviour and for trying to anticipate our part in social interactions with others that is held very widely in our society. We could say that in our daily lives we act as if there were such a thing as personality, and most of the time we get by reasonably well by doing so. But it is a big leap from this to saying that personality really exists in the sense of traits inhabiting our mental structures, or being written into our genetic material. The social constructionist position, in addition to questioning the concept of personality itself, is that whatever personal qualities we may display are a function of the particular cultural, historical and relational circumstances in which we are located.

The points that I have dealt with here are important ones and will come up again many times in later chapters, especially in the context of what it means to be a person and to have a self. You don't have to be a social constructionist to abandon traditional personality theory; behaviourists and social learning theorists did this a long time ago. But it is a useful starting point from which to explore some of the key features of social constructionism.

Health and illness

The common-sense view of health and illness

Health and illness have become areas of major interest for people in recent times. In western societies, we have become concerned about changes in disease patterns, such as the increased incidence of heart disease and the spread of HIV and AIDS. Furthermore, although we see illness as something that may befall us if we are unlucky, we are taking on board the idea that our own lifestyle choices, like diet, exercise and working practices, can affect our chances of developing major illnesses. Although we may grumble occasionally about the ineffective treatment we may have received from our GP, or feel frustrated that the laboratory tests have not revealed the cause of our continuing symptoms, we often explain such things by assuming that medical knowledge is, as yet, incomplete. We may argue that we just don't know enough about the intricacies of the body's internal organs and about what causes them to malfunction, producing the disease that underlies our symptoms.

Despite its imperfections, the understanding of health and illness that underpins modern medicine is widely accepted, and is referred to as 'biomedicine'. It is the view that the origins and treatment of disease are to be understood through the application of concepts from physiology, anatomy and biochemistry (Radley, 1994). Biomedicine adopts the methods of the natural sciences, and the onset of disease and its subsequent treatment are conceptualised in terms of causal relationships. So, for example, bacteria may invade the tissues in the throat causing a pathological condition we call tonsillitis. The treatment is to remove the cause by the use of antibiotics, which kill the bacteria.

But today we also accept that psychological and social factors can influence our susceptibility to disease. For example, Friedman and Rosenman (1974) proposed that a person's susceptibility to heart disease is affected by whether they are a 'Type A' or 'Type B' personality. Type A people were characterised as ambitious and competitive and easily aroused to anger by the everyday frustrations of their lives. The physiological and biochemical processes that accompany these frequent bouts of anger are thought to be responsible for a complicated chain of events which culminates in fatty acids being deposited in blood vessels, thus increasing the risk of heart attack (Williams, 1989). The role of psychology and sociology in understanding health and illness is therefore often seen as one of identifying possible features of our social and psychological functioning that may adversely affect the proper workings of the body.

The social constructionist case

Whatever the causes of the diseases that make us ill, it seems to us that there can be little ambiguity about our bodily condition – either it is disease-free, normally functioning and we are healthy or there is a presence of some disease or malfunction and we are ill. But a few examples will serve to show that the position is not as clear as this. Dental caries (tooth decay) can be said to be a pathology of the teeth – but how many of us who need regular visits to dentist would regard ourselves as ill or suffering from a disease? A person may have a medical condition for many months or years and yet suffer no symptoms. Are we to say that the person was in fact ill for this time and didn't know it? Is a woman who is unable to conceive ill? Or someone whose eyesight deteriorates in later life? Or someone born with malformed limbs? What about the person who experiences bodily symptoms for which no underlying organic pathology can be found? The point of these examples is that, accepting for the moment that the presence of 'disease' can unambiguously be established, this by no means leads us to an easy judgement about whether or not the person is ill. This is because illness is not a physiological matter – it is a social one. When we say that we or someone else is ill, we are making a judgement that only in part relates to their physical condition. Much of our judgement rests on cultural prescriptions, norms and values surrounding our ability to perform our usual activities. Radley (1994) gives the example of very common ailments such as colds and 'flu. A person may suffer from a variety of symptoms such as headache, sore throat, aching limbs and raised temperature. But are they suffering from a bad cold or is it 'flu? The diagnosis is less of a physical issue and more of a moral one. In our culture, we see ourselves as to some degree responsible for catching a cold; we may have gone out without our coat and got very cold or wet. By comparison, we think of 'flu as something that we are simply unfortunate enough to catch. This moral dimension has implications for the extent to which we can claim sympathy and exempt ourselves from our usual responsibilities. In a study of working-class women in Scotland, Blaxter and Paterson (1982) (cited in Hardey, 1998) found that they described themselves as 'healthy' if they were able to go to work and perform their usual everyday activities. They saw common ailments and 'women's troubles' as just part of normal life, and reserved the term 'illness' for serious conditions. A person was not ill if they just got on with their lives and didn't dwell on their symptoms; 'Illness was not so much the experience of symptoms as the reaction to symptoms' (Hardey, 1998: 33).

The status of the body as ill or healthy therefore depends upon social rather than biological criteria. Illness cannot be seen as a fixed entity but as something that necessarily varies according to the norms and values of the particular social group that one is studying. But the physical status of the body as functional or malfunctional can also be shown to be context-dependent. For example, a person may have lost the use of their legs through a spinal injury and must use a wheelchair. Typically, they may have difficulty getting into some buildings, getting up stairs and using some public facilities. They may find that in their own home they need help to use the bathroom and are unable to use their kitchen. They are 'disabled'.

It seems obvious at first that their physical impairment and their disability are the same thing. But once we provide ramps to buildings, stair lifts and make appropriate adjustments to bathroom and kitchen appliances the disability effectively reduces. We could argue that if we were to tailor the entire built environment specifically to the abilities of the wheelchair user, there would be no sense in which it would be meaningful to refer to them as 'disabled'. In fact, would we even regard their physical condition as impaired? Perhaps the rest of us would be seen as disabled by our lack of wheels? Or impaired by the encumbrance of a pair of unnecessary limbs? 'Disability' is therefore a function of the environment in which people are constrained to live, not a quality that belongs to them as persons. Makin (1995) terms this 'the social model of disability' in contrast to the medical model, which implicitly places the source of the problem within the disabled person.

Furthermore, this environment is inevitably fashioned according to the values and practices of some people rather than others. If we look at our environment and ask for whom it may be problematic in some respect, we immediately see that it is often those groups of people who have had less power in society. Apparently trivial examples show this up. Being unable to read the small print on food packets or take the lid off a vacuum-packed jar is not only a problem for those with specific disabilities but for many people of advancing age. Heavy-duty work gloves (for handling DIY materials etc.) don't come in small sizes, presenting a difficulty for many women and for men of small stature. We can give ourselves all kinds of reasonable explanations for the status quo, but in the end it comes down to the values of dominant groups. If the world was run by children, what sort of physical environment would we live in, and what difficulties would that pose for adults? So health, illness and disability are not only socially created; they are sustained by social practices that often serve the interests of dominant groups in society.

The cultural and historical specificity of biomedicine is also clear. As with the example of personality, it seems that the biomedical model is one that is not universal and is a fairly recent development in the history of western societies' attempts to understand illness. Anthropologists report medical belief systems in other cultures that are radically different from biomedicine. Young's (1976) study of the Amhara people (Ethiopia) contrasts a biomedical understanding of disease, which focuses upon the internal workings of the body, with an understanding that locates the disease in a social context. The Amhara believe that disease can be caused by a number of external events, for example eating food that has been poisoned or by being attacked by the spirit of an enemy. The cures for diseases, which are often herbal remedies, are seen not in terms of their effect on internal organs and systems, but operate to restore balance to the individual within the moral order of society (Radley, 1994). In our own society we are seeing an increasing use of 'alternative medicines', which are often based upon belief systems quite different to biomedicine, such as homeopathy, acupuncture and reflexology. This should caution us against the view that our own predominant, biomedical view of disease is the right one and all others false. To the extent that such therapies are effective, to maintain such a view we would have to argue that this effectiveness is some kind of placebo effect and explain their effectiveness within the terms of biomedicine.

So, all medical belief systems operate within a culture with norms, values and expectations that make sense of illness for people in that culture and set the criteria for what, locally, can count as illness. The variation in ways of understanding illness that exists across cultures and across the range of alternative medicines in our own society can also be seen historically. Radley (1994) describes how, up until the end of the eighteenth century, doctors saw the patient's emotional and spiritual life as directly relevant to their state of health, and the illness they suffered was not conceptualised as independent of the sick person themselves. With developments in the study of anatomy it became possible to think of illnesses as things attacking the body as a system of interrelated organs, with the result that the experience of the person as a whole became irrelevant to diagnosis. But the rise of biomedicine is not something that can be seen as simply a story of the progress of medical knowledge. It is a way of viewing the body that, it can be argued, is intimately connected to broader social developments. The study of the inner workings of the body in the anatomy laboratory took place in the context of a more general movement towards understanding the world by ordering and classifying it. Foucault (1973, 1976, 1979) has persuasively argued that such ordering and classifying, with respect to human beings, has played and continues to play a key role in controlling the populace. By classifying people as normal or abnormal, mad or sane and healthy or sick, it became possible to control society by regulating work, domestic and political behaviours. For example, the certified mentally ill may not vote and may be forcibly confined, those who cannot obtain a sick note from their doctor may have no choice but to work and those whose sexuality is deemed unhealthy or abnormal may be denied access to family life.

Furthermore, pathological entities themselves can be seen to be problematic. The above example of the distinction between colds and 'flu is an example of this. Bury (1986) cites the work of Figlio (1982), who studied the relationship of the condition 'miners' nystagmus' to social class and capitalism. The existence of this as a disease entity was not simply a medical matter. It was at the centre of conflicts over malingering and compensation for workers. As Burr and Butt (2000) have noted, in recent times we have seen the emergence of a number of conditions that were unknown in earlier times, for example premenstrual syndrome and ME (myalgic encephalomyelitis), and the medical status of these is similarly problematic and infused with cultural assumptions and moral prescriptions. Prior to 1973 homosexuality was a disease and was classified in the *Diagnostic and Statistical Manual of Mental Disorders* (DSM-III). Following changes in social attitudes and campaigning by gay activists the American Psychiatric Association voted to remove it; diseases are not simply objectively defined medical entities but social ones.

Summary

Defining illness and disease is not simply a matter of identifying the presence of pathology. It is a deeply social matter involving the interpretation of our experience within our particular cultural context of assumptions, norms and values as well as the economic structure of our society. It is also a matter of power relations. The body's 'deficiencies' only show up as such when persons are constrained to live in environments designed to suit the needs and activities of others. The biomedical conceptualisation of health and illness is only one perspective among many, and its predominance in western societies cannot be understood as simply the result of progress in scientific knowledge. The rise of biomedicine can be seen to be at least in part related to changes in the exercise of social control taking place over the last two hundred years.

Sexuality

The common-sense view of sexuality

Like our personalities and our health status, sexuality is an aspect of being a person that at first glance appears to be anything but socially constructed. We can often trace the origins of other things that we enjoy; for example it is often remarked that the British are a nation of tea-drinkers and despite the increase in coffee consumption in recent times it remains the case that for many Brits, myself included, there are times when only a cup of tea will do. But no one is born with a taste for this beverage. It develops through a long association with being offered 'a nice cup of tea' as a welcome to someone's home, or as a comfort in illness, or as a warm and relaxing way of starting the day. Often we cannot trace the origins of our sexual orientation, tastes and practices in the same way. They appear 'given' to us, beyond learning. Sex as a feature of human life seems to us little different from other basic needs, like the need for food, water and shelter. We talk of a 'sex drive', and this language paints a graphic picture of human beings as in the grip of a powerful and undeniable force.

The subjective feeling that sexuality is a 'given' of human nature is endorsed by popular biological and evolutionary theories. It is now almost common sense to think of sexual desire and behaviour as emanating directly from the imperative to reproduce, to continue the human species; it's where our 'sex drive' comes from. Men's and women's sexualities are understood as necessarily different because of the different roles they must play in this reproductive process. Evolutionary theory seems to explain men's promiscuous sexual behaviour through the logic of gene transmission. Likewise, it fits our perception of women as more selective in their choice of mate, since they must invest time and physical energy in the production of a child and therefore must ensure that their offspring come from 'good stock'. It provides a rationale for men's desire for younger women (they're likely to be more fertile) and for women's preference for 'good providers'.

Such theories underpin our ideas about what it is natural for women and men to desire. But as in many other areas of life, what is seen as natural is also seen as 'normal'. In the social sciences, to say that something is normal simply means that it is typical of the most usual characteristics or behaviour of a particular group of people. But the everyday use of this term, as well as the term 'natural', has developed moral connotations. We feel that we ought to behave in ways that are natural and normal, and with respect to sexuality this means penetrative, heterosexual sex.

The case for social construction

If sex was just about procreation it is unlikely that we would see much variation in human sexual practices. Advocates of biological and evolutionary accounts of sexuality treat human beings as similar in all important respects to other animals, but this ignores the immense variety in human sexual practices. When dogs, cats and other animals have sex they do it in the manner characteristic of their species, and it really doesn't vary too much. It is highly prescriptive. But humans have been, and continue to be, extremely inventive and imaginative in their sexual practices. Forms of sexuality are currently proliferating and sub-dividing in contemporary western societies – the sexual 'menu' is now a far cry from a binary choice between straight and gay. We can't even say that an individual person, let alone the human species, is characterised by a particular form of sexual practice. Most people ring the changes to some extent. And when it comes to what people find erotic, that which fuels their sexual desire, it is often difficult indeed to see any support for biological and evolutionary accounts. How might a fetish for lace or leather, shoes or stockings be explained? Furthermore, other people's sexual desires and fantasies are often mystifying, or even distasteful. When it comes to sex, one wo/man's meat is indeed another's poison. It is the meaning of leather or stockings to the person that makes them erotic; the role of meaning in sexuality is impossible to deny. And meaning making is something that is characteristically human. Our ability to invest our actions with meaning is what marks us out from other animals.

These meanings are socially created and socially shared. In order to go along with the view that the need for sex, like the need for food, is something that is 'hard-wired' into human nature, a biological imperative that we cannot ignore, we would have to deny – or at least to render pathological – the choices that many people evidently make about their sexuality. A person who decides to practise chastity or celibacy, whether for religious, health or other reasons, becomes a puzzle. We leave ourselves with a conundrum that we can only resolve by imagining, and without any evidence, that such people must be channelling their sexual drive in some other way, or repressing it – with potentially explosive future consequences. This problem does not present itself if we see sexuality as something that is powered by meaning rather than biological drive, and meaning itself is profoundly social. The person who lives in celibacy as part of their religious commitment is doing so in part because of the meaning of sex in their community and culture. The woman with a husband and children who later chooses to become a lesbian because she now sees heterosexuality as politically oppressive can only be understood when we recognise the meaning that heterosexuality holds for her. And we understand it further if we locate that meaning within a feminist perspective on the world that is predominant in the social circles in which she moves.

Like personality and illness, human sexuality is not a stable phenomenon. It is often pointed out that, a couple of hundred years ago, a woman of ample proportions and pale skin was the epitome of desirable femininity. The change to today's preference for a slender, tanned body is hard to understand within the view of sexuality as hard-wired and fixed but makes a good deal of sense once we locate sexuality within a socially shared meaning system that is intimately bound up with social structure and the economy. In times when access to the material resources for sustaining life was perhaps even more divided by class than today, a well-fleshed body, whose skin declared that its owner had never needed to toil in the fields, spoke of wealth and comfort. Today, a tanned body is more likely to signal enough disposable income to spend on holidays in the sun; but this too may be changing as such activities become more widely enjoyed by people of all classes, together with the increasing circulation of meanings linking exposure to the sun with illness. In addition to this historical instability, as mentioned above we are seeing an explosion in the forms of sexuality practised by people in contemporary western societies.

As Stainton-Rogers and Stainton-Rogers (2001) have pointed out, biological and evolutionary theories are highly speculative and could tell a plausible story to explain quite the opposite state of affairs from the gender differences we commonly see. If men preferred mature women who already have children, it could be argued that this is because they are choosing more experienced, and therefore potentially better mothers for their own future offspring. The attractiveness of such theories is that, to the extent that they purport to tell us what is natural and normal, they can be used to bolster our moral arguments about what kind of sexuality is permissible. Such theories are often wheeled out when people want to defend sexual or gender inequalities by suggesting that they are inevitable, or to derogate non-normative sexual practices. But they are on other occasions conveniently forgotten for the very same reasons. For example, heterosexuality is seen as natural and hard-wired – but a homosexual teacher is seen as a potentially corrupting influence upon children in his charge. They could 'learn' homosexuality from him.

Sexuality is, then, primarily a moral issue for human beings, not a biological one. It is hard to imagine people getting so worked up about our different tastes in food or drink. Why? Because the meaning that sexuality carries for us is intimately bound to the social and economic structure of the society we live in. Masturbation was seen as an illness in times when fertility and reproduction were crucial to capitalism's need for an increasing supply of workers. Our sexual practices have immediate bearing upon such fundamental issues as who bears children, how many and who cares for them; how families are constituted and what kinds of housing and other provision is needed for them; who is available for work and who takes care of the workers. To the extent that diversity and change in sexuality may sound the death knell of the form of society in which we currently live, those with an investment in the status quo may well find such diversity and change deeply threatening.

Summary

As with personality and illness, there is considerable diversity across people and across time in sexual desire and sexual practice. In the face of this we must distrust essentialist accounts of sexuality. The role of meaning in our sexual lives is paramount, and meaning is made by human beings together; it is social. Meaning, unlike biological material, is fluid, volatile and always open to change through this medium of social interaction. Furthermore, sexuality is an area of our lives where the meanings we have created are often imbued with value and come with prescriptions for action. They are moral meanings; they tell us how we ought to feel and behave. And finally, these moral meanings are not accidental. They make sense within the social and economic structure of the society we live in. To the extent that this society is one divided by numerous power inequalities, the meanings that are widely endorsed play a role in maintaining these power relations.

Conclusion

I have used these three examples of personality, health and illness, and sexuality to illustrate some of the main features of social constructionism. In the abstract, the theoretical tenets of social constructionism can seem to be counter-intuitive. At first sight, they appear to contradict what seems common sense in our understanding of ourselves. But by appealing to everyday experiences that are problematic for these common-sense understandings, I have tried to demonstrate why we should at least take seriously social constructionist ideas long enough to see if they offer us a more fruitful or facilitative vision of human beings. The major conclusion that I would like you to draw from this chapter is that a lot of the things we take for granted as given, fixed and immutable, whether in ourselves or in the phenomena we experience, can upon inspection be found to be socially derived and socially maintained. They are created and perpetuated by human beings who share meanings through being members of the same society or culture. This is, in short, what social constructionism is all about. In the next chapter, I shall put some flesh on the bones of the idea (outlined in Chapter 1) that it is language, both in its form and its use, that is central to the making, maintenance and contesting of meaning and that it is language that provides the framework for the kinds of thought that are possible for us.

Chapter 3

The role of language in social constructionism

In Chapter 2, I made a case for the view that much of the experience that constitutes us as people is socially constructed. In this chapter I shall present the view that language is at the heart of this construction process. I will present the arguments that language and our use of it, far from simply describing the world, both constructs the world as we perceive it and has real consequences. The terms 'structuralism' and 'poststructuralism' will be used here, with a brief explanation of them in relation to language.

Language is unique to human beings. Undeniably, other animals communicate with each other. Scent, sound, markings, gesture and posture are employed by animals to signal danger, occupation of territory, sexual overtures and so on, but do they warrant the name of language? These behaviours clearly do have meanings, to which other animals respond, for example by fighting, running away, copulating etc. But the difference is that these meanings appear to be fixed and stable. When a dog rolls over and displays its belly, this is a sign of submission. It has the same meaning for all dogs, and this meaning has remained stable for countless generations of dogs. As we shall see later on in this chapter, it is the insistence upon the nature of language as constantly changing and varied in its meanings that is the keystone of social constructionism, and language is seen as having a much more important role in human life than traditional psychology has given it.

Our traditional, common-sense view of the relationship between language and the person sees the one as a means of expressing the other. When I talk about 'myself', my personality or some aspect of my experience like health or sexuality, it is assumed that this self, personality or experience predates and exists independently of the words used to describe it. We think of language as a bag of labels which we can choose from in trying to describe our internal states such as thoughts and feelings. The nature of the person and their internal states seem to us to come first, and the job of language is to find a way of expressing these things to other people. In this way of thinking, then, people and the language they use are certainly closely bound up with each other; people use language to give expression to things that already exist in themselves or in the world, but the two are themselves essentially independent things. In the rest of this chapter, I will outline two major differences between traditional psychology and social constructionism with respect to language. These are the relationship between language and thought and the relationship between language and action. These are given different emphasis in the two forms of social constructionism that I earlier referred to as deconstruction and discursive psychology (Chapter 1), so I will also outline the particular issues raised for each of these social constructionisms. However, I will give considerable space to spelling out the ideas relating to language and thought, since they are quite complex.

Language and thought

Our common-sense understanding of the relationship between language and thought has been most radically challenged by deconstructionist social psychologists, who have drawn heavily upon structuralist and poststructuralist ideas. Within this view, the person cannot pre-exist language because it is language which brings the person into being in the first place. This sounds rather bizarre at first. It seems as if we are saying that human beings just wouldn't exist if they didn't have language. Didn't cave people and their forebears exist? But human beings, people as we know them today, inhabit a world of experience which it is hard to imagine being possible for the cave dweller. Our daily experience is crammed with our hopes and fears for the future, our desires and worries, embarrassments and disappointments. We examine our motivations, drives and unconscious wishes. It is hard to imagine that the early humans too used these concepts to understand themselves and their world, but hadn't yet developed the linguistic tools for describing them to each other. The alternative is that language itself provides us with a way of structuring our experience of the world and of ourselves and that the concepts we use do not pre-date language but are made possible by it. This is what is meant by the phrase, used frequently by writers in this area, that 'language is not transparent', i.e. we should guard against the common-sense assumption that language is nothing more than a clear, pure medium through which our thoughts and feelings can be made available to others, rather like a good telephone line or a window which has no irregularities in the glass which could distort one's view.

There are two implications of this. Firstly, that what we take being a person to mean (such as having a personality, being motivated by drives, desires etc., having loves, hates and jealousies and so on) is not part of some essential human nature which would be there whether we had language or not. These things become available to us, through language, as ways of structuring our experience. Secondly, it means that what we take being a person to mean could always have been constructed differently – and indeed we live in a world in which there is still an enormous diversity of languages and of ways of understanding personhood. The possibility of alternative constructions of the self and other events in one's world, through language, is fundamental to this social constructionist view.

I have suggested that our experience of ourselves, how we understand others and ourselves, does not originate in pre-packaged forms inside us. For example, psychoanalysts take the view that there are discrete and identifiable emotions, such as anger, envy and hatred, which are innate in all human beings. They are part of the way human beings are constituted, and the words we have attached to them are simply the labels we have chosen to refer to these emotional entities. A social constructionist view, by contrast, would say that, in English-speaking cultures, the words 'anger', 'hatred' and 'envy' and the concepts to which they refer pre-date any one person's entry into the world as an infant, and in the process of learning to talk we have no choice but to come to understand ourselves in terms of these concepts. This view would suggest that our experience of the world, and perhaps especially of our own internal states, is undifferentiated and intangible without the framework of language to give it structure and meaning. The way that language is structured therefore determines the way that experience and consciousness are structured.

Some examples will help to illustrate this point. Descartes, from whose name is derived the term 'Cartesian', radically changed the way people thought about themselves by suggesting that human experience was divided by a fundamental dichotomy – the physical versus the mental. He saw these as two separate realms of experience, with their own phenomena. For example, being in pain, eating one's dinner and feeling the cold could be said to belong to the physical realm. Dreaming, having a spiritual experience or coming up with a good idea belong to the mental realm. Although this was a novel idea at the time, it has quickly embedded itself in our language and thought, with profound consequences for how we understand our experience. The mental–physical dimension is one which is inescapable for us when we try to make sense of events. Is my headache physical, having an organic cause, or mental, being either imaginary or originating in psychological distress? Is depression a physical illness or a mental illness? Can a physical illness such as cancer be cured by having positive thoughts? The fact that these questions are often so difficult to answer should first of all alert us to the possibility that the mental–physical dichotomy may not be a very good way of trying to divide up at least some aspects of our experience. But more than this, it shows that once we have divided up the world in this way, we are left with conceptualising the mental and physical as separate but related. We are led to ask questions like 'does physical illness affect your state of mind?' or 'can positive thinking cure physical illness?' The very fact of the existence of the mental–physical dichotomy in our language and concepts spawns a particular kind of understanding of human beings, their experience and their potentialities.

Let's take another example. Homosexual ('homo' meaning 'same') practices have been known throughout history, and in some cultures homosexual love has been prized above all other forms of love. However, it is only relatively recently that the word 'homosexual' has appeared in our language as a noun rather than solely as an adjective. This means that it is now possible to talk about 'a homosexual', which is a person, rather than 'homosexual practices' which are something a person does. Almost as if by magic, the linguistic trick of turning an adjective into a noun has created a certain kind of person. Interestingly, this can be seen as part of the general move toward seeing people in terms of what they are rather than what they do, described in Chapter 1. Because we can *say* 'a homosexual' we can *think* in terms of 'a homosexual'; we can imagine the existence of certain kinds of people that we can call homosexuals. And such language and thinking is inevitably lived out by us in our everyday dealings with each other. The power of language to bring about a change in our thinking is sometimes explicitly utilised by those seeking social change. For example, the Union of the Physically Impaired Against Segregation (UPIAS) makes the distinction between impairment (lack of or deficiency in a body part) and disability (the disadvantage to which a person is subjected due to their impairment). The term 'disabled people' thus signals that a person's disability is socially constructed through the values and practices of their society. It takes the responsibility for change off the shoulders of the disabled person and places it in the realm of social practices, organisation and the law.

Language and structuralism

The idea that the structure of language determines the lines along which we divide up our experience is at the heart of what is referred to as 'structuralism'. In fact structuralism implies rather different things in different disciplines, but for our purposes we will take it as referring to the ideas that originated with Saussure's study of structural linguistics (Saussure, 1974), and which were later reworked and extended to become 'poststructuralism'.

The key concept in Saussurean linguistics is that of the sign. Signs can be thought of as the things that populate our mental life, things we may refer to, talk to others about, muse upon, try to describe and so on. 'Intelligence', 'dog', 'marriage', 'teaspoon', and 'art' are all signs, and they all have two parts to them. There is the thing referred to (dog, intelligence) and there is the word, the spoken sound, used to refer to it. Saussure gives these two parts different names – the spoken sound is the 'signifier', and the thing it refers to is the 'signified'. I have intentionally included in my list of signs some rather abstract ones. 'Intelligence', 'art' and 'marriage' are different from 'dog' and 'teaspoon', in that we do not think of them as having the same kind of concrete existence or 'thingness' that dogs and teaspoons apparently have. However, they all qualify as 'signs' because in each case the signified is not a concrete object, but a concept. So that when we use the words 'dog' and 'teaspoon' we are referring to the concepts of dog and teaspoon, the meanings that these terms embody. If we watch a child in the process of acquiring language, we can see that this is so. At first, they may point to the family pet, and their parent may say, 'Yes, "dog!"' 'Dog', the child repeats. Later, the child sees a cat or a pig and proudly announces 'Dog!', to which the adult might reply, 'No, that's not a dog, that's a cat [pig]'. Unless we believe that the child truly doesn't notice any surface dissimilarities between these animals, we must conclude that what they are doing here is working out what features and characteristics the concepts 'dog', 'cat' and 'pig' encompass.

Saussure's major contribution was in his assertion that the link between the signifier (spoken sound) and the signified (concept) is an arbitrary one. At first sight this appears to be a rather obvious assertion. Of course we all know that there is nothing inherent in the sound of the word 'dog' that makes it a singularly appropriate label for the animal, and we only have to observe the fact that other languages use different words for 'dog' or 'pig' to be satisfied that the words we use to refer to concepts are just a convention – any word would do as long as everyone uses the same one. But Saussure is saying more than this. He is also saying that the concepts themselves are arbitrary divisions and categorisations of our experience. We have divided up our world into things we have called 'dogs', 'pigs', 'marriage', 'intelligence' and so on, and these divisions are arbitrary. It is quite possible that in some cultures separate concepts for 'dog' and 'cat' do not exist. In English-speaking cultures we have the words 'sheep' and 'mutton', and they refer to different concepts, but in French there is only one word, 'mouton'. Whatever differences we see between the concepts 'sheep' and 'mutton', as English-speakers, simply do not exist for the French. So when Saussure talks of the arbitrary linking of signifiers to signifieds, he is saying that, with the aid of language, we have divided up our world into arbitrary categories.

It is important to recognise here that 'arbitrary' doesn't imply accidental or random. The objects of our mental world do not exist 'out there' ready for us to attach our arbitrary labels to them, and although in principle our conceptual world could have been divided up very differently – and it is in this sense that the divisions we do have are arbitrary – the concepts we operate with are tied in with the kind of society we live in and are therefore not random (see Chapter 2). Signs themselves can have no intrinsic meaning. The meaning we give to the concept 'dog' does not reside within that concept itself, otherwise this would be a slide back into the idea that the things in our social world already exist 'out there', and are just waiting around for human beings to 'discover' them and label them within their language. The idea of making a division between things lies in the rules you use to say what makes them different from each other. Any category or concept can only ultimately be described by referring to yet other categories or concepts from which it is different. The concept 'dog' only has meaning by reference to its difference from other concepts such as 'cat' or 'table'. The meaning of a sign resides not intrinsically in that sign itself, but in its relationship to other signs. To give another example, it is not anything intrinsic to the signifier 'professional' that gives it its meaning, but rather its difference from and contrast with other signifiers of class such as 'manual worker' and 'trader'. This is what Saussure's structuralism is saying, then: language does not reflect a pre-existing social reality, but constitutes and brings a framework to that reality for us. It is the structure of language, the system of signifiers and signifieds and their meanings as constituted in the differences between them, which carves up our conceptual space for us. However, Saussure also believed that once a signifier became attached to a signified this relationship, though arbitrary, became fixed. This means that the words we use may have arbitrary meanings, but once words become attached to particular meanings they are fixed in that relationship, so that the same word always has the same meaning. This explains how all the users of a particular language are able to talk to each other, to deal in the same currency of concepts (signifieds), by using the same words (signifiers).

But the problem with this is that it doesn't explain two things. It doesn't explain how the meaning of words can change over time, and it doesn't explain how words can carry numerous meanings, depending upon who is speaking, to whom and to what purpose. Some examples will illustrate this. The words 'It's been a lovely sunny day today' have one meaning when spoken by the TV weather reporter, but quite another when spoken by acquaintances who feel they cannot pass each other on the street without a polite exchange. The word 'gay' in the past used to mean 'happy and joyful', and still can, but now also has a homosexual meaning and the meaning we take from it depends upon the context in which it is used, who is using it and why.

Language and poststructuralism

This is the point that writers after Saussure have focused upon, and it is for this reason that they are referred to as poststructuralist.

'Post', in this sense, means 'coming after and adding to' rather than 'rejecting'. This argument – that the meanings carried by language are never fixed, always open to question, always contestable, always temporary – is fundamental to poststructuralism and has major implications for our understanding of the person, their identity and the possibilities for personal and social change. This sounds like a rather large claim for such an apparently innocuous and insignificant piece of theory, but it leads us to a number of radical conclusions, which I will spell out.

It will be helpful to begin with two points upon which both structuralism and poststructuralism appear to be in agreement. Firstly, it is clear that both structuralism and poststructuralism see language as the prime site of the construction of the person. The person you are, your experience, your identity, your personality, are all the effects of language. This means that we can only represent our experiences to ourselves and to others by using the concepts embedded in our language, so that our thoughts, our feelings and how we represent our behaviour are all pre-packaged by language. Even this notion that we have three different categories of psychological event called thoughts, feelings and behaviour is itself a function of language, and it is quite possible, and I would think probable, that there are cultures and languages in which these categories are not present. For example, according to Lutz (1982) the Ifaluk have no word which translates as 'emotion'.

But this process of construction cannot be accomplished by individuals on their own. We must not lose sight of the fact that language is a fundamentally social phenomenon; it is something that occurs between people, whether they are having a conversation, writing a letter or a book, or filling in their tax return. It is in such exchanges between people that the construction of the person can take place. Every time we telephone a friend, visit our bank manager, take part in a seminar, read a magazine or tell someone we love them we, and the other people either actively or implicitly involved in that exchange, are in the process of constructing and reconstructing ourselves. It is from all the myriad forms of language exchange between people that the person emerges.

This leads to the second point shared by structuralism and poststructuralism, which is their anti-humanism. Humanism refers to a set of assumptions about human beings which is central to much of western philosophy. In particular, it refers to the idea that the person is a unified, coherent and rational agent who is the author of their own experience and its meaning. Humanism is essentialist; it assumes that there is an essence at the core of an individual which is unique, coherent and unchanging. But it also says that the individual's experience and the meaning it holds originates within the person, in their essential nature. 'Essential nature' here could refer to a number of things such as personality traits, attitudes, masculinity and so on. Within this view, the person's experience, their thoughts, feelings and behaviour, the sense they make of social events, all these arise from say, whether they are an extravert or an introvert, whether they hold prejudiced attitudes, or how masculine they are. By their insistence upon language as the fount of the meaning of experience, structuralists and poststructuralists have moved the psychological centre of gravity out of the individual person into the social realm. This means that if we are looking for explanations of the social world, either in terms of what individual people do and feel or in terms of groups, classes or societies, we should not look inside the individual, but out into the linguistic space in which they move with other people.

This anti-humanism also rejects the idea of the coherent, unified self, and this is a logical conclusion from the previous arguments. If the self is a product of language and social interactions, then the self will be constantly in flux, constantly changing depending upon who the person is with, in what circumstances and to what purpose – something that is, to some degree at least, borne out by our usual experience. The constructive force of language in social interaction ensures a fragmented, shifting and temporary identity for all of us. The subjective feeling we have of continuity and coherence can itself be seen as an effect of our language-based social interactions with other people and is an effect which is more illusory than real.

This is the point at which the poststructuralist view of language becomes very important. As I mentioned earlier, the departure from structuralism is based on the view that meaning is never fixed. Words, sentences, poems, books, jokes and so on change their meaning over time, from context to context and from person to person. Meaning is always contestable; the meaning of a term, a passage in a book, or a question addressed to us is always 'up for grabs'. This means that, rather than language being a system of signs with fixed meanings upon which everyone agrees, as Saussure argued, it is a site of variability, disagreement and potential conflict. And when we talk about conflict, we are inevitably dealing in power relations. So with the poststructuralist view of language we are drawn into a view of talk, writing and social encounters as sites of struggle and conflict, where power relations are acted out and contested. Let's work through these ideas a bit more slowly, with some examples. Take the question 'Does he take sugar?', a good example because most people are familiar with it as an emblem of the stereotyping of disability. Addressed to the parent of a young child, the question probably would not incite much interest. There are a number of assumptions implicit in the question. It assumes perhaps that the child is not in a position to know its own taste, or maybe to communicate it reliably to another person, or alternatively that it cannot be trusted to make a sensible decision. Addressing the question to the child's parent assumes that the parent is likely to be more reliable in any or all of these respects. It also demonstrates the parent's position of power relative to the child; the parent is probably able to determine whether or not the sugar goes into the child's drink irrespective of its own wishes. So implicit in this very small question are a lot of assumptions about the nature of young children, the nature of adults and a demonstration of the power relationship between children and their parents.

The meaning of this question, then, when addressed to the child's parent, would not usually, in our culture at least, be taken as insulting, demeaning or otherwise offensive. But when addressed to the wife of a blind man it certainly can be. The meaning of the question has changed because the situation and people are different. What is demeaning is the implication that the blind man stands in relation to his wife in the same way that the child does to the parent. It represents him as incapable of rational thought or communication and as relatively powerless. This representation could be contested – the blind man could say, 'I usually get my own – I take two in coffee and one in tea, thank you'. Or his wife could reply, 'Perhaps you had better ask him'. Both serve to contest the assumptions carried in the question, to reject the meanings it offers. Analysing the question in this way may even lead to a re-evaluation of parent–child relations. For example, some people may feel uncomfortable about the image of children it presents and with the relatively powerless position it gives them and may decide in future to treat them more like adults in some situations. This is a form of consciousness-raising.

If language is indeed the place where identities are built, main-tained and challenged, then this also means that language is the crucible of change, both personal and social. A person may feel trapped, restricted or oppressed by their identity as, say, 'mother', 'homosexual' or 'mental patient'. Poststructuralist theory would see language as the major site where these identities could be challenged or changed. If our experience of ourselves and of our lives is only given structure and meaning by language, and if these meanings are not fixed but constantly changing, sought after and struggled for, then our experience is potentially open to an infinite number of possible meanings or constructions. What it means to be a woman, to be a child or to be black could be transformed, reconstructed, and for poststructuralists language is the key to such transformations.

All this does not mean to say that change is easy, or that we can just talk our way out of damaging identities or oppressive social relations. What people say and write is not divorced from the things they do, either as individuals or as groups (social practices), or from the way that society is organised and run (social structure), and I will have more to say later about what the relationship between language, social structure and social practices might look like. But it does mean that what we say, the way we represent things to each other, matters crucially. If language provides the structure and content of our thought, then in a fundamental way what we say is what we think. Arguments over whether the head of a committee should be given the genderless title of 'chairperson', or whether we should outlaw terms such as 'blackleg' and 'blacklist' because of their racist connotations lose their apparent triviality in this light.

Language, performance and social action

Discursive psychologists have also been very interested in the way that different constructions of people and events are brought into being. But they have focused less upon the way that language structures our thinking and more upon the way that it is used by people in spoken interactions. At the beginning of his book *Discourse and Cognition* Edwards says that his approach is one where 'the primary and defining thing about language is how it works as a kind of activity, as discourse' (1997: 1). Potter (1996a) asks how descriptions are produced so that they will be regarded as 'factual' and how these descriptions then enable particular actions to be carried out. Discursive psychologists are therefore primarily interested in our situated use of language, that is, how people actively construct accounts to try to build defensible identities or to have their versions of events legitimated or endorsed by others in the interaction. The following is a fictional example of the use of language in a struggle to build defensible identities. It is an interchange between a woman and a man in a car. The woman is driving.

Him: There's nothing coming after the blue van . . . you can pull out. Oh, you've missed it now. You just keep looking the other way and I'll tell you when it's OK to go.

Her: Thanks – but if you'd just keep your head back I'd be able to see perfectly well anyway.

Him: There's no need to be like that – I was only being helpful.

Her: I don't really need you to help – I'm perfectly capable of getting us to the supermarket without constant instructions. I bet you wouldn't do it if I were a man.

Him: What's that supposed to mean? You're always complaining that I don't help you enough, and then when I do try to be helpful, you just throw it back in my face.

Her: You know perfectly well what I mean. If I were a man you wouldn't dream of suggesting that I'm incapable of driving down the road without your assistance. You only do it to assert your masculinity.

Him: That's complete rubbish, and you know it. You're just spoiling for a fight, and you drag that feminist stuff in just to score points. Well that's the last time I'm going out of my way to be helpful to you – if you don't want my help, then that's fine.

There is very obviously a struggle after meaning here. Both parties are engaged in an effort to define what the other was doing, and to have their version of events given the stamp of 'the truth'. The meaning of these interchanges between the couple is being strongly contested. He is claiming that his words were an act of generosity, and she that they were an attempt to 'feminise' her and bolster his masculinity. He is struggling to produce for himself the identity of a thoughtful, helpful man – perhaps a 'New Man', and is fighting off the implied identity of chauvinist. She is trying to bring off her identity as a capable, thinking woman and to resist a representation of herself as in need of male advice and direction. Both parties are engaged in a linguistic struggle to build, maintain or reject the identities on offer in this situation.

Language as performative and action-oriented

Our talk therefore has specific functions and achieves purposes for us in our interactions with each other. Discursive psychology builds upon the earlier traditions of 'speech act' theory and ethnomethodology. Speech act theory, usually associated with the philosopher Austin, was an attempt to get away from the idea that the prime function of language is to describe some state of affairs, some aspect of reality. Austin (1962) pointed out that some sentences or utterances are important not because they describe things but because of what they do. Potter and Wetherell (1987) give some examples:

> For instance, the sentence:
>
> I declare war on the Philippines
>
> is not a description of the world which can be seen as true or false but an act with practical consequences; when uttered in the right circumstances it brings into being a state of war. Austin called sentences of this kind performatives. Other examples are:
>
> I name this ship The Lady Penelope
>
> Beware of the bull
>
> I sentence you to six months hard labour
>
> In each of these cases, the primary role of the sentence is not description as such but to make certain things happen; they are sentences performing acts.
>
> (Potter and Wetherell, 1987: 13)

Speech act theory therefore draws attention to language as a human social practice. This view of language as functional rather than descriptive is also common to the sociological tradition of ethnomethodology. The word 'ethnomethodology' simply means the study of the methods (methodology) used by the people (ethno). It is the study of the methods that ordinary people use to produce and make sense of everyday life. Again, rather than view the things that people say as simple descriptions of reality, ethnomethodologists look at the functions that the person's talk has within an interaction and the effects it achieves for them. Both for speech act theory and for ethnomethodology the things that people say become the object of study themselves rather than being taken as a route to discovering some aspect of an assumed underlying reality, like a person's attitudes or the causes of a particular event. For a brief account of the links between speech act theory and ethnomethodology see Potter and Wetherell (1987), Chapter 1.

This approach to talk gives rise to a number of questions, which are very different from those of traditional psychology. It leads us to ask what functions a person's talk might have for them, what is at stake for them in the interaction, what purposes they are trying to achieve, and what discursive devices they employ to bring about the desired effects. It is therefore 'action-oriented'. It encourages us to catalogue the range of discursive devices and rhetorical skills that are brought into play for specific purposes and to ask how people construct their talk to achieve the effects they do. Discursive psychologists have studied a range of such discursive practices such as justifications, disclaimers, attributions and blamings.

Interpretative repertoires

Potter and Wetherell (1987) put forward the concept of the interpretative repertoire as a way of understanding the linguistic resources that people draw upon in constructing their accounts of events. Interpretative repertoires can be seen as:

> the building blocks speakers use for constructing versions of actions, cognitive processes and other phenomena. Any particular repertoire is constituted out of a restricted range of terms used in a specific stylistic and grammatical fashion. Commonly these terms are derived from one or more key metaphors and the presence of a repertoire will often be signalled by certain tropes or figures of speech.
>
> (Wetherell and Potter, 1988: 172)

And:

> By interpretative repertoires we mean broadly discernible
> clusters of terms, descriptions and figures of speech often
> assembled around metaphors or vivid images . . . They are
> available resources for making evaluations, constructing
> factual versions and performing particular actions
> (Potter and Wetherell, 1995: 89)

Thus, interpretative repertoires can be seen as a kind of culturally
shared tool kit of resources for people to use for their own
purposes. Identifying an interpretative repertoire is rather like an
archaeologist inferring the past existence of a particular type of
widely used chisel or spear by observing a number of different
instances in which it appears to have been used. The functions that
these repertoires serve for people are seen as generally enabling
them to justify particular versions of events, to excuse or validate
their own behaviour, to fend off criticism or otherwise allow them
to maintain a credible stance in an interaction. Different repertoires can construct different versions of events. Willig (2001) gives
the following example:

> A newspaper article may refer to young offenders as 'young
> tear-aways', while a defending lawyer may describe his or her
> clients as 'no-hope-kids.' The former construction emphasises
> the uncontrollability of young offenders and implies the need
> for stricter parenting and policing, whereas the latter draws
> attention to the unmet psychological and educational needs of
> young offenders and importance of social and economic
> deprivation.
> (Willig, 2001: 95)

However, one person may use different and apparently contra-
dictory repertoires in their talk, depending upon their moment-to-
moment accounting needs (e.g. Potter and Wetherell, 1995; Billig,
1997a). Also, the same repertoire may be used by different people
to achieve different ends (see Chapter 9). Repertoires, then, do not
belong to individual people and are not located inside their heads.
They are a social resource, being available to all who share a
language and a culture, and are seen as a tool kit from which
people can assemble accounts for their own purposes.

Although what people say, the repertoires that they draw upon, may have implications beyond the immediate social situation they are engaged in, such implications and consequences may be unintended by the speakers themselves. There is a distinction between the person's reasons for using particular discursive forms and their social psychological consequences. When people speak, they may not be aware of the associations and implications that their choice of words brings with it. Furthermore, people's use of interpretative repertoires and their efforts to construct events in a particular way may be conducted at a non-conscious, non-intentional level. When people use repertoires, they are not necessarily acting in a machiavellian fashion, but just simply doing what seems appropriate or what comes naturally in that situation.

Language and social action

Although it is the discursive psychologists who have paid most attention to the action-orientation of language, this is not to say that deconstructionists have always treated language as if it were disconnected from the world of action. As pointed out in Chapter 1, a key feature of social constructionism is a recognition of the fact that different constructions of the world sustain different kinds of social action. To the extent that our constructions of the world are founded upon language, as has been argued throughout this chapter, then language underpins the forms of action that it is possible for us to take. This seems to be a conclusion compatible with both deconstruction and discursive psychology. Deconstruction typically focuses upon language as a system of signs and symbols existing at the level of society or culture. Within this view, our culturally shared representations of the world often have far-reaching implications for how we treat people. For example, as noted in Chapters 1 and 2, as a society we often describe people who hear voices as mentally ill and refer them to psychiatrists and psychologists who then have power over many aspects of their lives. If we constructed them as seers or prophets, we might instead visit them for advice about the future. Discursive psychologists' focus upon situated language use brings different kinds of examples to the fore, like the fictional car journey described above. To the extent that the man in this scenario succeeds in building an account of himself as helpful, the woman will feel less able to challenge his behaviour or legitimately ask him to change how he behaves when in the car with her.

Summary

The main thrust of this chapter has been to suggest that, rather than view language and thought as two separate phenomena which can affect each other, they are inseparable and that language provides the basis for all our thought. It provides us with a system of categories for dividing up our experience and giving it meaning, so that our very selves become the products of language. Language produces and constructs our experience of each other and ourselves. Structuralist writers have shown the arbitrariness of the way human experience is carved up by language, that it could always have been different. There is nothing about the nature of the world or human beings that leads necessarily to the conceptual categories present in any language. But in their insistence upon the shifting, transitory and contestable nature of the meaning of language, and therefore of our experience and identity, poststructuralism has identified language as a site of struggle, conflict and potential personal and social change. Discursive psychologists have emphasised the performative and action-oriented nature of language. They have investigated the way that accounts are built in interactions to suit particular purposes – fashioning identities, justifying our actions, blaming others and so on – and argue that people draw upon a shared cultural resource of tools, such as interpretative repertoires, for these purposes. Both deconstructionists and discursive psychologists therefore endorse the view that language constructs rather than represents the world and, in different ways, hold the view that how we describe ourselves, other people and events has consequences for our action, either as individuals or as a society.

Both deconstructionists and discursive psychologists use the term 'discourse' to refer to the linguistic subject matter that is the focus of their research and theoretical interests. They also use the terms 'discourse analysis' to refer to their approach to the empirical study of written and spoken texts. However, due to their different focus the terms 'discourse' and 'discourse analysis' have different meanings in each case. As we saw above, for discursive psychologists the term 'discourse' refers to the situated use of language in social interactions. But for those adopting a more deconstructionist approach its meaning is more complex, and in Chapter 4 I will outline what this meaning of discourse involves. I will address the different forms of discourse analysis in Chapter 8.

Chapter 4

What is a discourse?

As outlined in the previous chapter, when used by discursive psychologists the term 'discourse' refers to an instance of situated language use. This is very often a conversation or other spoken interaction, but it can also be written texts of all kinds. Such spoken and written texts are analysed by discursive psychologists to examine the way that language is used in building successful accounts for the speaker or writer. The question underlying such analysis is typically one of process; the aim is to make visible how certain representations of events or persons are being achieved.

When used by those taking a more deconstructionist stance, what I am calling macro social constructionism, the term 'discourse' has a somewhat different meaning, a meaning that extends its focus of interest beyond the immediate context in which language is being used by a speaker or writer. Whereas discursive psychology seems to emphasise the freedom of the speaker to draw upon language as a cultural resource for his or her own ends, macro social constructionism emphasises the way that the forms of language available to us set limits upon, or at least strongly channel, not only what we can think and say, but also what we can do or what can be done to us. The use of the term 'discourse' here, then, incorporates not just language but practice too. As outlined in Chapter 1, this approach has been heavily influenced by the work of the French historian and philosopher Michel Foucault, and for this reason this analytic approach is often termed 'Foucauldian'. It has often been taken up by those interested in issues of identity, subjectivity, personal and social change and power relations (e.g. Henriques et al., 1984; Willig, 1999a; Parker and the Bolton Discourse Network, 1999). In this chapter, I will outline what is meant by 'discourse' within this approach, and show how it is intimately connected to social structure and social practices. In this view, then, 'discourse' is certainly a lot more than just 'talk', or even 'language'.

What is a discourse?

Discourses are 'practices which form the objects of which they speak' (Foucault, 1972: 49). This apparently circular statement sums up the relation between discourses and the world of 'things' that we inhabit. A discourse refers to a set of meanings, metaphors, representations, images, stories, statements and so on that in some way together produce a particular version of events. It refers to a particular picture that is painted of an event, person or class of persons, a particular way of representing it in a certain light. If we accept the view, outlined in the last chapter, that a multitude of alternative versions of events are potentially available through language, this means that, surrounding any one object, event, person etc. there may be a variety of different discourses, each with a different story to tell about the object in question, a different way of representing it to the world.

Let's take an example to illustrate what is meant by a discourse. Foxhunting as an 'object' could be said to be represented in at least two radically different discourses. The 'foxhunting as pest control' discourse could be said to represent foxhunting as a natural method of keeping the fox population down to manageable numbers. Within this discourse, foxhunting is not immoral but is ultimately in the best interests of both humans and the fox, and its long tradition can be said to testify to its 'tried and tested' effectiveness. People drawing upon this discourse in their talk might be expected to say things like 'If it wasn't for the hunt, the fox population would run out of control' or 'The fox is a pest to farmers, who lose thousands of pounds each year in attacks on livestock.' Consistent with these statements might be a letter to a national newspaper extolling the virtues of foxhunting, or a poster advertising the annual hunt ball.

A different discourse of foxhunting could be 'foxhunting as the contravention of basic morality.' From the vantage point of this discourse, people might be expected to say things such as 'Animals have basic rights to life, just like humans', or 'The hunting and killing of animals is uncivilised and is unworthy of human beings'. You might also find photographs of foxes being savaged by the

dog pack in newspapers or magazines, or of animal rights pro-
testers carrying placards bearing slogans. These photographs too
are manifestations of the discourse, even though they are not
spoken or written language, because they can be 'read' for meaning
in the same way and appear to belong to the same way of representing 'foxhunting' (putting the word in scare quotes serves to
point to the fact that the nature of the object is contentious).
You might like to suggest further possible discourses of 'foxhunting', such as 'foxhunting as healthy outdoor sport' or
'foxhunting as pastime of the idle rich'. The point is that numerous
discourses surround any object and each strives to represent or
'construct' it in a different way. Each discourse brings different
aspects into focus, raises different issues for consideration, and has
different implications for what we should do. So discourses,
through what is said, written or otherwise represented, serve to
construct the phenomena of our world for us, and different
discourses construct these things in different ways, each discourse
portraying the object as having a very different nature from the
next. Each discourse claims to say what the object really is, that is,
claims to be the truth. As we shall see, claims to truth and
knowledge are important issues, and lie at the heart of discussions
of identity, power and change.

Notice that what is absent from this account is any reference to
notions such as 'opinion' or 'attitude'. I suggested above the kinds
of things that people might say about foxhunting, and to say that
such statements issued from the person's opinions or attitudes
would be completely opposed to a social constructionist view.
Attitudes and opinions are essentialist concepts of the 'personality'
kind. They invite us to think of structures residing inside the person
which are part of that person's make-up and which determine or at
least greatly influence what that person does, thinks and says. The
presence of a positive or negative attitude is inferred from what a
person says, but the attitude itself is a hypothetical structure which
cannot itself be directly observed. But such essences have no place
in a social constructionist understanding of the person, and have
no status as explanations of the things people say. Let us be clear
about the status of the things people say and write, from a
Foucauldian perspective: these things are not a route of access to a
person's private world, they are not valid descriptions of things
called 'beliefs' or 'opinions', nor can they be taken to be manifestations of some inner, essential condition such as temperament,

personality or attitude. They are manifestations of discourses, outcrops of representations of events upon the terrain of social life. They have their origin not in the person's private experience, but in the discursive culture that those people inhabit.

The things that people say or write, then, can be thought of as instances of discourses, as occasions where particular discourses are given the opportunity to construct an event in this way rather than that. Pieces of speech or writing can be said to belong to the same discourse to the extent that they are painting the same general picture of the object in question. Of course, the same words, phrases, pictures, expressions and so on might appear in a number of different discourses, each time contributing to a rather different narrative. To go back to the foxhunting example, the words 'sentimentality over vermin is misplaced' could appear as part of the 'hunting-as-tried-and-tested-pest-control' discourse, or as part of the 'hunting-as-pastime-of-the-idle-rich' discourse. Words or sentences do not of themselves belong to any particular discourse, in fact the meaning of what we say rather depends upon the discursive context, the general conceptual framework in which our words are embedded. In this sense, a discourse can be thought of as a kind of frame of reference, a conceptual backcloth against which our utterances can be interpreted. So there is a two-way relationship between discourses and the actual things that people say or write: discourses show up in the things that people say and write, and the things we say and write, in their turn, are dependent for their meaning upon the discursive context in which they appear.

A discourse about an object is said to manifest itself in texts – in speech, say a conversation or interview, in written material such as novels, newspaper articles or letters, in visual images like magazine advertisements or films, or even in the meanings encoded in the clothes someone wears or the way they do their hair. In fact, anything that can be 'read' for meaning can be thought of as being a manifestation of one or more discourses and can be referred to as a 'text'. Buildings may 'speak' of civic pride, like the town halls and factories of the industrial revolution, or of a yearning for the past as in the current trend towards vernacular building. Clothes and uniforms may suggest class position, status, gender, age or subculture and as such can be called texts. Given that there is virtually no aspect of human life that is exempt from meaning, everything around us can be considered as textual and 'life as text' could be said to be the underlying metaphor here. To return to the quote that I used to introduce this section, discourses are 'practices which form the objects of which they speak'; it should now be clear that objects and events come into existence for us as meaningful entities through their representation in discourse. This is what is meant by the claim 'there is nothing outside the text' (Derrida, 1976: 158). When they make this claim, social constructionists are not denying the existence of a material world but are pointing out that our engagement with the world of things and events is dependent upon the meaning that discourses give these:

> Discourse, Foucault argues, constructs the topic. It defines and produces the objects of our knowledge. It governs the way that a topic can be meaningfully talked about and reasoned about. It also influences how ideas are put into practice and used to regulate the conduct of others.
>
> (Hall, 2001: 72)

Discourse, knowledge and power

If discourses regulate our knowledge of the world, our common understanding of things and events, and if these shared understandings inform our social practices then it becomes clear that there is an intimate relationship between discourse, knowledge and power. Foucault was centrally concerned with this relationship, and it is worth spending a little time fleshing out some of his main ideas, since they have been taken up with such enthusiasm by many writers wishing to import poststructuralist ideas into social psychology. Our common-sense understanding of the relationship between knowledge and power is the notion that knowledge increases a person's power. For example, by gaining the knowledge offered by higher education, a person increases their access to good jobs, good pay and high status. But Foucault's conception of the relationship between knowledge and power is quite different from this, as we shall see.

I have already gone into detail about how a discourse analysis of the world puts forward the view that events, people, social phenomena and so on are subject to a variety of possible constructions or representations. Some constructions will have a greater tendency to be seen as common sense or more truthful than others, although this can be expected to vary greatly with the specific culture, its location in history and the structure of its society. For example, in contemporary western societies it is commonplace for the versions of natural events provided by science and medicine to be given greater credence than those offered by religion, magic or superstition and to be given the stamp of truth. However, this certainly has not always been the case, and is not true of all cultures in the world. Behaviour which a few hundred years ago would have been taken as evidence of possession by evil spirits is today thought of as mental illness. Even where scientists have not been able to put forward adequate accounts of phenomena, such as psychokinesis and mind reading, these things are often taken to have an underlying rational explanation which science, given time, will uncover. What we call knowledge then simply refers to the particular construction or version of a phenomenon that has received the stamp of truth in our society. Even within the discourse of science, what we may regard as the truth with respect to, say, a healthy diet, adequate parenting or disease prevention has changed markedly over a short time span and such changes cannot simply be seen as the result of progress in medical science.

For Foucault, knowledge, the particular common-sense view of the world prevailing in a culture at any one time, is intimately bound up with power. Any version of an event brings with it the potential for social practices, for acting in one way rather than another, and for marginalising alternative ways of acting. In the example above, 'evil spirits' can be 'exorcised', but 'mental illness' may require 'treatment' in a mental hospital. What it is possible for one person to do to another, under what rights and obligations, is given by the version of events currently taken as knowledge. Therefore the power to act in particular ways, to claim resources, to control or be controlled depends upon the knowledges currently prevailing in a society. We can exercise power by drawing upon discourses, which allow our actions to be represented in an acceptable light. Foucault therefore does not see power as some form of possession, which some people have and others don't, but as an effect of discourse. To define the world or a person in such a way that allows you to do the things you want is to exercise power. When we define or represent something in a particular way we are producing a particular form of knowledge, which brings power with it. To construe the world in terms of those people who are mad and those who are sane, thereby producing one particular knowledge, brings with it a power inequality between those groups.

Given that there are always a number of discourses surrounding an event, each offering an alternative view, each bringing with it different possibilities for action, it follows that the dominant or prevailing discourse, or common sense, is continually subject to contestation and resistance. For Foucault, power and resistance are two sides of the same coin. The power implicit in one discourse is only apparent from the resistance implicit in another. If power is what you exercise in drawing upon discourses, Foucault's view of power, then, certainly has nothing in common with the idea that power is in evidence when one person can force another to do what they want them to, that is, when their resistance is overcome. Sawicki (1991), elaborating upon Foucault's views, points out that repression and the need to resort to force is rather to be taken as evidence of a *lack* of power; repression is used when the limits of power have been reached.

Disciplinary power

Foucault therefore rejects the view of power as an essentially repressive force, seeing it instead as at its most effective when it is productive, when it *produces* knowledge. In particular, he believes that over the last hundred years or so we have seen the rise of a number of institutional and cultural practices that have as their product the individual that we know today. Changes in the nature of society, such as increases in population, the change from an agricultural to an industrial economy and so on, brought with them social practices which allowed certain discourses or knowl-edges of the person to rise to prominence. These discourses have produced the individual of contemporary western industrial society; the person we feel to be inhabited by drives and motiva-tions, possessed by traits and characteristics, and whose freely chosen actions are monitored by conscience. And these knowledges are very powerful, in that they manage the control of society and its members efficiently and without force, through what he calls 'disciplinary power'.

Foucault (1976) demonstrates how this came about. He argues that in the eighteenth century, due to the growth in numbers of people and the consequent problems of public health, housing conditions and so on, there began to emerge the concept of 'population'. Until then, those living under the rule of the monarch might have been thought of as 'a people' or 'loyal subjects', but the idea of a country having a population, had different implications. 'Population' brings with it estimates of the country's labour power, its organisation and the wealth it is capable of generating. It raises issues of population growth and the resources needed for meeting that growth. In short, the concept of population was a relatively sophisticated way of conceptualising the inhabitants of a country that brought with it questions of management and control. Foucault sees the body, and especially sexuality, as a major site of power relations, and describes how this came about as follows:

> At the heart of this economic and political problem of population was sex: it was necessary to analyse the birth-rate, the age of marriage, the legitimate and illegitimate births, the precocity and frequency of sexual relations, the ways of making them fertile or sterile, the effects of unmarried life or of the prohibitions. . .Things went from ritual lamenting over the unfruitful debauchery of the rich, bachelors and libertines to a discourse in which the sexual conduct of the population was taken both as an object of analysis and as a target of intervention.
>
> (Foucault, 1976: 25–6)

In other words, sex became an area of intense interest to the state. Those in positions of authority, in the state or the church, took on the role of inquisitors and had the power to extort confessions about sexual practices from the men and women under their supervision. One of the interesting points about Foucault's analysis here is that it was only at this point that the ideas of 'sexual perversion', 'unnatural practices' and 'sexual immorality' became a possibility. With the power to say what practices were permissible and which not inevitably came the idea of normality. The practice of scrutinising the population's sexual behaviour and of encouraging people to confess their sexual 'sins' developed into a powerful form of social control as people began to internalise this process. Thus, people were encouraged to scrutinise their own behaviour, to ask questions about their own normality and to adjust their own behaviour accordingly. The powers of the inquisitor, the power to encourage self-examination and confession, have now passed into the hands of the present-day bearers of authority, such as the medical profession and psychiatrists in particular. Practices such as psychoanalysis view sexuality as the key to self-understanding. They encourage us to believe that in order to resolve our personality and relationship problems, we must discover the true nature of our sexuality. In this way personal life is psychologised, and thus becomes a target for the intervention of experts.

Foucault completely reverses our usual understanding of sexuality in the nineteenth century. The present-day orientation toward sexual liberation is commonly thought to be a reaction against earlier sexual repression, against a time when sex was not spoken about or otherwise openly represented in social life. This era is usually thought of as a time when there was a pervasive silence on the subject of sex. Foucault regards this 'repressive hypothesis' as a myth. Instead, he says that the nineteenth century saw an explosion in discourses of sexuality. Never before was sex so much scrutinised, classified, theorised and controlled. The fact that sex was not mentioned in polite society does not alter the fact that, in a diversity of ways, sexuality was rapidly being discursively constructed during this period. For example, the practice of covering the legs of furniture spoke volumes about sexuality as a powerful, shameful force.

From this perspective, the nineteenth-century burgeoning of the sexology literature is seen not so much as an increase in knowledge about sexuality as a proliferation of classifications and divisions with which the population could be categorised and controlled. And it wasn't only in the area of sexuality that such a move toward surveillance and normalisation was taking place. Psychiatry developed the category of sane/insane, later extending this to become innumerable varieties of abnormality (psychosis, neurosis, manic depression, schizophrenia etc.). The development of criminology transformed crime into the study of 'criminals', certain kinds of people who were predisposed to criminal behaviour. The power of surveillance as a method of social control is epitomised, according to Foucault (1979), by Bentham's Panopticon. This was a nineteenth-century invention in which prison cells were arranged around a central watchtower. From this chamber, a supervisor could keep a watchful guard over the inmates. In their cells, no prisoner could be certain that they were not being observed, and so they gradually began to police their own behaviour. Foucault's point here is that, as with the confessional, the practice of surveillance became internalised by those who were watched and in principle this is all members of society. People came to monitor and control their own behaviour according to the prevailing standards of normality. This is essentially what we mean today by self-discipline. Sarup (1993), in a very clear and readable brief account of Foucault's ideas, draws parallels between the Panopticon and both the Christian God's infinite knowledge and the computer monitoring of individuals in advanced capitalism. Thus Foucault believes that there has been a radical shift in the way that western societies are managed and controlled. This was a shift away from 'sovereign power' in which the sovereign controlled the populace by the power to punish, coerce or kill them, towards 'disciplinary power', in which people are disciplined and controlled by freely subjecting themselves to the scrutiny of others, especially experts, and to their own self-scrutiny. Such disciplinary power, he believes, is a much more effective and efficient form of control.

Looked at against this background, the position of psychology itself becomes highly dubious. In this light, the practice of psychology becomes seen not as a liberatory project in which knowledge discovered about human beings is used to improve their lives, but one more cog in the machine of social control. In fact the term 'psy-complex' (e.g. Ingleby, 1985; Rose, 1985) has been coined to refer to all the practices and professions with a 'psy' prefix, such as psychology, psychotherapy and psychiatry, which play a central role in the surveillance and regulation of people in contemporary society. The practice of surveillance requires information about people. This information can then be used to establish norms for healthy or morally acceptable behaviour, against which any person can be assessed or assess themselves. The history of psychology is littered with such products: intelligence tests, personality inventories, tests of masculinity, femininity and androgyny, child development tests, measurements of attitudes and beliefs and so on. All this information about ourselves constitutes, from a Foucauldian perspective, the production of knowledges which can be used to control people while making it appear as though it is in their own interests, and with the stamp of 'science' to give such knowledges authority. Rose (1990) undertakes a Foucauldian analysis of the rise of psychology as a social science and demonstrates the way that psychology is implicated in modern forms of disciplinary power, and Parker (Parker, 1998b; Parker et al., 1995) has developed a critical deconstruction of psychotherapy and psychopathology.

The invisibility of disciplinary power

One of the key points raised in the last section is the idea that the discourses, which serve as a framework to people's everyday experience of themselves and their lives, their subjectivity, serve purposes of social control. However, this process is not recognised by us as such. The argument appears to be that, on rational grounds, if people really understood that they were being controlled they wouldn't stand for it. Foucault saw this as an essential aspect of the operation of power: 'Power is tolerable only on condition that it masks a substantial part of itself. Its success is proportional to its ability to hide its own mechanisms' (Foucault, 1976: 86). So discourses offer a framework to people against which they may understand their own experience and behaviour and that of others, and can be seen to be tied to social structures and practices in a way which masks the power relations operating in society. Let's take an example to see what this might look like.

The discourse of 'romantic love' is one which we are all subject to. We are surrounded by film and TV images of true love, young love, adulterous love, love-at-first-sight and unrequited love. Singers sing of it, magazines publish letters about it, and each of us at some time has asked ourselves the question whether we are 'in' it, ever have been or ever will be. As a way of formatting our thoughts, emotions and behaviour the discourse of romantic love must surely be one of the most prevalent in modern society. What are the images and assumptions of this discourse, what does it say? Firstly, it represents itself as a natural feature of human nature, and one that has a function in (almost exclusively heterosexual) bonding. Love appears as the emotional cement which strengthens the sexual relationship between men and women. If we really love someone, it means that we care about them and their welfare, and that we to some extent bear responsibility for that welfare. It also means that sexual services can be expected to form part of the relationship, and that these are freely given. Secondly, love is the foundation for marriage and family life, and marriage is seen as the appropriate and natural culmination of a romantic alliance. Falling in love is therefore seen as the precursor to a caring, sexual relationship – marriage – in which men and women take responsibility for each other's welfare and that of their family (see Averill, 1985 for a social constructionist analysis of love).

However, as discourses 'romantic love', 'marriage' and 'the family' may be seen as ways of talking about our lives, ways of constructing them, living them out and representing them to ourselves that mask inequitous social arrangements. In other words, we may be entering into forms of life which are not necessarily in our own interest, but are in the interests of relatively powerful groups in society, because the discourses available for framing our experience obtain our consent. Of course feminists, though not necessarily calling themselves social constructionists, were among the first to develop critiques of notions such as romantic love. From a Marxist view, marriage and the family play a crucial role in the maintenance of capitalist economy. It is vital that men, as workers, are able to appear each day in the marketplace ready to sell their labour power. They need to be fed and clothed, to have their health attended to and to be relieved of other family responsibilities like taking children to school or to the dentist and doing the shopping. Women therefore play a central role both in this daily reproduction of the labour force, and in its renewal from generation to generation in the form of children who will in their turn become workers. But it is also vital that women provide these services free of charge. If women did not marry, have children and provide their caring and sexual services free of charge, activities such as cooking, laundering, child care and so on would have to be paid for by employers via the wage packet. The idea of the family wage, that a man should be paid enough money to support not only himself, but a dependent wife and children, serves further to legitimate women's position as provider of free services to her husband and family. But if you were to ask a selection of men and women why they think people get married and what they think marriage is about, it is unlikely that these ideas would feature in their accounts. The discourse of romantic love serves to re-cast this economic arrangement into a narrative of a mutually beneficial, caring relationship freely entered into for personal, emotional reasons. Men and women get married because they love each other, and women care for their husbands and families because they love them.

In effect we have here two accounts, two different constructions, with conflicting stories to tell about marriage and the family – the 'romantic love/marriage/family' group of discourses and the 'Marxist discourse', and it is the former version of events that is understood as common sense. In Foucault's terms, the power exercised through these discourses in persuading women to willingly give away their services, and in persuading men that the money they receive in their wage packet is a fair exchange for the work they have done, is so successful because of the extent to which it has been possible to obscure its operation by the discourses of love, marriage and family life.

Discourse, social structure and social practices

Discourses have implications for what we can do and what we should do. Prevailing discourses of femininity often construct women as, say, nurturant, close to nature, emotional, negatively affected by their hormones, empathic, and vulnerable. From this it is only a short step to the recommendations that women are particularly able to care for young children, and that they should do so, that they are unsuited to careers in top management or positions of responsibility, and that they should avoid potentially dangerous activities such as walking home alone at night or hitchhiking. Prevailing discourses of the individual paint a picture of human beings as separate, disconnected units naturally differing from each other in terms of their motivation, talents, intelligence, determination and so on, so that, within a market economy, competitiveness and ambition secure the survival of the fittest, according to their natural abilities. But why do these particular versions of femininity and the individual enjoy such widespread popularity and acceptance? Why do some versions or ways of representing people or events appear as truth and others as fiction?

Discourses are not simply abstract ideas, ways of talking about and representing things that, as it were, float like balloons far above the real world. Discourses are intimately connected to institutional and social practices that have a profound effect on how we live our lives, on what we can do and on what can be done to us. For example, Willig (2001) points out that as 'patients' within a biomedical discourse our bodies can be legitimately exposed and invaded by doctors and nurses as part of the practice and institution of medicine. In our society we have a capitalist economy and we have institutions such as the law, education, marriage and the family, and the church. These things give shape and substance to the daily lives of each of us. They offer us positions and statuses: the capitalist economy makes us into 'workers', 'employers' or 'unemployed'. The institutions of marriage and the family mean that people can be 'married', 'single' or 'divorced' and they can be 'mothers' or 'fathers' or 'childless'. The institution of education provides 'educated' and 'uneducated' people and so on. Each of these ways of structuring society is put into practice every day by the things that people do, by social practices. Capitalism is being put into practice every time a worker 'clocks in' or collects a wage packet or unemployment benefit. Education is put into practice when children sit in classrooms or truant. The family is put into practice when mothers cook dinner for their husbands and children, or when they take time off work to care for a sick child. And all of these social structures and social practices are variously ensured or encouraged by the law and other state controls such as the benefits system and religious laws. The contract of employment between worker and employer ensures the practices of clocking in and collection of wage packets. The law can punish parents if their children do not attend school. The lack of state benefits or provision of childcare means that many women with children who might otherwise choose to work outside the home cannot afford to do so, and that some women who might prefer to stay at home with their children are forced to go out to work.

Discourses are intimately tied to the structures and practices that are lived out in society from day to day, and it is in the interest of relatively powerful groups that some discourses and not others receive the stamp of truth. If we accept that men, relative to women, are still in a more powerful position in society, then we can say that prevailing discourses of femininity serve to uphold this power inequality. Discourses such as 'education as a meritocracy' and career success as 'survival of the fittest' serve to justify the greater wealth and opportunity of the relatively powerful middle class by representing education and capitalism as unbiased, egalitarian institutions. Discourses representing education and capitalism as systems of social control and exploitation are less likely to enjoy widespread acceptance as common-sense truths.

However, there are two cautions to be sounded at this point. Firstly, we should beware of coming to the conclusion that prevailing discourses are ensured their dominant position for eternity, or that other competing discourses cannot complete a successful 'takeover bid'. For example, the twentieth century has seen a gradual emergence of alternative discourses of femininity, and more recently of masculinity, which are gaining more ground.

What can be said of women or men, or how they can be portrayed in stories, images and so on, is undergoing change and these changes go hand in hand with changes in the way society is organised. Paid work, and therefore a degree of financial independence, is available to more women than it was a century ago, and the traditional nuclear family is no longer the predominant household form. Secondly, discourses do not simply map on to particular political arrangements. The version of woman as nurturant, close to nature and empathic is also used by some feminists who wish to see the ascendancy of feminine ways of being, and attacks on the notion of madness are used simultaneously by the anti-psychiatry movement as well as those who wish to close down the mental hospitals and replace them with doubtful 'community care' for financial reasons.

Additionally, power is not a one-way street. A discourse may have complex power implications for those attempting to use it. For example, Wendy Hollway (1981, 1984) identifies what she calls the 'male sexual drive discourse'. This is a system of representations of male sexuality, ways of talking and thinking about it, which constitutes the prevailing, common-sense view. It constructs male sexuality as the manifestation of a powerful biological drive. Men therefore are seen as having a basic need for sex, which they cannot ignore, and which must be satisfied. It has been commonplace for men who rape to be treated sympathetically by the courts, in recognition of their assumed undeniable sexual requirements. The male sexual drive discourse can therefore be seen as a potential source of power for men, who may sexually assault women with some impunity or benefit from the controlling effect that the pervasive threat of rape has upon women generally. The male sexual drive discourse not only constructs male sexuality as driven by a biological imperative, but represents women as potential triggers, which can set it in motion. Accordingly, rape victims considered to have dressed provocatively have been seen as bringing on the attack. But this discourse itself thereby endows women with a certain measure of power. Women have the power to elicit men's desire, and are therefore a potential source of danger to men. A man whose sexual drive is awoken may feel himself to be on board a runaway train. His usual sense of self-control may frighteningly evaporate in the presence of an attractive woman, someone who has the power to trigger urgent desires and who also has the power to satisfy him or deny him satisfaction. It may still be the case that this particular discourse affords men relatively more power than women, but the example serves to demonstrate that power is never absolute.

It is important to note that Foucault certainly does not see the emergence and rise to prominence of particular discourses or knowledges as the result of intentional machinations by powerful groups. Powerful people do not, as it were, think up and then disseminate discourses that serve their purposes. Rather, the practical and social conditions of life are seen as providing a suitable culture for some representations rather than others, and the effects of these representations may not be immediately obvious or intended. Nevertheless, once a discourse becomes available culturally, it is then possible for it to be appropriated in the interests of the relatively powerful. Historically then, we can trace back the emergence of a discourse into a culture and try to uncover the social, physical and economic changes that provided the breeding ground for it, but we should be careful not to tie these into a causal relationship. Foucault cautioned against seeing certain social conditions as necessarily producing particular discourses. One could always look back and see how a particular discourse had emerged, but one could not look into the future and postulate that certain types of future society would be accompanied by any specific representations of human life. He was therefore opposed to the wholehearted recommendation of some discourses rather than others on the assumption that they would be more likely to bring about a better society. He saw the possibilities for the appropriation of discourses as being entirely unpredictable and their possible future effects as open ended. He refused to make any universal political or moral judgements, and this was in part because he saw that, historically, what looked like a change for the better has sometimes turned out to have undesirable consequences. His prime focus was therefore upon what he called the 'archaeology of knowledge', which entailed this tracing back to uncover the conditions which allowed a certain discourse or knowledge to emerge. His point was that if we can understand the origins of our current ways of understanding ourselves, we can begin to question their legitimacy and resist them. In doing this, he also aims to bring to the fore previously marginalised discourses, to give voice to those whose accounts of life cannot be heard within the prevailing knowledges – the voices of the mad, the delinquent, the abnormal, the disempowered. These marginalised voices and discourses are seen as important sources of resistance for us all in challenging the legitimacy of the prevailing knowledges through which we understand ourselves and our lives.

Summary

Discourses make it possible for us to see the world in a certain way. They produce our knowledge of the world. If we think of knowledge as one possible account of events, one that has received the stamp of truth, then to the extent that this version brings with it particular possibilities for acting in the world then it has power implications. For Foucault, then, knowledge and power always go together as a pair. Where there is knowledge, there is power. The two are so inseparable that they are often written as 'power/ knowledge' or referred to as the 'power/knowledge couple'. Foucault argues that in relatively recent history there has been a shift from 'sovereign power' to 'disciplinary power', in which the population is effectively controlled through our own self-monitoring processes. This form of power is so efficient because people enter into the process willingly. It is therefore based on the assumption that people don't recognise that they are being controlled, believing their self-monitoring and surveillance to be their own choice and for their own good. Psychology itself is implicated here, to the extent that it has provided various ways of assessing and categorising people which can then be used to create norms for what we consider to be a well-balanced, healthy personality.

Conceptualised in this way, power is not a property of any person or group, but is something that in theory anybody can exercise through discourse. This means that we should be wary of seeing power as residing in a particular group of people or institution such as the middle class, men or the state, as power resides everywhere. Foucault was therefore quite opposed to Marxism, which sees power as lying in the hands of capitalist employers. His point was that in making broad generalisations of this kind we tend to mask the vast array of differences between people and their situations and the many different kinds of power relations in which they are caught up. We risk leaving the varied, local power struggles between people unnoticed in our preoccupation with what he calls 'totalising discourses'. One of the implications of this is that some power at least is available for exercise by each and every one of us, and we can use this power in our struggle to change ourselves and our lives. In fact power and resistance always go together for Foucault. Prevailing discourses are always under implicit threat from alternatives, which can dislodge them from their position as truth. In fact you could say that if it weren't for this resistance there would be no need to constantly reaffirm their truthfulness. For example, if the notion that 'a woman's place is in the home' were really secure in its position as prevailing truth, there would be no need to keep asserting it. This opens up for people at least the possibility of change through resistance. Foucault recommends that in order to take advantage of the unstable nature of knowledge and power, we need to be made aware of how we came to see ourselves as we do, a process that he calls the 'archaeology of knowledge'.

In the last two chapters I have presented the social constructionist case for the importance of language in our experience of the world. But let us be clear about the radical nature of the social constructionist case. Social constructionism is not claiming that language and discourse merely have a strong influence upon our perception of reality. What we know as reality is itself a social construction. It is at this point that some people begin to doubt the social constructionist position. Both discursive psychology and Foucault's analysis of knowledge and power make the concept of 'truth' highly problematic. Truth becomes revealed not as some irrefutable state of affairs ultimately discoverable through the application of scientific method, but a fluid and unstable description of the world created through discourse. Reality, likewise, becomes unstable and multiple, dependent upon the historically and culturally situated perspective of the perceiver. The claim that 'nothing exists outside the text' often provokes the reaction that social constructionism is clearly fanciful. If I stub my toe on a stone it hurts, and this is so whether the word 'stone' exists or not. Surely social constructionists are not denying the existence of stones or any of the other things that make up the material world? And what about other, less material things such as oppression, wars and the Holocaust? Are these supposed to be just an effect of discourse? Didn't they really happen?

Such questions go right to the heart of current debates in social constructionism about the status of the real and the material world. In the next chapter I will therefore outline the nature of the issues that have fuelled this debate and indicate the extent to which I think the disagreements are capable of resolution.

Chapter 5

Is there a real world outside discourse?

The absence of an ultimate truth seems to be the foundation upon which the theoretical framework of social constructionism is built. Within this framework it is enormously difficult to say that some ideas or ways of thinking about the world are correct or true and others false. If we accept the possibility of many different realities constructed within different historical and cultural contexts, we have no way of asserting that one of these is the right one. There are no absolute, historically and culturally transcendent standards against which we can confidently judge local variations. This is the position of relativism; different constructions of the world can be judged only in relation to each other and not by comparison with some ultimate standard or truth. The consequence is that this relativism appears to undermine our attempts to morally ground our action, our choices and politics. How can we justify our political preferences if there is no way of asserting that some groups of people really are oppressed by others, or even that we can justifiably argue that people belong to certain 'groups' anyway? The groups and their oppression become just one way among many potential ways of constructing the world.

It is also difficult to conceptualise the relationship between discourse and reality. The claim that 'discourse is all there is' is a logical conclusion of the argument that language does not label discrete entities in the real world that exist independently of it. All that language can do, then, is to refer to itself. Language is a 'self-referent' system. This means that any sign (see Chapter 3) can only be defined in terms of other signs existing in the same language system. For example, if I was asked to define a 'tree', I could only do this by contrasting the concept 'tree' with other concepts, to demonstrate the category. I could say 'a tree is living rather than inanimate, but not sentient like an animal, and is different from a shrub in that it has one main stem.' But all I am doing here is referring to other signs (animate, sentient, shrub) which themselves can only be defined in terms of yet more signs from the same language system. There is no way out of this into the 'real' world that might exist beyond language. Whatever the nature of the 'real' world, we cannot assume that the words in our language refer to it or describe it.

Social constructionism seems to lead to the claim that nothing exists except as it exists in discourse, i.e. the only reality that things have is the reality they are given in the symbolic realm of language, that 'there is nothing outside of the text' (Derrida, 1976: 158). This appears to deny that there is any material base to our lives, and the things that have a tremendous effect upon us such as financial resources, living conditions, war, natural disasters or health are reduced to being simply the effects of language. Understandably, many people react to such assertions with disbelief and indignation. Surely suffering and death are real, and the physical objects that surround us are not figments of our imagination? Surely, these things would exist in the same way regardless of how we represent them in language?

These questions regarding truth and reality are problematic ones for social constructionists, and there is quite a lot of disagreement between different social constructionists in their views on such matters. In fact the debate has generated such heat it was given a focus in a special edition of the journal *Theory and Psychology*, 11(3) in 2001. In addition, the positions of relativism and realism cannot be identified in any simple way with the different forms of social constructionism outlined in earlier chapters. In this chapter I will try to tease out some of the theoretical issues that might help us to understand the nature of the claims that are being made by social constructionists and the disagreements between them.

Social constructionism is not the only body of theory to find the concepts of reality and truth problematic. When social construc-tionists talk of the way in which discourses can be employed to keep people willingly in a condition of oppression by obscuring power relations, they have sometimes drawn upon the sociological notion of ideology. Ideology, too, has raised questions about truth and reality, and since it may also help to illuminate the issue of the relationship between discourse and power, addressed in Chapter 4, some discussion of it is warranted here. I will talk about four ways of thinking about ideology, noting the issues that each of these raise for social constructionism, before going on to examine the issues of truth and reality specifically within social constructionism.

Discourse and ideology

Ideology as false consciousness

The basic assumption underlying this classic Marxist view is that there is a real, material state of affairs, which is that employers exploit their employees, but that people do not recognise and challenge this reality because it is obscured by widely accepted ideas and beliefs. People are therefore said to be living in 'false consciousness' because their understanding of their position is distorted. The ideology serves to mask the contradiction in society between the exploitative economic relationship and the need for some kind of minimum consent from those who are disadvantaged.

For social constructionists, this version of ideology enables us to take a critical stance to the discourses and narratives prevalent in society and ask what effects they are bringing about, but it also brings with it some difficult problems. In the example I used earlier, a woman's love for her husband and family and her desire to care for them are real and cannot be reduced to illusions or misconceptions. A big problem for Marxist ideology is the image of the person that it necessarily imports; human beings become potentially irrational creatures committed to a way of life which is not in their best interest. How is it possible for people to be self-deceived in this way, and what kind of psychology must we adopt in order to understand this self-deception? It is this problem that has led to the popularity of psychoanalytic theory among Marxists. Psychoanalysis can accommodate false consciousness because it says that the real reasons for people's actions and choices often lie in the unconscious and are not readily available for rational examination. Social constructionism has the same problem; if discourses mask an underlying reality of which people are kept ignorant, what kind of status do individuals' accounts of their feelings, motivations and desires have? This question of how and why discourses come to be 'lived out' in the consciousness of us all from day to day has not really been adequately answered. In Chapter 6 I will outline the questions about psychology and subjectivity that need answering, and look at some of the approaches that have emerged.

The idea of 'false consciousness' also brings essentialism with it. Clegg (1989), drawing on Laclau (1983), says that the category of false consciousness is tenable only if the person has a fixed, true identity which they are capable of recognising. Clegg goes on to show the implications that this has for the concept of ideology. Rather than ideology being the misrecognition of the person's true interests and true identity, it becomes instead the non-recognition or denial of the person as decentred, fragmentary and unstable. This means that all forms of talk, representation and social practice which insist that human beings have a particular nature which is somehow inevitable or natural, for example individuality, sexuality, personality and so on, are ideological.

Secondly, the 'false consciousness' notion of ideology raises the issues of reality, truth and relativism. If we say that people are living in a false consciousness, we are assuming that there is a reality, in which they are oppressed, which lies outside of their understanding of the world, i.e. it is a version of events that is more valid or truthful. This at least involves a value-laden assessment of what is truly in a person's interests, and raises questions about who has the right to make such judgements. But the idea that there is one version of events that is true, rendering all others false, is also in direct opposition to the central idea of social constructionism, i.e. that there exists no truth but only numerous constructions of the world, and that which becomes regarded as truth depends upon culturally and historically specific factors. This view is certainly that espoused by Foucault, who insisted that the term ideology assumes that there is a truth, and that we should instead speak of 'regimes of truth', where one regime is no more correct than another. Given that an explicit aim of the social constructionist is to deconstruct the discourses which uphold inequitous power relations and to demonstrate the way in which they obscure these, it is difficult to see how it is possible to do this without falling back upon some notion of reality or truth that the discourses are supposed to obscure. A further problem such relativism poses regards the status of social constructionist accounts themselves. If all accounts, including scientific and other theories, are equally valid, how can social constructionist accounts justifiably have any special claim to truth? The relativism inherent in social constructionism appears to put its very own premises in doubt.

Ideology as knowledge in the service of power

A more useful way of thinking about ideology, for the social constructionist, is to see it as knowledge deployed in the service of power. This view detaches ideology from questions of truth and falsity. A version of events, or a way of representing a state of affairs, may be true or false, but it is only ideological to the extent that it is used by relatively powerful groups in society to sustain their position. Thus ideas in themselves cannot be said to be ideological, only the uses to which they are put. The study of ideology is therefore the study of the ways in which meaning is mobilised in the social world in the interests of powerful groups (Thompson, 1990). This view allows us to say that discourses may be used ideologically. The discourses themselves can therefore be said to be neither oppressive nor liberating, and this is a point which Foucault was at pains to make clear. Foucault held that just about any discourse could theoretically be used towards good or bad ends, and that there was no way of predicting the final outcome of the struggles in which they may be deployed. Every discourse is potentially dangerous. Bury (1986) gives a good example. Attacks on the medical profession's power to define illness and allocate resources have, in Britain, begun to look rather different. The New Right of the 1980s and 1990s attacked medical autonomy as part of a more general argument for individualism and choice in a view of the health services as consumer goods. The irony is that those radicals calling for alternative medicine find themselves arguing for the very same values, consumer choice and free market competition, which underpin contemporary capitalist society.

Ideology as lived experience

The third view of ideology, which also has something to offer social constructionism, helps us to go beyond the assumption, implicit in the previous two accounts, that ideology is concerned only with what people *think*. The French philosopher Althusser was concerned to stress that ideology is 'lived experience'. Ideology is present therefore in not only what we think, but what we think about, what we feel, how we behave, and the pattern of all our social relationships. Althusser uses the term 'ideological state apparatuses' to refer to the mechanisms by which people are manipulated and controlled by ideology. Schools, the church, the media, the family and so on are all regarded as ideological state apparatuses, and the ideas and ways of thinking that these apparatuses entail cannot be separated from their practices. For example, the ideas of sin, humility, obedience to a higher authority and so on cannot be separated from the practices of going to confession, prayer and kneeling before the altar. Even the structure of the church building itself, which may have, say, a spire 'pointing' to heaven is part of this ideology. So for Althusser, ideologies have a material nature. They comprise a package of material things, practices and ideas that are woven into each other. Thus ideas and representations are never solely ideal (existing only in the realm of thought). An ideology always exists in an apparatus and its practices.

This view has a tendency to see ideology as existing everywhere, which to some extent deprives it of its analytical cutting edge; if everything is ideological, the concept doesn't have much analytical power. Nevertheless, Althusser is surely right to widen the scope of the concept to the ways in which ideology pervades everyday life. If, say, British nationality is an ideological matter it must be reasonable to look at the way we represent Britishness in phenomena as disparate as chocolate boxes with Constable's *Haywain* on the front, Jubilee mugs, the last night of the Proms and the World Cup. We can therefore think of the ideological workings of discourses as located not only in our language, but also in the social practices in which we engage as a society. This view of ideology therefore mirrors the concept of discourse as incorporating not only representations in language but also social practices and social and institutional organisation.

Ideology as dilemmatic

Billig et al. (1988) hold that our thought, its content and processes, is provided by wider, socially shared concepts and issues. The concepts, values and beliefs of the society into which we are born shape what we will think about, but they also shape what we see as the two sides of an argument or issue. For example, in our society we might wonder whether traditional or progressive education is better for children, or whether we should blame the poor or the state for poverty. According to Billig et al., thinking itself is characterised by this 'dilemmatic' nature, i.e. it takes the form of a dilemma, a two-sided question to which there is no easy answer. Whatever we are thinking about, it is always, either explicitly or implicitly, part of a two-sided, or many-sided, debate taking place in our thoughts. We therefore think in terms of dilemmas, and what Billig et al. call 'ideological dilemmas' simply refers to thinking which is shaped by prevailing ideologies in our society. For example, the ideology of 'the individual' has pervaded our mental life, and in our thinking it is manifested in terms of dilemmas such as whether we should give priority to the freedom of the individual or to the overall good of society. Billig et al. see ideologies, like all other ideas, as being themselves inherently dilemmatic. Ideologies cannot therefore be thought of as coherent, unified systems of ideas, but always consist of a dilemmatic opposition. So that the ideology of the individual already contains within it its opposite, i.e. collectivism.

There are important implications of this idea for social constructionism. It suggests that, although the content of our thoughts is provided by wider social concepts and values, we do not simply absorb them uncomplicatedly and live them out in our lives. First of all, ideologies are not coherent, unified systems anyway, but always at least two-sided and as such do not present a story that can be lived out in this way. And second, the nature of human beings is such that our very thinking processes involve us in debate, argument, weighing up pros and cons and so on. In this account, human beings are not like sponges, soaking up ideas from their social environment, but are rhetoricians, arguers, people who are constantly engaged in exploring the contrary implications of ideas. The person here is an active thinker, someone capable of exercising choice and making decisions about the strengths and weaknesses of values and ideas.

Taking the useful aspects of all of these views of ideology, then, we can think of discourses as systems of meaning, ways of representing ourselves and our social world, which constitute not only what we think and say, but what we feel and desire and what we do. Discourses can be seen as having the potential to be deployed ideologically, that is in the service of power and in the interests of the relatively powerful groups in society. Science itself, and of course the social sciences such as psychology, has been analysed as an ideology which is constructed through various rhetorical devices and linguistic practices (Billig, 1990; Kitzinger, 1990; Potter, 1996a) and which is used in the services of relatively powerful groups in society. The scientific concepts of race and intelligence are good examples. But at the same time there may be room for the person to exercise some degree of choice in the discourses they take up and use, and in later chapters I will return to the issues of agency and choice. But the questions about reality and truth that are thrown up by this brief discussion of ideology are problematic ones for social constructionism, and I will spend the rest of this chapter outlining these difficulties and examining their implications.

Discourse, truth and reality

The debates between social constructionists concerning the status of reality and truth are sometimes grouped together under the generic title of the 'realism–relativism debate'. This may give the impression that there are two sharply divided camps, each characterised by a single and coherent argument. In fact there are many subtle variations and overlaps in the arguments, so that it is more accurate to talk of various 'relativisms' and 'realisms'. Furthermore, as we shall see, the picture is muddied further by the fact that most realists acknowledge the power of language to construct the world in some respects, and most relativists do not deny the possibility of a real world existing independently of our talk about it. The heat generated by the debates comes from the concern, on both sides, with how one is able to take up a moral or political position, which can inform one's action. I shall discuss a number of positions that may be regarded as relativist and realist and then consider further analyses from writers who have tried to find a way out of the impasse by transcending or reframing the debates.

Relativisms

It is those who espouse some form of relativism who are likely to be accredited, rightly or wrongly in their own view, with Derrida's claim that 'there is nothing outside of the text' (Derrida, 1976: 158). If 'discourses form the objects of which they speak' (Foucault, 1972: 49), then language creates all the objects of our consciousness, whether these are material, physical things like buildings, trees and computers or more abstract things like intelligence, friendship and happiness. In her concise and very accessible book, *Discourse*, Mills (1997) notes that 'There has been a great deal of rather pointless debate about whether Foucault is in fact denying the existence of the real when he stresses the formative powers of discourse' (p. 50), and that Foucault drew fire from historians in particular for seeming to deny the reality of historical events. But Mills points out that this is a misunderstanding of Foucault's aim, which was to draw attention to the way that discourse brings some aspects of our world into view as objects for us and hides other aspects from us. She characterises Foucault's position here as similar to that of Laclau and Mouffe (1985):

> The fact that every object is constituted as an object of discourse has nothing to do with whether there is a world external to thought, or with the realism/idealism opposition. An earthquake or the falling of a brick is an event that certainly exists, in the sense that it occurs here and now, independently of my will. But whether their specificity as objects is constructed in terms of 'natural phenomena' or 'expressions of the wrath of God', depends upon the structuring of a discursive field. What is denied is not that such objects exist externally to thought, but the rather different assertion that they could constitute themselves as objects outside any discursive condition of emergence.
>
> (Laclau and Mouffe, 1985: 108, cited in Mills, 1997: 50)

Foucault, Mills argues, therefore does not deny the existence of a reality beyond discourse, but that discourse 'causes a narrowing of one's field of vision, to exclude a wide range of phenomena from being considered as real or as worthy of attention, or as even existing' (Mills, 1997: 51). She gives a good illustrative example of the way that the world does not come ready-made in categories of events and types of object, but that order is imposed on the world through our linguistic description of it. It is a lengthy example, but worth quoting in its entirety:

> An example of this constitution of objects through discourse is the changes in the way the borderline between animals and plants has been drawn differently at different historical periods. In the nineteenth century, bacteria were placed within the category 'animal', whereas now they are located in a separate categorisation of their own. Several organisms have been switched from one category to another, for example, algae, diatoms and other micro-organisms. In fact, the

categories 'plant' and 'animal' are constantly being redefined by which living things are placed in each categorisation – a *post hoc* categorisation system which is discursive rather than one which is determined by the 'real' nature of plants and animals. Plants and animals, in fact, share many elements, but the fact that we separate them into two groupings means that we concentrate on the differences we perceive between these two categories rather than on their shared features. The fact that the boundary has shifted shows clearly that there is no natural ready-made boundary between animal and plant life, but that humans have thought it necessary to draw this boundary. It might be more useful for the differences between animals and plant[s] to be thought of on a cline or continuum, but within current systems of thinking about this subject it is considered necessary to classify plant and animal life as separate. This could be related to the fact that we have moved away from the nineteenth-century polymath ability to undertake multi-disciplinary work; instead, at present, botany and zoology are seen as two separate sciences with separate departments in universities and as separate disciplines with different methodologies and spheres of interest.

(Mills, 1997: 53. Italics in original)

I would agree with Mills in her assessment of Foucault's position. He does not deny the materiality of events, but says that our only way of apprehending reality is through discourse, which determines our perceptions of reality. In a sense, Foucault brackets off the question of reality. Since we can never have direct access to a reality beyond discourse we cannot concern ourselves with its nature.

Discursive psychologists have also bracketed reality for similar reasons. If language is a self-referent system of signs, as discussed in Chapter 3, then when we think about and talk about the world we can never break out of this system into the 'real' world outside of discourse. Like Foucault, discursive psychologists have sometimes been criticised for seeming to deny the existence of a reality beyond the text, and like Foucault they have drawn fire from those who find such a claim preposterous. Surely death is inescapable regardless of anything we might say or do? Surely the physical things in our world, like tables and chairs, exist independently of our thoughts and talk about them? We bang on the very table before us in order to demonstrate the point. Such arguments led to the publication of a now classic paper entitled 'Death and furniture: The rhetoric, politics and theology of bottom line arguments against relativism' (Edwards et al., 1995). In this paper the authors claim that such arguments, including the table-thumping that often accompanies them, are themselves rhetorical constructions used to build particular accounts of the world:

> The realist thumps the table. What a loud noise! Much louder than talk! Much more gritty. Much more real. And yet we insist that this noise, being produced in *this* place, at *this* time, in the course of *this* argument, *is* an argument, *is* talk. As an argument, it takes the form of a demonstration: '*This* (bang!) is real. *This* (bang!) is no mere social construction. Talk cannot change *that* it is or *what* it is. See how its reality constrains my hand (bang!), forcing it to stop in its tracks. Hear the inevitable result (bang!) of the collision of two solid physical objects. Need I say more?
>
> (Edwards et al., 1995. Italics in original)

Edwards et al.'s insistence upon the rhetorical nature of such demonstrations should not be regarded as an amusingly clever attempt to side-step the question of reality. Like Foucault, discursive psychologists are not denying the existence of a material world or that this materiality may have unavoidable consequences for people. But they are pointing out that, once we begin to *talk* about or otherwise signify or represent the material world then we have entered the realm of discourse; and at that moment we have engaged in social construction. What makes something a table, or a rock or anything else that might be appealed to for its materiality, is not a natural essence but the social and cultural world:

> But then, rocks are cultural too, in that they are thus categorized, included in the definition of the natural world, classified into sedimentary and igneous, divided into grains of sand, pieces of gravel, pebbles, stones, rocks, boulders, mountains, domesticated in parks and ornamental gardens, protected in wildernesses, cut, bought, used and displayed as 'precious stones', and include as a sub-category 'girls' best friends'; not to mention coolant for vodka!
>
> (Edwards et al., 1995)

The example provided earlier by Mills (1997) is in a similar vein. The point is that what signifies as a 'rock' or a 'table', and what features of it make it count as a member of such a category, depends upon local and context-bound human purposes. The material world certainly exists, but it is not simply reflected in our talk or other forms of signification.

Edley (2001), drawing on Edwards (1997), has tried to illuminate the debate by proposing that there exist two senses in which the term social constructionism is used: ontological and epistemic. Ontology is the study of being and existence in the world. It is the attempt to discover the fundamental categories of what exists in the world. Epistemology is the study of the nature of knowledge and how we come to know the world of things. The epistemic sense of social constructionism rests on the notion that 'as soon as we begin to think or talk about the world, we also necessarily begin to represent . . . Talk involves the creation or construction of particular accounts of what the world is like' (p. 437). This is essentially the argument put forward by Edwards et al. (1995). But when social constructionists who take this position say that 'there is nothing outside the text' they are not, says Edley, making an ontological claim, that is a claim about the nature or existence of a world beyond discourse. When used ontologically, the term social constructionism refers to the way that real phenomena, our perceptions and experiences, are brought into existence and take the particular form that they do because of the language that we share. This does not make these phenomena or things unreal, fictitious or illusory; they are no less real for being the products of social construction. Edley concludes:

> Contrary to the view of some critical realists, most social constructionists do not see language as the only reality. When they travel to conferences or go on holiday, for example, they consult their map books just like everyone else. They do not suppose that, say, Nottingham appears in the middle of the M1 motorway because it says so on the page and neither do they imagine that it somehow springs into existence at the moment it is mentioned. The way that constructionism upsets our common-sense understandings is much more subtle than this. Instead, a constructionist might point out that Nottingham is a city by virtue of a text (i.e. by royal decree) and that its boundaries – where it begins and ends – are also a matter

for negotiation and agreement. The argument is not, therefore, that Nottingham doesn't really exist, but that it does so as a socially constructed reality.

(Edley, 2001: 439)

Kenneth Gergen is often the social constructionist writer most identified with the position of relativism due to his assertion that linguistic descriptions of things and of mental events are divorced from the world of material reality (e.g. Gergen, 1989). If we cannot judge the accuracy or validity of our descriptions of the world by an appeal to reality, then we should celebrate rather than mourn the limitless multiplicity of possible perspectives to which this gives us access. However, he too claims that his relativism has been persistently misunderstood (Gergen, 2001a). Like the discursive psychologists, he refutes the accusation that he denies the existence of a reality beyond discourse. He also allows that language can be used to refer to reality for practical purposes. This seems to echo the philosophical tradition of pragmatism, in that the truthfulness of theories and accounts is of less interest than their usefulness in the business of dealing with the world of events; our descriptions of the world are true only in the sense that, for the moment, they successfully enable us to go about our business in the world. Hruby (2001) explicitly takes this view, arguing that the value of our theories and models is not based on how truly they reflect reality, but how useful they are in allowing us to make predictions about phenomena.

But Gergen is emphatic that our talk about the world is in no way constrained by the latter's material properties. He suggests (Gergen, 1998, 2001b) we regard realism and constructionism as two different forms of discourse, which any of us can use in appropriate circumstances. As such, we should not be pitting them against each other, but instead setting value upon the very process of argumentation. The continual possibility of debate and argumentation is, for Gergen, the ultimate value of a relativist position. This comes to the fore in the issue of morality and political action, and this is the position also adopted by Edwards et al. (1995):

There is no contradiction between being a relativist and being somebody, a member of a particular culture, having commitments, beliefs and a common-sense notion of reality. These are the very things to be argued for, questioned, defended, decided, without the comfort of just being, already and before thought, real and true. The idea that letting go of realism entails that all these commitments must fall is no more convincing than the idea that life without God is devoid of meaning and value . . . the death of God has not made the rest of the world disappear, but has left it for us to make. What we are left with is not a world devoid of meaning and value . . . but precisely the reverse. It is a foregrounding of meanings and values, to be argued, altered defended, and invented.

(Edwards et al., 1995)

So, if we understand knowledge, reality and truth as human constructions, we have even more responsibility to think, argue and make up our minds about our own views and then defend them. Potter (1998) is emphatic that the criticism levelled at relativism is that it leads to a position of 'anything goes' is quite unfounded. People, he argues, whether they are relativists or not, are often emphatic about 'what goes' for them. Gergen (1999) says '. . . while constructionist arguments do invite moral and political deliberation, they do not champion one ideal over another . . . Constructionism may invite a posture of continuing reflection, but each moment of reflection will inevitably be value-saturated' (p. 231) and 'The major challenge, then, is not the existence of values, but how we are to manage in a world of pandemic value conflict . . . The existence of the single voice is simultaneously the end of conversation, dialogue, negotiation' (p. 233). Gergen argues that the constructionist focus on multiple realities leads to practices that invite interchange and mutual understanding.

In the context of therapy and counselling, the liberatory possibilities entailed in simply exploring the implications of the diversity of discourses to which a person is subject has also been noted. Davies (1998) contests the claim that deconstruction cannot lead to empowerment and action. She describes an example from her own practice in which a woman was enabled to make important decisions about the welfare of her child by being shown how the discourses positioning her could, to various degrees, be seen as 'optional' and resistible. And Burr and Butt (2000) argue that our 'vocabulary of self' can be challenged and changed by exploring and elaborating non-dominant discourses.

Realisms

First of all, it is probably safe to say that no one who counts themselves as any kind of social constructionist would espouse the position of what is termed naïve realism. Naïve realism is 'an unquestioning faith in the reality of what we perceive' (Wetherell and Still, 1998: 99). Those social constructionists who call themselves realists take the view that, to a greater or lesser degree, our perceptions can only ever approximate to reality. Social constructionists who disagree with at least some of the assumptions of a relativist position are more likely to refer to themselves as 'critical realists'.

Hruby (2001) describes the critical realist position succinctly. It is the belief that 'there is a coherent and dependably consistent reality that is the basis for our sensations, even if our sensations do not resemble the causative phenomenal bases, or "onta" that prompt them, or demonstrate the same presumed cohesion or consistency' (p. 57). So that, although our perceptions and sensations do not mirror reality, and although they are often volatile and changeable, nevertheless they do reference the real world in some way; they are not independent of it, produced entirely through our symbolic systems such as language.

Liebrucks (2001) adopts a position that maintains a transcendent reality while allowing for different perspectives on that reality. He argues that, in order for there to be discrepancies in the accounts of an object or phenomenon offered by different people occupying different cultural and historical positions, we must presuppose that these people are in fact looking at the same thing: 'after all, their descriptions could not seem discrepant were they not supposed to be descriptions of the same matter.' Liebrucks thus argues that the world is not socially constituted at a different place depending upon time and place, but that each of us sees different aspects of the same world; we each look at it from a different perspective. Liebrucks therefore wants to maintain a realist position while accepting a plurality of perspectives. Nevertheless, he makes a distinction between the 'things' of the material world, that are subject to the laws of natural science regardless of our talk about them, and the 'things' that form the subject matter of psychology. While he sees the material world as having a nature independent of human thought and language, psychological entities are indeed socially constructed and relative to time and place; and it is of course these psychological entities, such as mental illness and gender differences, that most social constructionists have been at pains to deconstruct.

Willig (1999a) begins by acknowledging the benefits of social constructionism but considers that these benefits are not enough. She welcomes social constructionism's challenge to the apparent reality and inevitability of psychology's objects of study, such as intelligence and mental illness. Since positivistic science represents such objects as having an existence independent of human values and practices, they have been able to be used to oppress and marginalise certain people. Willig agrees that the value of social constructionism is that it is able to deconstruct such objects and to show how they could always have been constructed differently. However, she goes on: 'I would argue that what is needed is an account that not only suggests that things could be different but is capable of explaining why things are as they are and in what ways they could be better' (p. 38). She is arguing for a social constructionism that, in addition to challenging our assumptions about the world, can also function as social critique. Critical realism, she says, maintains that the things we observe and experience are 'generated by underlying, relatively enduring structures, such as biochemical, economic or social structures' (p. 45). Drawing on Parker (1992), she argues that the existence of these structures and the events that they produce means that some ways of making sense of them, some constructions, are more likely than others. They do not determine our constructions, but 'afford' some constructions more readily than others. Parker (1992, 1998a) argues for an epistemological relativism. This is the view that the knowledge we have about the world, our ideas about it, are constructed; and for Parker, this construction is socially achieved through discourse. But he combines this with an ontological realism (ontology is the study of what exists), arguing that our social constructions are nevertheless based on reality as it is actually structured.

Parker suggests that we should extend the category of 'ontological status' to include all the aspects of our physical and social environment that structure our action. We are born into societies in which life is lived out in a certain kind of physical space, such as houses, offices, schools and factories, which are physically and socially organised in ways that impose constraints on what it is possible to do and say:

In a capitalist economy, for example, industrial workers are physically located for much of the time together with others, and certain types of collective action make sense. In patriarchal societies in the West, women are physically located in homes for much of the time and certain types of collective action do not make sense. In a world organised by structures of imperialism, victims outside and inside the industrial centres can only act, accept or resist, in particular ways.

(Parker, 1992: 36)

This means that if the character of daily life for men is such that they spend much of their time in close physical proximity and are located in the workplace alongside other 'workers' in different accommodation to 'managers', representations and accounts which focus upon 'fraternity' and 'solidarity' may well emerge. These accounts go hand in hand with the action which such arrangements also make possible, such as joining a trade union and going on strike. For women, whose daily lives typically isolate them from each other, or at least do not provide many opportunities for women to come together in large numbers, such accounts and action are unlikely, and some feminists have suggested that the lack of a focus for organising (in the same sense as the trade unions) makes it difficult for women to take collective action to improve their position in the world.

Thus, for Parker, there is a reality that exists outside of discourse, and this reality provides the raw material from which we may structure our understanding of the world, through discourse. This reality consists not only of the physical properties of our bodies and the possibilities and constraints of that bodily life, but also the properties and organisation of the physical and social environment in which we live. While reality does not determine knowledge, it lays down important restrictions on the variety of ways open to us to construct the world.

Collier (1998) takes perhaps the most extreme stance within the position of critical realism, since he rejects even the milder pragmatist view that truth and reality can be defined in terms of what models of the world currently 'work' for us. He is emphatic that both our subjective experience and our use of language are grounded in independently existing properties of the real world. Collier focuses upon 'practice', our practical, often physical, engagement with the world around us. He argues that, while it may be possible for our use of language to become distanced from the real world and its nature, so that language can misrepresent the world, this can never be the case for our practice. Our practical engagement with the world will always, sometimes brutally, remind us of its nature. He is critical not only of idealism, the philosophical position that claims that only minds and their ideas exist, but also those who lean toward a pragmatist understanding, arguing that pragmatism is just a way of conserving our comfortable beliefs in the way the world appears to us rather than challenging our own assumptions. It allows us to invest in our own particular view of the world, because it works for us, regardless of the problems such a view might throw up for other people, those who might be oppressed or marginalised by our view. Collier claims that non-realism (relativism or pragmatism) is a licence for dogmatism. If there is no truth, then no one can be wrong – we can all be smugly confident in our own belief: 'There are open practices which let reality hit them in the face, and transform themselves in the light of it; and there are closed practices which project their own conception of reality and won't see it questioned. Pragmatism is the philosophical normalization of closed practices; realism is the philosophical normalization of open practices' (pp. 51–2). Collier argues that political beliefs, and consequent action, must start with our convictions about the nature of the material and social world. Our practice will lead us to an appreciation of the structures underlying social phenomena, and for Collier the important structure is capitalism. We will come to see the reality of this structure simply because any attempts to act as if capitalism were not a major force in determining the shape of people's lives will be brutally disconfirmed.

There appears, then, to be something of a stalemate in the debate over morality and politics between advocates of relativist and realist positions, with the various positions suffering from different weaknesses. Burkitt (1999) criticises the polarising of micro and macro forms of constructionism such that 'a world of conversation and discursive dialogue is posited against a material world that might, or might not, be "out there"' (p. 76). His particular concern is the understanding of power: either power is seen as nothing more than an effect of discourse during social interactions, or it takes the form of social and institutional practices that do not depend upon discourses for their existence, although they are intimately related to them. He argues that both micro and macro constructionism, on their own, offer inadequate understandings of power. Burkitt (1999) sees macro constructionism as inadequate in that it does not acknowledge the role of the person in authoring their own history and therefore cannot really understand how people can escape the determining effects of discourse. On the other hand, micro constructionism either does not consider power at all or sees it as located only in the strategies used by people in interaction to represent themselves in advantageous ways. The latter does not acknowledge the ways that such representations inevitably derive their leverage from inequalities and patterns of domination in wider society. For example, claims that one is 'normal' and that another is 'perverted' depend for their effectiveness, in any interaction, upon wider inequalities between people of different sexual orientations. Willig (2001) sums up the impasse succinctly:

> Critical realists have accused relativists of being unable to take up a moral or political position in relation to anything at all. It is argued that if everything is discursively constructed, then we have no grounds for adjudicating between different views. As a result, all views are equally valid and 'anything goes'. Relativists, in turn, have pointed out that realists' commitment to 'bottom line' arguments means that certain truth claims are ruled out of bounds and cannot be challenged. A principled questioning of all truth claims is, therefore, not possible within a realist framework. It is this, however, relativists argue, which is required to promote a genuine spirit of enquiry.
>
> (Willig, 2001: 124)

There appears to be no obvious way out of this impasse, at least within the terms of the debate as they have been drawn up. However, there have been attempts to conceptualise the problem in terms that may allow some forward movement, although it is probably too early to judge the success of these.

Reframing the debate

For the present purposes, I will group alternative conceptualisations into two categories: those advocating some form of synthesis of realist and relativist proposals, and those suggesting that the opposition 'reality vs construction' is a false one, although there is no reason to suppose that these approaches are incompatible.

Willig (1999a) talks of social and physical arrangements providing the conditions of possibility for the emergence of discourses, but without determining them. 'Conditions of life, as experienced by the individual through discourses, provide reasons for the individual's actions. It follows that from a non-relativist social constructionist point of view, meanings are afforded by discourses, accommodated by social structures and changed by human actors' (p. 44). Willig therefore tries to maintain the equal importance of social structure, discourses and individual action. Nevertheless, she begins with 'social and physical arrangements', which would appear to privilege the material world and to cast discourse and its effects as secondary phenomena of these.

In similar vein, Nightingale and Cromby (2002) argue that social constructionism need in no way be threatened by a critical realist belief in a world that exists independent of our representations of it. Like Liebrucks (2001), they argue that objects must have differential properties, to which language must, in some way, refer, although language may only be able to partially and imperfectly capture the nature of the real world. They argue for the 'co-constitution' of personal experience by both the nature of material reality and the constructive force of language. This is a position that appears to privilege neither structural conditions, as in Collier's view, nor language, as in Gergen's. In a dialectical fashion, material conditions generate, but do not determine, social constructions which in their turn ground actions and decisions which then have real consequences. So that although material conditions provide the ground in which discourses may take root, once constructed those discourses channel action which itself then transforms the nature of the real world.

Burkitt (1999), although he does not refer to himself as a critical realist, also argues for some appreciation of a material reality existing beyond discourse and he transforms the realism/relativism debate by considering social constructionism as a material, as well as a linguistic, practice. He takes issue with the argument that the 'expressive order' of language, social conventions and moral rules can be uncoupled from the 'practical order' of the material world (Harré, 1993). Burkitt argues for a social constructionism that recognises both the material and the discursive, both agency and social constraints. He says that it is not discourse alone that constructs the world. People create artefacts, which then transform our reality, from telescopes to prosthetic devices. 'Reality' is therefore not a constant, but an ever-changing realm that is both discursively and practically constructed by people. Furthermore, material and social conditions place limitations on the constructions or accounts of events that can be built. Burkitt therefore manages to disrupt the tendency to place social construction and materiality in opposition, since the act of social construction may take place through material means (the production of artefacts).

He also allows room for the person to have an active role in change through the part they play in producing artefacts and thus 'transforming the real', and in then taking advantage of opportunities to create new constructions based upon this transformed reality.

I have elsewhere argued (Burr, 1998) that one of the reasons why constructionists have become caught up in these arguments is that there is some confusion and misunderstanding about the different senses in which the term 'reality' is being used. For example, Gergen (1998) appears to use the terms 'realism' and 'constructionism' as opposites. But the debates surrounding realism and relativism suggest that the term 'reality' can imply different contrast poles, with quite different implications. I identified three contrasts to the term 'reality': (1) reality (as truth) versus falsehood; (2) reality (as materiality) versus illusion; and (3) reality (as essence) versus construction. The reality–construction dimension sometimes gets mapped on to the other two, so that:

> . . . constructionism is taken as also implying illusion and/or falsehood. There is therefore a tendency to talk of things being either real or 'merely constructed'. The constructed world thus construed is somehow less tangible, less trustworthy. It is a sham. I think that this is what is in part what is going on in the table-banging disputes described by Potter. Critics of constructionism here appear to be contesting the idea that the world is a figment of our imaginations and has no materiality (dimension 2), which was never constructionism's claim.
>
> (Burr, 1998: 23)

Summary

In terms of micro and macro social constructionism, deconstructionist versus discursive, it seems safe to say that discursive psychology takes a relativist stance, and that deconstructionist (Foucauldian) social constructionism, while relativist in its

theoretical foundation, has provided an acceptable social constructionist starting position for those who lean towards a more critical
realist analysis. The latter are more likely to make use of the
concept of ideology in their analyses, while discursive psychologists
are less likely to focus on questions about power and inequality in
their research, being more concerned with the micro-processes of
the manufacture of accounts in interaction.

Those adopting a relativist position do not deny the existence of
a material reality but question the possibility that we can directly
know it and certainly find problematic the idea that reality is
somehow reflected in our talk and other symbolic systems. Critical
realists give more credence to this idea, but differ in the specific
ways they conceptualise the relationship between reality, knowledge and language. For critical realists there is a structural reality
to the world, usually described in terms of power relations, which
in some way underpins, generates or 'affords' our ways of understanding and talking about it. To over-simplify the positions for
the moment, the relativist view tends toward a 'bottom up'
approach, which sees language as generating the reality that we
know. The realist position tends toward a 'top down' view which
sees reality producing our knowledge and descriptions of the
world. The heat in the debate between realism and relativism has
largely been generated by concern over morality and politics.
However, both relativism and realism can provide a defensible case
for adopting and arguing for a moral and political viewpoint.
Equally, they can both be shown to be vulnerable to attack in this
respect.

It seems unlikely that further progress on the nature of the
relationship between reality, knowledge and language, and the
implications of this for morality and politics, will be made within
the terms of the debate as it has been typically framed. For this
reason I am inclined to welcome the appearance of analyses which
attempt to transcend the terms of the debate. Michael (1999),
drawing on Rose (1993), has suggested that setting up the debate as
a contest between two irreconcilable opposites – an 'either/or'
opposition – is a typical, but often unhelpful, form of analysis in
patriarchal societies. But this dualistic thinking is not limited to the
realism/relativism debate. We meet it in various guises, for example
mind/body and individual/society. In each case, a debate is generated which invites us to decide which of the two terms should be
privileged. Part of the difficulty of resolving the realism/relativism

debate lies in the fact that it tends to bring the individual/society dualism with it. Do individuals have the agency to construct the world through their discourse, or are we all the products of social structures beyond our control? For the psychologist, these debates throw up some important questions. How should we now understand what it means to be a person? Are our personal experience and our identity in our own hands or are we entirely products of discourse? Do we use discourse or does it use us? If we are discourse users, what kind of psychology do we need to understand what this means? If we are simply products of discourses arising out of social structures is psychology redundant? Is our bodily existence part of a material reality that 'grounds' our accounts of our experience, or is that too a social construction?

In the next chapter, I will address this problem of the psychological subject. Social constructionism takes us so far from psychology's traditional understanding of what constitutes a person that we must begin to rebuild ourselves according to a different model, and the first step in doing this is to work out the implications that the various forms of social constructionism have for us as persons.*

---

* I am indebted to Dallas Cliff for material used in this chapter.

Chapter 6

Discourse and subjectivity

As we have seen, social constructionism makes us radically question many of the assumptions underlying traditional psychology. It claims that the knowledge that psychologists have produced about people must be regarded as historically and culturally contingent; there is no human nature that transcends time and place. Whatever it is that we have become, this is socially constructed and not part of some essential nature. And language, rather than simply being the way we talk about and describe ourselves and the world, is one of the most important sites of this construction process. It is now time to address the question of what kind of person we must now envisage as the subject of social constructionism. It is clear that the model of the person that is at the centre of traditional psychology just will not do. But what, within social constructionism, might it mean to be a person? What kinds of properties, processes or content are implied? In this chapter and the next, I will examine these implications, and also discuss some of the areas where social constructionism has so far struggled to come up with an adequate understanding.

The different forms of social constructionism that I have talked about appear to be in agreement on some basic assumptions about the person. They abandon essentialism in favour of construction; they replace traditional psychology's emphasis upon coherence and unity with fragmentation and multiplicity; and they remove the forum for psychological life out of the individual's head and into the social, interpersonal realm. Social constructionism, then, replaces the self-contained, pre-social and unitary individual with a fragmented and changing, socially produced phenomenon who comes into existence and is maintained not inside the skull but in social life. However, the way that these assumptions cash out in a model of personhood varies between the different forms of social constructionism. In the present chapter, I will focus on the production of identity and subjectivity through discourse. Although it is tempting to contrast the model of the person within macro with that in micro social constructionism, the picture, as usual, is a little muddier than this with some positions seeming to have a foot in both camps. Nevertheless, it will be noticeable to the reader that the emphasis of the present chapter, at least at the outset, is more upon macro social constructionism.

The person in discourse

Let us begin by stating the social constructionist case in its most extreme form. All the objects of our consciousness, every 'thing' we think of or talk about, including our identities, our selves, is constructed through language, manufactured out of discourses. Nothing has any essential, independent existence outside of language; discourse is all there is. A discourse provides a frame of reference, a way of interpreting the world and giving it meaning that allows some objects to take shape. 'Weeds' and 'flowers' only have an existence as different objects by the application of language, by viewing plant life through a particular pair of spectacles, which we might label the 'gardening' discourse or the 'agriculture' discourse. Even plant life as distinguishable from, say, animal life exists only within the frame of reference of language. So not only is language more important than psychologists might have thought, but language is all there is.

Now this presents us with a radically different view of personhood and personal agency. Firstly, we are accustomed to thinking of ourselves as having a certain kind of personality, as holding beliefs and opinions and making choices and that these have originated in our own minds – we are their 'author'. But social constructionism denies us psychological properties such as personality, attitudes and opinions drives and motivations; these things are only present in discourse, an effect of language. We experience ourselves as if these things had a concrete existence in the world, but they are all brought into being through language. They are examples of objects formed through discourses.

Terms such as personality, attitude, skill, temperament, and so on present a particular vision of humankind. Through the use of these terms we are invited to think of human beings as if they were endowed with varying amounts of different qualities, whether inborn, acquired through life experience or learned. Together they contribute to what might be called the discourse of individualism, a way of representing people as unique combinations of psychic material which determine the kind of life a person is likely to lead. For example, a nurturant person may well end up caring for children or taking up a career in nursing. But according to the social constructionist these qualities only exist within the discourse of individualism which makes it possible for us to think in terms of personalities and attitudes. It brings these phenomena into view for us, but the words do not in themselves refer to real entities or psychological properties.

Discourse and identity

If we are not to talk of personality as a meaningful way of understanding ourselves, what concepts are available to us instead? One that is frequently used by social constructionist writers is that of identity. 'Identity' avoids the essentialist connotations of personality, and is also an implicitly social concept. When you identify something, say a plant or an animal, you give it an identity. To say 'that's a weed' or 'there's a wild animal' is not to detect some essential feature or nature of the thing you're looking at. 'Flower' versus 'weed' is a dimension only relevant if you are a gardener. 'Edible' versus 'inedible' might be the, albeit not articulable, dimension used by sheep and cows. And 'wild' versus 'tame' is a distinction that surely only has meaning for humans, since 'tame' implies an encounter and relationship with human beings. The point is that it is you that is doing the identifying, and the identity you confer has more to do with your purposes than the nature of the thing itself. The same applies to the things that make up human identities, such as masculine/feminine, hetero/homosexual, sane/ insane, black/white, working/middle class and so on – these may be seen as socially bestowed identities rather than essences of the person, and this is why the term identity is often found in social constructionist writing.

Our identity is constructed out of the discourses culturally available to us, and which we draw upon in our communications with other people. A person's identity is achieved by a subtle interweaving of many different threads. There is the thread of age, for example they may be a child, a young adult or very old; that of class, depending on their occupation, income and level of education; ethnicity; gender; sexual orientation and so on. All these, and many more, are woven together to produce the fabric of a person's identity. Each of these components is constructed through the discourses that are present in our culture – the discourses of age, of gender, of education, of sexuality and so on. We are the end product, the combination, of the particular versions of these things that are available to us. A young, black, unemployed man will have his identity constructed out of the raw materials of the various discourses surrounding age, ethnicity, work and masculinity. And the different components have implications for each other. The discourses of age, for example, represent people at various stages of life in different ways. Old age is often associated with loss of personal competencies such as memory and motor skills and of status and power, with decline and an absence of development. But alternative discourses of old age can paint a picture of wisdom, respect and serenity. Similarly, youth is variously represented as the time of progress, development and change, a period of identity crisis, or as a period of dangerousness and non-conformity. The version of youth that a person can live out is affected by the discourses of ethnicity, gender, class and so on that they are also subject to. The youth who is black, unemployed and male is likely to be represented or constructed out of rather different discourses of youth than the youth who is white, middle class, employed and female.

For each thread of our identity there is a limited number of discourses on offer out of which we might fashion ourselves. For example, the discourses of sexuality on offer in our present society offer a limited menu for the manufacture of sexual identity. Some newer, more recent discourses of sexuality are gaining ground; for example there are emerging a variety of lesbian and gay sexualities, many of which have been consciously constructed. However, two well-established discourses in particular call upon us to identify ourselves with respect to them: 'normal' sexuality, usually embodying notions of naturalness and moral rectitude; and 'perverted' sexuality, which more or less includes anything else. The dichotomy of hetero- and homosexuality is overlaid on this, such that heterosexuality is usually represented as normal, natural and right, and homosexuality as perverted, unnatural and wrong; the two dichotomies are not synonymous, since some heterosexual practices are also seen as perversions. Given these representations of sexuality that are culturally available to us, we have no choice but to fashion our identity out of them. Our sexual activities (or lack of them!) can have no form of representation to ourselves or to the people around us other than in the form of these discourses, and so we must inevitably adopt the identity of straight or pervert, of hetero- or homosexual: the discourses of sexuality available within our language leave us with very few other alternatives. It is also worth pointing out here that the very use of the terms hetero- and homosexuality, like normal and perverted, creates the illusion that all varieties of homosexuality and lesbianism, and all forms of heterosexuality, are functionally equivalent, and that homosexuality is in some simple way just a mirror image of heterosexuality.

Surrounding any aspect of a person's life, then, are a variety of alternative discourses, each offering a different vision of what it means to be, say, young, educated, employed, or disabled and so on. Sometimes there is no problem with combining identities supplied by these discourses. For example, a young person just entering higher education might effortlessly adopt the identity of student, because the prevalent discourses of youth and education have much in common. Youth as a time of development, exploration and of mental and physical agility fits well with the discourse of education, which represents it as a process of self-development and preparation for adulthood. But a middle-aged person returning to education after a long period of employment or child care might be expected to have difficulties with the identity of student because our usual ways of talking about and representing middle age do not include concepts of development or of mental and physical prowess.

The discourses of science and of gender are also good examples of this. Science and masculinity pose few problems for each other. Science is thought of as logical, objective and value-free. Masculinity embodies rationality and an ability to keep one's emotions out of one's reasoning. The man who becomes a scientist can expect few identity problems. But for women there is a potential area of conflict or confusion. Prevailing discourses of femininity speak of emotionality, illogicality and intuitiveness – not the stuff of science. Women who want to do science are faced with the problem of how they can bring off their identity without appearing to be either unwomanly or a poor scientist.

For each of us, then, a multitude of discourses is constantly at work constructing and producing our identity. Our identity therefore originates not from inside the person, but from the social realm, a realm where people swim in a sea of language and other signs, a sea that is invisible to us because it is the very medium of our existence as social beings. However, to say that identities are socially constructed through discourse does not mean to say that those identities are accidental. It is at this point that social constructionism can bring to bear a political analysis of the construction of personal identity.

Resistance through discourse

Sexuality offers an illustrative example of the way that discourses and the identities they offer are tied to material power relations (see Chapter 4) but at the same time offer possibilities for resistance. The prevailing discourses which construct homosexuality and lesbianism are primarily those of unnaturalness, perversion and sickness. At their most charitable, they characterise the homosexual as suffering from an unfortunate illness. At their least charitable, these discourses represent the homosexual or lesbian as morally reprehensible or even evil. They serve to place homosexual and lesbian relationships outside the orbit of what is considered normal and natural, though by now it should be clear that these terms themselves are not unproblematic, and allow them as only marginal forms of illegitimate social life. Why should it be that the images on offer for representing homosexuality are so pejorative? To the extent that the heterosexual nuclear family is the keystone of our present capitalist economy, then homosexuality and lesbianism pose a threat to this status quo. Those who stand most to benefit from society as it is presently arranged have a vested interest in marginalising family forms which appear to question the naturalness and moral righteousness of heterosexual, married family life.

But Kitzinger (1987, 1989) shows how lesbians whom she interviewed were able to resist this marginalising tendency by drawing upon the discourses of 'romantic love' and of 'self actualisation'. Kitzinger identifies these as being part of a broader liberal humanist discourse. This discourse presents a picture of the human being in which every person has an equal right to happiness and self-fulfilment. It stresses the person's individuality and uniqueness, and his or her need to make their own decisions about how they ought to live their life. Liberal humanism could be said to be a heavily legitimated discourse in our society. Within the liberal humanistic framework, which stresses the essential personhood of the lesbian and the relative unimportance of her sexual preference, these women were able to bring off accounts of themselves as more similar to than different from other ordinary women. The lesbian, within liberal humanist discourse, should be accepted as part of the rich variety of humanity.

However, Kitzinger goes on to suggest that using this discourse can be counter-productive politically, since we end up endorsing its legitimacy. If it is true that discourses of love and family life serve to obscure oppressive relations in society, between workers and employers, between women and men, and between hetero- and homosexuals, then these women are doing nothing to ultimately help either the general state of affairs or their own oppression. She concludes with the rather pessimistic view that '. . . the oppressed are actively encouraged to construct identities that reaffirm the basic validity of this dominant moral order' (Kitzinger, 1989: 95).

There are a couple of points that are worth drawing from this. Firstly, it demonstrates the way in which identities are struggled after by people. We are all in the process of claiming and resisting the identities on offer within the various prevailing discourses, and it is when we look at those who appear to be on the margins of mainstream society that we see this struggle writ large. However, Kitzinger's concluding remarks could seem to suggest that no matter how hard you try to break out of the discourses maintaining your relatively powerless position in the world, the whole discourse system closes in around you and you end up caught up in it again sooner or later. I don't think that this is what she is saying, but she does demonstrate that discourses which are threatening to the status quo, and therefore to those who benefit from it, such as political lesbian or radical feminist discourses which explicitly challenge existing social institutions, will be strongly resisted and marginalised. The process of constructing and negotiating our own identities will therefore often be ridden with conflict, as we struggle to claim or resist the images available to us through discourse.

Discourses do not interlock neatly with each other, cleanly sealing off all possible cracks and weaknesses. There are weak points, places where they may be attacked, and points at which other discourses pose a real threat; they are always implicitly being contested by other discourses. This is Foucault's point about power and resistance always operating together (see Chapter 4). Where there is power there is also resistance.

Subject positions and speaking rights

The concept of subject positions is used by some social constructionist writers to refer to the process by which our identities are produced. The philosopher Althusser had a very similar idea when he talked about how we come to take on board ideologies. His central thesis was that ideology 'interpellates' or 'hails' individuals as subjects. It shouts to us 'Hey, you there!', and makes us listen as a certain type of person. When we recognise ourselves as the person hailed in the ideology, we have already become that person. The idea of positions within discourse is rather similar. Discourses address us as particular kinds of people (as an old person, as a carer, as a worker, as a criminal and so on) and furthermore we cannot avoid these subject positions, the representations of ourselves and others that discourses invite. Our choice is only to accept them or try to resist them, and if we accept or are unable to resist a particular subject position we are then locked into the system of rights, speaking rights and obligations that are carried with that position.

According to Willig (1999b) 'individuals are constrained by available discourses because discursive positions pre-exist the individual whose sense of "self" (subjectivity) and range of experience are circumscribed by available discourses' (p. 114). Gillies (1999) uses the example of addiction discourse to represent the behaviour and experience of people who smoke. This discourse calls such people into the subject position of addict, with the result that those people then come to understand their behaviour and to experience themselves in those terms. The subjectivities open to us through positions in discourse may be oppressive and leave us little potential for changing our situation. Gillies argues that the discourse of the smoker as addict is disempowering because the possibilities for change and for taking control of one's life seem small.

Parker (1992) gives an illustrative example of how these subject positions also entail possibilities and limitations on action and speaking rights. A badge displaying the words 'Dialogue on Diarrhoea' highlights a health problem for many third world countries, and is sold as part of a campaign to increase awareness and raise funds. Directed at western industrialised societies, it may be addressing us through one of a number of different discourses, each entailing different subject positions for us and different rights and obligations. A medical discourse typically contains positions of those who offer treatment through their medical knowledge (doctors and nurses) and less knowledgeable patients who receive their care. Through this discourse we are addressed as potential carers, but only to support the work of the 'medically qualified', for example by volunteering our practical aid or undertaking medical training. In a medical discourse those without medical training will be addressed as patients or as non-medics, positions which carry lesser rights to take decisions, make diagnoses, use medical terminology and so on.

The idea of subject positions within discourse has been used in the area of gender and sexuality. Hollway (1984, 1989) identifies a number of heterosexual discourses, which contain different positions for women and men. Drawing on her own interview material, she identified three discourses: the 'male sexual drive' discourse, the 'permissive' discourse and the 'have/hold' discourse. The male sexual drive discourse centres on the idea that men's sexuality is directly produced by a biological drive, a drive that exists in order to propagate the species. The position implicitly offered for women in this representation of sexuality is as its object; a woman is the object that precipitates men's natural sexual urges, and may be seen as 'trapping' a man by the power of her sexual attraction. The male sexual drive discourse is regularly encountered in our culture, and is often used to legitimate men's behaviour such as infidelity or rape (Ehrlich, 1998). The positions offered to men and women within this discourse can be seen to be very different, involving very different rights and obligations and possibilities for action.

By contrast, the have/hold discourse legitimates quite a different set of behaviours. It centres on the Christian ideals of monogamy, partnership and family life, and retains the link, seen in the male sexual drive discourse, between sexuality and reproduction. It positions women as primarily seeking a long-term emotional commitment through relationships with a husband and children, her sexuality being primarily bound up with her desire for motherhood and family life. Representations of men within this discourse focus on their preparedness, or lack of it, to commit themselves to a long-term relationship and to become subject to the obligations it brings. Within this discourse, then, the gender roles are in a sense reversed. Women are the pursuers and men the 'catch'. Hollway suggests that, for men, the resolution of the conflict between the male sexual drive discourse and the have/hold discourse is to manufacture a divide between the 'good' girls whom they marry and the 'bad' girls whom they visit in whorehouses.

Positioning in interaction

The notion of positioning (Davies and Harré, 1990; Van Langenhove and Harré, 1994; Harré and van Langenhove, 1999) has also been taken up in a way that acknowledges the active mode in which persons endeavour to locate themselves within particular discourses during social interaction; in this respect, this view is more in keeping with micro social constructionism. A man accused of rape may, in his courtroom defence, position himself within a discourse of male sexuality that locates him as a victim of uncontrollable biological urges. In everyday interactions we take up positions vis-à-vis other people which sometimes turn out to be problematic. Within prevailing discourses governing close relationships, one person may take up the position of 'lover' in an interaction, which implicitly calls the other person into a reciprocal position and all that entails. However, the other may accept this position or reject it, perhaps by striving to position themselves as 'friend'.

The concept of positioning recognises both the power of culturally available discourses to frame our experience and constrain our behaviour while allowing room for the person to actively engage with those discourses and employ them in social situations. Davies and Harré (1990, 1999) suggest that these two aspects of positioning are operating at the same time. They see the human subject as simultaneously produced by discourse and manipulators of it. The positions available within discourses bring with them a 'structure of rights'; they provide the possibilities and the limitations on what we may or may not do and claim for ourselves within a particular discourse.

We may ourselves adopt a position by drawing upon a particular discourse, or we may assign positions to other speakers through the part that we give them in our account. For example, a person may treat someone's remark as 'offering sympathy', and respond to it by adopting the position of 'victim'. However, the original remark may not have been intended in this way, and the speaker may not wish to be positioned as 'one who would offer sympathy in such cases'. The result may be that an attempt is made to redefine the speaker's first remark and therefore offer new positions for both speakers. Thus subject positions of many kinds are drawn into the play from moment to moment, and these may be offered, accepted, claimed or resisted by the participants. And it is these subject positions, offered, claimed or accepted, that define us as persons:

> An individual emerges through the processes of social interaction, not as a relatively fixed end product but as one who is constituted and reconstituted through the various discursive practices in which they participate. Accordingly, who one is, that is, what sort of person one is, is always an open question with a shifting answer depending upon the positions made available within one's own and others' discursive practices and within those practices, the stories within which we make sense of our own and others' lives.
>
> (Davies and Harré, 1999: 35)

Davies and Harré also reserve a place for the individuality of the person; one's personal history and unique life experiences will influence the extent to which we want to occupy and feel able to occupy particular positions within interactions.

Defining the situation

It follows that in any interchange between people, there is a constant monitoring of the 'definition of the situation' that each participant is struggling to bring off. Participants' understanding of 'what kind of interaction this is' will radically affect their perception of what subject positions are available to them and whether they wish to claim or resist those positions. The following was reported as an example of the negotiation of roles, but can also be viewed as a struggle for viable positions within a medical discourse.

> Davis (1961) observed how a physiotherapist tried to convert a person with a temporary physical handicap into a *patient*. The therapist emphasised the disability's seriousness, to persuade the person to relinquish 'normal' roles usually played in favour of total patienthood. The person responded by emphasising the

handicap's temporary character and the imminent prospect of recovery. The person attempted to establish friendly relations by providing personal details about self, asking the therapist personal questions, extending social invitations and in other ways attempting to avoid becoming 'only' a patient. The therapist could not play a completely professional role unless the person became a complete patient, however, so that offers of friendship and intimacy were rejected. But the therapist still could not afford to be viewed as cold and distant by either patient or colleagues. A 'distant cordiality' was maintained as a role relationship emerged from the negotiation

(Jackson, 1998: 124–5. Italics in original)

Different constructions of an interaction can offer radically different subject positions, which in turn entail different sets of rights and obligations for the participants. And such positioning is not necessarily intentional, though it sometimes is. People may therefore become enmeshed in the subject positions implicit in their talk without necessarily having intended to position each other in particular ways. But we can recognise and develop an awareness of the potential implications of the discourses we adopt in our dealings with others. As well as being less likely to position others in ways we did not intend, we may also gain for ourselves a useful strategy in our own struggles with personal identity and change.

Positions and power

This concern with the details of positioning in the interpersonal context is about how positions offered, accepted or resisted in everyday talk are the discursive practices by which discourses and their associated power implications are brought to life. When we position ourselves or others during conversation, we are doing something that has effects which go beyond that immediate social event. Everyday conversation, even down to the apparent inconsequentiality of exchanges about the weather or how your children are getting on at school, are therefore far from trivial and represent an important arena where identities are fashioned and power relations played out. In fact, the claim that such talk is trivial can be used as a powerful device. Feminists who believe that language is central to women's oppression have often made this point. For example, a woman who complains that suggestive comments from her male work colleagues constitute sexual harassment may have her complaint defused by the response that the comments were 'only a bit of fun' or 'just a joke' and that therefore the problem lies not in their comments but in her lack of a sense of humour. The success of such a strategy depends upon these comments being represented as trivial and therefore harmless. Real oppression, if it exists, is represented as lying elsewhere, perhaps in the laws regarding employment and pay, a site apparently removed from the day-to-day commonplaces of conversation. If we are going to take seriously the view that language is a crucial site of identity negotiation and of power relations, then we can no longer afford to view as trivial the arguments over whether words such as 'blackleg' or 'mankind' should be outlawed.

The concept of positioning, then, affords a way of looking at both how people are subject to discourse and how this subjectivity is negotiated in interpersonal life. Walkerdine (1981) gives a good example, which illustrates this dual nature of positioning. Using her own recordings of child–teacher interactions in a nursery school, she shows how children and teachers are engaged in a struggle to position themselves and each other in different discourses, and the power effects that are brought about by this positioning. She quotes an exchange between the nursery teacher, Miss Baxter, and two 4-year-old boys, Sean and Terry. I have reproduced the entire episode here:

> The sequence begins when Annie takes a piece of Lego to add on to a construction that she is building. Terry tries to take it away from her to use himself and she resists. He says:

> *Terry:*   You're a stupid cunt, Annie.

> The teacher tells him to stop and Sean tries to mess up another child's construction. The teacher tells him to stop. Then Sean says:

> *Sean:*   Get out of it Miss Baxter paxter.
> *Terry:*   Get out of it knickers Miss Baxter.
> *Sean:*   Get out of it Miss Baxter paxter.
> *Terry:*   Get out of it Miss Baxter the knickers paxter knickers, bum.

Sean:	Knickers, shit, bum.
Miss B:	Sean, that's enough, you're being silly.
Sean:	Miss Baxter, knickers, show your knickers.
Terry:	Miss Baxter, show your bum off.
	(*they giggle*)
Miss B:	I think you're being very silly.
Terry:	Shit Miss Baxter, shit Miss Baxter.
Sean:	Miss Baxter, show your knickers your bum off.
Sean:	Take all your clothes off, your bra off.
Terry:	Yeah, and take your bum off, take your wee-wee off, take your clothes, your mouth off.
Sean:	Take your teeth out, take your head off, take your hair off, take your bum off. Miss Baxter the paxter knickers taxter.
Miss B:	Sean, go and find something else to do, please.

(Walkerdine, 1981)

Walkerdine uses this example to show how as individuals we are constantly subject to an interplay of different discourses, each with its own structure of rights, obligations and possibilities for action, and each carrying identity and power implications. She is primarily arguing against a traditional Marxist analysis of education, which would see the teacher as uncomplicatedly in a position of power over the children, who have relatively fewer rights and freedoms. In such an analysis, the children are straightforwardly oppressed by education, and by its representative here, the teacher. But in this example, the children are seen to temporarily seize power and to render their teacher relatively powerless by their ability to draw upon the discourse of sexuality and to position themselves and their teacher within it. The two boys, by their sexual comments, temporarily locate themselves as male and their teacher as female within a discourse of sexuality, which affords them some supremacy. Miss Baxter ceases to signify primarily as a teacher, the relatively powerful position in the teacher–child educational pairing, and for a time becomes positioned as 'woman' in a discourse of sexuality, thus rendering her as 'sex object' to the young boys.

The teacher's response to their talk appears weak and ineffective ('I think you're being very silly') and does not help her to resist the subject position she is being offered. Walkerdine explains the teacher's response in terms of the prevailing discourse of nursery education within which she experiences herself as a teacher.

Nursery education is seen as a process of allowing the child's natural potential to unfold through the teacher's nurturance and guidance. Free expression, denying the distinction between work and play, is seen as the process by which the child can develop naturally. Within this framework, the teacher is there to monitor the child's unfolding development, and to gently steer it in appropriate directions. A strict, regimented or controlling teacher is out of place here, and Miss Baxter's later comments about the children's talk explain her response:

> The kind of expressions are quite normal for this age . . . As long as they're not being too silly or bothering anybody, it's just natural and should be left . . . coming out with that kind of expression is very natural.
>
> (Walkerdine, 1981: 169)

The boys' talk, within this discourse of nursery education, was represented as part of a natural developmental phase, and therefore to be simply monitored rather than resisted by the teacher. One could say that prevailing discourses of sexuality and of nursery education came together in this episode and provided an opportunity for the young boys to reverse the usual power relations operating in school settings. This example nicely shows how the positions offered, accepted or resisted are not just of importance in understanding how people manage social interactions, but how positions are drawn from discourses which are constantly operating as it were 'behind the scenes' of all social interactions. Opportunities for identity negotiation and for grasping power occur as we position ourselves and others within a variety of discourses in the shifting flow of social interaction.

The discursive positions on offer to us during social interaction may therefore play a central role in the extent to which we are able to negotiate satisfactory identities for ourselves, and in our ability (physically and morally) to behave and to take action as we would like. To the extent that material conditions and social practices are inextricably bound up in discourse, then our ability to, say, earn a living, go out at night, tell people what to do or refuse to do what others say depends upon the positions in discourses that we can take up or resist. It follows therefore that an understanding of positioning and an ability to use it skilfully could be important tools in a person's efforts to change themselves or their circumstances.

Positions, positioning and subjectivity

The social constructionist attack on essentialist psychology has left us with an empty person, a human being with no essential psychological characteristics. However, we certainly feel ourselves to be the bearers of personality traits, to be the holders of attitudes, and to experience emotions, drives and motivations. Our subjective experiences and individual differences still need to be explained, though in new ways. For example, how can we explain why some people show emotion more readily than others, or why they become mentally ill? Why do some people hunt foxes and others try to stop them? What is happening when we 'fall in love'?

One answer is that our subjective experience is provided by the discourses in which we are embedded. It is as if we internalise the ways of representing human life present in discourses, as with the discourse of 'the individual', and our subjective experience flows from that. It is a complete reversal of our common-sense understanding, in which our subjective experience comes first and we then describe it and label it with language. Language, in the form of discourses, provides our subjective experience of the world. However, this claim does not really answer in detail questions like the ones I have posed above, and I think it is a fair criticism of the macro form of social constructionism that our experience of personhood and subjectivity is left unexplained.

Davies and Harré's account of positioning is a little more helpful in this respect. Positions in discourse are seen as providing us with the content of our subjectivity. Once we take up a position within a discourse (and some of these positions can entail a long-term occupation by the person, like gender or fatherhood) we then inevitably come to experience the world and ourselves from the vantagepoint of that perspective. Once we take up a subject position in discourse, we have available to us a particular, limited set of concepts, images, metaphors, ways of speaking, self-narratives and so on that we take on as our own. This entails both an emotional commitment on our part to the categories of person to which we are allocated and see ourselves as belonging, such as male, grandfather or worker, and the development of an appropriate system of morals (rules of right and wrong). Our sense of who we are and what it is therefore possible and not possible for us to do, what it is right and appropriate for us to do, and what it is wrong and inappropriate for us to do thus all derive from our occupation of subject positions within discourse.

Some subject positions are more temporary or even fleeting and therefore who we are is constantly in flux, always dependent upon the changing flow of positions we negotiate within social interaction. Thus, in this account, our subjective experience of ourselves, of being the person we take ourselves to be, is given by the variety of subject positions, some permanent, some temporary and some fleeting, that we take up in discourse.

Agency and change

The possibility of agency

If people are products of discourse, and the things that they say have status only as manifestations of these discourses, in what sense can we be said to have agency? The actions, words and thoughts of human beings appear to be reduced to the level of by-products of larger linguistic entities of which we may be largely unaware. Our hopes, desires and intentions become the products of cultural, discursive structures, not the products of human agents. And not only are we unaware of this state of affairs, but we continue in the belief that human beings can change themselves and the world they live in through the force of their (apparently) independently developed and freely chosen beliefs and acts. We look around us and see the world changing, and imagine that human intention and action is at the root of it, but this is an illusion. There is a real danger that we can become paralysed by the view that individual people can really do nothing to change themselves or their world. The problem of how human agency might be addressed within a social constructionist framework has not been neglected, but neither has it been resolved.

For writers such as Althusser and Foucault, the constitutive role of discourse takes centre stage. Althusser believed that all of us live out the requirements of the prevailing ideologies while doing so under the illusion that we have freely chosen our way of life. In fact, according to Althusser, ideology *is* the experience of being the authors of our own actions. We are simply the bearers of social structures, but experience ourselves as agents. For Foucault too, the human subject appears to be described in terms of the ways in which discourses manifest themselves in texts and practices; discourses live themselves out through people. This way of conceptualising human beings, which amounts to little more than seeing them as puppets operated by structures they cannot see, has been called 'the death of the subject', and refers particularly to the fact that such conceptualisations make it virtually impossible to admit any notion of human agency, i.e. that people are the authors of their own thoughts and actions. This is nicely explained by Craib (1984):

> It is assumed instead that people are the puppets of their ideas, and their actions are determined not by choice and decision but are the outcome of the underlying structure of ideas, the logic of these ideas. If, for example, I am a Christian, I do not speak about Christianity, rather Christianity speaks through me; some structuralists reach the extreme of saying that people do not speak but rather they are spoken (by the underlying structure of the language), that they do not read books but are 'read' by books. They do not create societies but are created by societies.
>
> (Craib, 1984: 109)

This is an extreme position. If human beings and the things that form the objects of their knowledge are constructed through discourse, then this seems to afford more agency to discourse than it does to people. Certainly, if we are to characterise the experience and behaviour of human beings as nothing more nor less than the manifestations of prevailing discourses then there really does not seem to be much point in suggesting that people can change their situation or that of others by their own intentions and actions. However, this is a very extreme view, and one denied, at least implicitly, by social constructionists who are concerned with change. Even Foucault, who is often considered to lie at the 'human-beings-as-manifestations-of-discourse' end of the continuum, may have been misrepresented in this respect. It is true that he rejected humanism, the idea that because we experience ourselves as having goals, purposes and intentions that we are the sole source and free agents of our actions. But, as Sawicki (1991) points out, this may not necessarily close the door on human agency. She sees Foucault's notion of the person as still allowing for some kind of agency. Although the person, the subject, is constituted by discourse, this subject is yet capable of critical historical reflection and is able to exercise some choice with respect to the discourses and practices that it takes up for its own use. Within this view, change is possible because human agents, given the right circumstances, are capable of critically analysing the discourses which frame their lives, and to claim or resist them according to the effects they wish to bring about. Foucault proposed that change is possible through opening up marginalised and repressed discourses, making them available as alternatives from which we may fashion alternative identities. This is a form of consciousness raising, and the purpose of it is not to impose another, though different, identity upon us, which would be just as oppressive, but simply to free us from our usual ways of understanding ourselves. This view thus sees the person as simultaneously constructed by discourse and using it for their own purposes.

Positioning and change

A first step toward personal change, within this framework of discursive positioning, might be to recognise the discourses and positions that are currently shaping our subjectivity. The example described by Davies (1998) (see Chapter 5) is illustrative here. Such a recognition can be beneficial in itself, by relocating problems away from an intra-psychic domain and into a societal one. For example, 'depression' is a term which locates problems within the internal psychology of the individual. A woman may complain of depression, feeling that she cannot cope with her life. Perhaps she feels that she is a bad mother because she frequently loses her temper with her young children, or that she is an inadequate daughter because she is reluctant to care for her own elderly mother. But in re-casting the problem at a societal level rather than at the level of the individual a different analysis emerges. Such an analysis may suggest that the woman sees herself as oppressed rather than depressed. The discourses of motherhood, femininity, family life and so on actively encourage women to engage in practices which are not necessarily in their own psychological, social and economic best interests. Thinking of oneself as oppressed rather than depressed fosters a different view of oneself and of how to attack one's problems. It may not solve those problems; the woman in the example will still have to decide what to do about her elderly mother, but she may not feel so conflict-ridden and guilty. An examination of the discourses and positions available to us may help us to work towards occupying positions in discourses which are less personally damaging. The woman who fears she is a bad mother may be helped by recognising the 'good mother' as a discourse with political implications. The popular representation of the good mother as one who spends time with her children when they are young and who sacrifices her own needs to theirs helps to keep women out of full-time employment and ensures their economic dependency upon men. But different and competing discourses of motherhood, and of 'good motherhood', exist. The task is therefore one of finding ways of resisting being positioned in personally damaging motherhood discourses, and how to claim positions in discourses, which are beneficial. In short, it means finding ways that you can 'do' good motherhood that are acceptable to you. For example, we might represent the essential task of motherhood as 'helping one's children to become self-reliant'. While preserving the idea that mothers should nurture and guide their offspring, such a representation allows a mother to go out to work and still claim the position of 'good' rather than 'bad' mother.

However, this is not to say that such changes can be accomplished easily. To the extent that prevailing or dominant discourses are often tied to social arrangements and practices which support the status quo and maintain the positions of powerful groups, then in challenging such discourses and resisting the positions they offer we are also implicitly challenging their associated social practices, structures and power relations. We can therefore expect to find some degree of resistance to our attempts at change. For example, a woman may want to become more assertive, but behaving in an assertive manner is not consistent with dominant discourses of femininity and womanhood. One could say that the absence of assertiveness and other instrumental qualities from the femininity package-deal means that such psychological repertoires are not easily available as a resource to women, and makes it easier for men to hold the reins of society. So in 'becoming more assertive' a woman is implicitly taking on more than a struggle to change the nature of her social interactions within her immediate social circle. However, recognition of this can at least help us to anticipate, understand and counter such resistance when it occurs.

On an interpersonal level, we can work towards change firstly by becoming more aware of the positions we are being offered and that we offer to others in our interactions with them. We can then devise strategies for how unacceptable positions might be resisted and positions in alternative discourses taken up. This would involve deciding how to change one's response to particular conversational gambits, or when to remain silent (silence may well be a particularly useful way of resisting positions we do not want to accept).

Summary

The person can be described by the sum total of the subject positions in discourse that they currently occupy. The fact that some of these positions are fleeting or in a state of flux means that our identity is never fixed but always in process, always open to change. The subject positions that we occupy bring with them a structure of rights and obligations; they legislate for what 'that kind of person' may or may not reasonably do or say. But not only do our subject positions constrain and shape what we do, they are taken on as part of our psychology such that they provide us also with our sense of self, the ideas and metaphors with which we think, and the self-narratives we use to talk and think about ourselves. As such, we have an emotional commitment to and investment in our subject positions which goes beyond mere rule following.

The extent of our personal choice and agency in taking up subject positions is a matter for debate. Those writers concerned to apply discourse theory to issues of personal and social change are generally committed to the view that the person has some negotiating power and room for manoeuvre. They stress the choices that are available to the person in how they may take up or resist the positions on offer to them, and to this extent the person can be seen as a negotiator of their own identity.

The view of macro social constructionism by comparison, taken to the extreme, sees human subjects as secondary to and as products of the discourses that structure their lives. The content of such a being is hard to imagine; indeed whatever psychological processes are attributed to it can only have the status of by-products. They can never have much explanatory value when it comes to understanding what people are like or why they behave in the ways they do. According to this view, once we have laid bare the structures and discourses which are currently producing human social life, there will be nothing left to explain. This view is problematic for a number of reasons (see Craib, 1984 for a good account of the arguments concerning agency), but it is also paradoxical when it comes to the application of its own research programme. In order to understand society and social life, we must identify and lay bare the discourses that are currently pulling our strings. However, if this is the case, how is such a task possible? How can we stand outside of and regard the very structures that are producing us? The very project of discourse analysis becomes problematic. The alternative view, that we both actively produce and manipulate, *and* are products of discourse allows us the possibility of personal and social change through our capacity to identify, understand and resist the discourses to which we are subject.

Chapter 7

The person in dialogue

In the previous chapter I examined some of the implications for being a person that arise from seeing people as occupying subject positions in discourse. The idea of subject positions is utilised by those working within both macro and micro forms of social constructionism; within macro social constructionism the emphasis is upon the constitutive force of the subject positions carried within particular discourses, and within micro social constructionism the emphasis is upon the ability of the person to negotiate subject positions within particular interactions. In this chapter I am going to continue with this examination of the nature of the person within social constructionism, focusing further upon the implications of those forms of social constructionism that emphasise the importance of dialogue and social interaction. This includes discursive psychology as well as a number of other approaches that emphasise social *relationships* as well as the process of social *interaction*.

Discursive psychology

The view of people as users and manipulators of language and discourse for their own purposes was outlined in Chapter 3. Let us begin with a brief overview of this approach. Discursive psychologists are primarily interested in our situated use of language, that is, how people actively construct accounts in interaction. They emphasise the performative and action-oriented nature of language, investigating the way that accounts are built in interactions to suit particular purposes and suggest that people draw upon a shared cultural resource of tools, such as interpretative repertoires, for these purposes. These repertoires enable people to justify

particular versions of events, to excuse or validate their own behaviour, to fend off criticism or otherwise allow them to maintain a
credible stance in an interaction. People draw upon a collection of
metaphors and linguistic devices, which could be used by virtually
anyone in order to bring about a particular desired representation
of an event. Repertoires, then, are not the property of individuals
and should not be seen as belonging to them like characteristics
or traits.

Psychological states vs public performances

To the extent that we share a common stock of linguistic skills we
can go about our business of constructing accounts to fit the purpose at hand. For example, as we grow up and become more
sophisticated users of language, we become adept at such rhetorical
skills as blaming someone, making an excuse or offering a justification. We come to understand just when to represent ourselves as
angry, jealous or wounded, and we come to know exactly how such
representations may be constructed (see Edwards, 1997 for a discursive psychological account of emotion). For example, we know
that, in our culture, it is assumed that we may sometimes be
overcome by powerful feelings, leading us to speak or behave
improperly. So that if we wish to justify or excuse our behaviour
we may mobilise this representation of emotion in our talk. This
approach to talk gives rise to research questions that are very
different from those of traditional psychology. It leads us to ask
what functions a person's talk might have for them, what is at
stake for them in the interaction, what purposes they are trying to
achieve, and what discursive devices they employ to bring about
the desired effects. It encourages us to study the discursive devices
and rhetorical skills that are used in interaction, such as justifications, disclaimers, attributions and blamings, and to ask how
people construct their talk to achieve the effects they do.

But this concern with the performative role of language for
people also brings with it important theoretical implications. Language had implicitly been regarded by psychology as an expressive
medium, as a way of indicating and communicating to other people
what is inside us, our thoughts and our feelings. But discursive
psychology places a big question mark above such familiar entities
as memories, attitudes and emotions. For discursive psychology,
our talk about the things we remember, think and feel does not

refer to entities or states inside us. Their existence cannot be inferred from such talk. If the things that people say are social acts, governed by the moment-to-moment requirements of social interactions, then they cannot also be simple expressions of internal states. The reality of these, other than their construction in discourse, is unknowable and so discursive psychologists prefer to bracket such questions about the possible nature of these things and concentrate instead on how we fabricate and mobilise them in our talk.

Indeed, when we begin to examine the way that psychological entities such as emotions and memories make their appearance on the social stage, the discursive psychologists' case can be convincing. For example, Stearns (1995) points out that our expression of anger is heavily dependent upon the social context: whether it is our partner or boss with whom we are angry, whether we are in a public or private place and the size and nature of the misdemeanour. In a sense, we therefore make a judgement about how angry we should be. Cross-cultural differences in the degree and mode of the expression of anger further suggest that our linguistic expression is not a simple product of an internal state. Thus, our expression of anger is less an outpouring of feeling and more a culturally regulated and normative mode of managing and putting into practice our society's system of rights and obligations – its moral code. Expressions of anger, and other emotions such as jealousy (see Stenner, 1993) and love, are therefore some of the resources we have for justifying our actions, blaming others, getting our own way and so on; they are tactical moves which have real consequences for us.

But we only regard some of our bodily expressions as emotions. As Harré and Gillett (1994) point out, stretching and yawning are expressions of 'feeling tired' but are not seen as the expression of an emotion. Emotions, they argue, tend to be displays that express a judgement and accomplish social acts:

> For example, when one feels or displays envy, this is an expression of the judgement that someone has something that one would oneself like to have. In the case of malign envy, one judges oneself to have been demeaned or depreciated by the possession of that good by the other. To take another example, because a display of anger, irritation or annoyance expresses a judgement of the moral quality of some other person's action,

such a display is also an act of protest, directed toward the offending person.

(Harré and Gillett, 1994: 146–7)

However, expressing a judgement does not imply a cognitive process, which we then express in emotional behaviour. The expression *is* the judgement; it is the form it takes. Cognitive or emotional structures do not mediate between private feelings or thoughts and public expressions:

> . . . discursive phenomena, for example, acts of remembering, are not manifestations of hidden subjective, psychological phenomena. Sometimes they have subjective counterparts; sometimes they do not. There is no necessary shadow world of mental activity behind discourse in which one is working things out in private.
>
> (Harré and Gillett, 1994: 27)

The same approach has been applied to cognitive states and functions, like attitudes and memory.

A now classic attack on the traditional view of attitudes was provided by Potter and Wetherell (1987) in their groundbreaking book *Discourse and Social Psychology: Beyond attitudes and behaviour*. One of Potter and Wetherell's main concerns was to raise a question mark over the traditional concept of attitudes by subjecting it to a social constructionist analysis. When social scientists interview a person about an issue, say unemployment, immigration or the health service, they commonly assume that the replies the person gives to their questions are in some way a representation of something that lies inside that person's head, i.e. their attitude or opinion on that issue. The language that the person uses, the account that they give, is taken to unproblematically express the attitude that lies within. Potter and Wetherell argue that attitudes in this sense do not exist, and that we only have to look at the degree of variation to be found within any respondent's interview transcript for proof of this. An attitude refers to a coherent and relatively stable orientation to an issue or object, and therefore we should expect that when a person is questioned about their attitudes there will be a high degree of coherence in what they say. However, Potter and Wetherell show that this is usually not the case. Using their own transcripts from two interview studies, one concerning race relations in New Zealand and the other about the handling of a riot by police, they point out that variability within accounts is the rule rather than the exception. In other words at various points in the interview, depending upon what question the interviewer was currently asking, respondents would typically give accounts that appeared to be quite incompatible with each other if considered as manifestations of the same underlying attitude. A good example of such variation is given in Wetherell and Potter (1988), from interviews about race relations in New Zealand. They give the following quotes from their interview transcripts:

> I do this bible class at the moment, not highly religious, I just think children ought to know about religion . . . and last night we were just discussing one of the commandments, love your neighbour, and I had this child who said 'What would happen if you got a whole load of Maoris living next door to you?' and I said to him 'That's a very racist remark and I don't like it', and he shut up in about five seconds and went quite red in the face, and I realized afterwards that obviously it wasn't his fault he was, turned out to be thinking like that, it came directly from his parents.
>
> (Wetherell and Potter, 1988: 174)

> The ridiculous thing is that, if you really want to be nasty about it, and go back, um, the Europeans really did take over New Zealand shore, and I mean that Maoris killed off the Maorioris beforehand, I mean it wasn't exactly their land to start with, I mean it's a bit ridiculous. I think we bend over backwards a bit too much.
>
> (Wetherell and Potter, 1988: 175)

Both extracts come from the same interview, from a single respondent, and Wetherell and Potter argue that it would be impossible from this to determine the person's attitude toward the Maoris. Could this person be described as tolerant or prejudiced? Would they be in favour of or against multiculturalism? The 'attitude' displayed here is neither coherent nor stable. Wetherell and Potter suggest that, rather than take what people say as an expression of internal states or underlying processes we should rather look at what people are doing with their talk, what purposes their accounts are achieving. And since a person may be trying to bring about different effects with their talk at different points in the interview it is not surprising that we find the variation that we do.

This view therefore problematises the view that there are internal structures to the person that we could call attitudes and instead looks at what people say as intentional, socially directed behaviour which performs certain functions for them.

Edwards and Potter (1995) and Edwards (1997) perform a similar reframing of memory. They claim that traditional psychology sees remembering as 'a kind of distorted re-experiencing, overlaid or altered by subsequent experience and by the machinations of inner cognitive structures and processes, with the report serving merely (and directly) as evidence of those underlying processes' (Edwards and Potter, 1995: 35). Experience tells us that we are unlikely to find an absolute version of the truth against which we can measure the accuracy of accounts. When people are asked to provide an accurate account of an event much 'memory work' is done to build 'an acceptable, agreed or communicatively successful version of what really happened' (Edwards and Potter, 1995: 34).

Edwards and Potter (1995), following Neisser (1981), studied transcripts of John Dean's testimony in the Watergate hearings. Neisser had argued that these transcripts can be used to judge the accuracy of Dean's memory. But Edwards and Potter see Dean's account, in which he described his efforts to accurately recall events, as an example of the very effective use of a rhetorical strategy used to negotiate a credible position for himself:

> Dean's presentation of himself as having a good memory, as being unwilling to take credit that belongs to others, as only following the authority of others, as telling the truth, all serve to enhance his reliability as a prosecution witness, to bolster his own disputed version of things, and to mitigate his own culpability under cross-examination
>
> (Edwards and Potter, 1995: 19–20)

Here, the question of the accuracy of Dean's account is not seen as a relevant issue. Rather, the researchers are concerned with *how* Dean constructed his account and made it effective. Traditional psychology's view of qualitative data such as interview transcripts has been to regard these as evidence of intrapsychic processes and states, like memories. So discursive psychology both reframes the status of language in psychology and also considers psychology's usual subject matter, i.e. internal states and structures, somewhat irrelevant.

The psychological subject in discursive psychology

Discursive psychology thus radically departs from traditional North American psychology, which has concerned itself with internal states such as cognitions, emotions, attitudes and motivations in the belief that these lie behind the things that people do and say. However, discursive psychology does not deny that people experience emotional states or memories, only that these can be assumed to lie behind our linguistic expression of them in a causal way; it brackets these off, arguing that we cannot know about them; at least we cannot find out anything about them from our study of what people say.

Discursive psychologists have taken the phenomena that we usually think of as private, psychological events and states such as attitudes, emotions and memories and removed them into the public, social realm. Their arguments for doing this are convincing, but the model of the person that is implied in discursive psychology is ambiguous. The person here is an active and skilful participant in social life, busily engaged in constructing accounts for various purposes, but it is hard to answer the question of why accounts might be constructed in one way rather than another without recourse to concepts such as self, belief or motivation. We are left without any clue as to who is doing the constructing and why.

Harré (1983, 1985, 1989, 1995a, 1995b, 1998, and 1999) also locates his theoretical approach within discursive psychology, and has used it to reframe a variety of psychological and physiological phenomena as social and performative, such as emotion, coughing, memory, and practical skills. He also provides a way of understanding the role of neurological and physiological functioning in psychological phenomena, and his approach is therefore rather more inclusive and integrated than other discursive accounts. In traditional psychology, the role of biology has often been reductionistic. That is, psychological events like thoughts and emotions have been reduced to and explained in terms of the activity of the brain, endocrine system and so on. Harré's discursive approach sees neurological functions as a necessary requirement for these psychological events without seeing these functions as causing or constituting them. He uses the example of a skill to illustrate this. Surely it is not unreasonable to believe that, say, laying a stone wall can be entirely and adequately described by a series of physiological events? However, Harré points out that when we begin to look at any skill, such as playing the piano or carving wood, we are immediately back in the social, linguistic realm. Certainly, particular physiological capacities and neurological functions must be present in order for us to perform certain tasks. But to demonstrate a skill means to have performed in accordance with some culturally and historically specific definition, and to have had one's efforts accounted for in skill-type language. We can begin to see that thinking of even simple skills as the straightforward manifestation of physiological events is very shaky. We are immediately drawn into issues about who decides what constitutes a skill, how it is deemed to have been performed, and under what circumstances claims to skilful performance are accepted or rejected.

But Harré's major contribution to an understanding of the person in discursive psychology has been his account of the self as a linguistic phenomenon. In traditional psychology, the self is a rather vague concept but it is generally taken to refer to the psychological properties of an individual that in some way lie behind their actions. The self is what motivates and directs the person's conduct. The self is therefore a very problematic concept within social constructionism, and particularly for discursive psychology, because of its essentialism and its location within the boundary of the individual. Harré reframes the self as a function of language; he argues that the assumption of the self as an entity, an object that can be studied, is a mistake that we make because of our language. We often use words to refer to the objects around us; we point to an animal and say 'there's a lion', and we make requests such as 'please pass the brown sauce'. In these cases, the words 'lion' and 'brown sauce' have what Harré calls an indexical function; they point to, refer to, existing objects. The words are labels for things. However, he says that we make a fundamental error when we assume that other, more psychological words such as 'I' and 'me' are indexical in the same way. It is as if we non-consciously reason that since the words 'I' and 'me' exist, then specific entities referred to by those terms must also exist; there must be an 'I' and a 'me' in the same sense that there are lions and brown sauce. He believes that our language, which has the personal pronoun 'I' (many languages do not use words such as 'I', 'she', 'they' and so on to accompany their verbs), misleads us into this fundamental but erroneous belief. The simple existence of the word 'I' allows us to foster the belief that we are autonomous individuals, that each of us is represented by a coherent, unified self, and furthermore that this self contains mechanisms and processes, the subject matter of psychology, that are responsible for our actions.

According to Harré (1995c, 1999), what the word 'I' actually does is to specify a location for the acts performed by a speaker:

> To be a person is to be a singularity, to be just one person. This is not a ubiquitous fact that students of human life have discovered. It is part of the grammar of the 'person' concept . . . Personhood is so bounded by the singularity of each human being's embodiment that neither more nor less than one person per body is permitted to stand.
>
> (Harré, 1999: 103)

'I' draws attention to the body of one particular speaker who occupies a unique location, both physically and socially, and it also commits that individual to the consequences of their utterance. When I say, for example, 'I promise I will fix the car tomorrow', this utterance is not a report on an internal thought or feeling but a public commitment, a moral act, that is simultaneously tied to myself as speaker; it is me, and no other, who has made the promise.

Instead of looking at the words 'I' and 'me' as if they represented real entities, and then going on, as psychologists have traditionally done, to ask questions about the nature of those entities, Harré instead argues that we make use of such words in conversation to perform actions in a moral universe. Within discursive psychology generally the person as social actor is seen as primarily struggling to represent themselves in an acceptable way with respect to their culture's local moral rules:

> Looking still more closely at our conversation shows the enquirer that I, and in other languages the first-person inflection, is used to perform a moral act, an act of commitment to the content of the utterance in the appropriate moral universe . . . The human individual is, above all, in those societies that recognize autonomy, a moral phenomenon . . . 'I' is a word having a role in conversation, a role that is not referential, nor

is the conversation in which it dominates typically descriptive fact-stating. It is a form of life, a moral community that has been presupposed by the uses of the first person, not a kind of hidden inner cognitive engine.

(Harré, 1989: 26)

Harré's use of the concept of 'positioning' (see Chapter 6) stresses the construction of subjectivity and personhood during the ebb and flow of real interactions, while acknowledging the power of prevailing discourses to constrain and shape our sense of self.

The person as moral actor

Discursive psychology stresses the active, performative role that language has, and sees the goal of such performances to be primarily one of accounting for our conduct within a moral framework, i.e. within the specific system of rules of conduct of one's local culture. 'Local', in this context, could, for example, mean western industrialised society, the culture of a particular nation, or a group sub-culture. It simply refers to the sets of rules and conventions about right and wrong and correct behaviour within which the person is currently operating. The person is primarily located within a local moral order within which they have to negotiate a viable position for themselves. The functions which their constructed accounts serve for the person are primarily those of offering explanations and excuses, making justifications, apportioning blame and making accusations. The person is therefore an actor in a moral universe, concerned with negotiating for themselves a credible, and creditable, moral position.

For example, Wetherell and Potter (1988) identify three of the repertoires used by interview respondents in their study of racism in New Zealand. The 'culture fostering' repertoire presents the view that Maori culture should be encouraged and protected both for the sake of its uniqueness and distinctiveness and in order to provide Maori people with a sense of their own historical and cultural roots. A second repertoire, that of 'pragmatic realism', stressed the promotion of things that are useful and relevant to modern-day life, and the third repertoire, 'togetherness', advocates the view that there should be no divisions or barriers between people; we should all see and treat each other simply as people, regardless of colour or cultural background. Wetherell and Potter suggest that these repertoires are used by their respondents to create accounts which relieve them of a moral responsibility for action and which effectively justify and validate the status quo. The respondents can be seen to be concerned to position themselves acceptably with respect to the moral rules and expectations of their culture. The person is therefore located as an actor or performer in a moral sphere, a person whose prime aim in constructing their account is to construct themselves and their actions as morally justifiable.

Although he does not describe himself as a discursive psychologist, Kenneth Gergen's view, at least in some of his earlier work, shares many of the same assumptions as discursive psychology and can certainly be placed within the area of micro social constructionism. In addition to a focus upon the skilful use of language by interactants, Gergen (1989) builds into his account some notion of power differences, something that is often absent from discursive psychology. Gergen sees the person as motivated by a desire for 'speaking rights' or 'voice', and to have their interpretation of events accepted as the truthful one. The person who is able to 'warrant voice' is therefore a skilled operator with a good understanding of warranting conventions. But in order to warrant one's actions, to give a socially acceptable account of them according to context, it is also necessary to draw upon a variety of different representations of selfhood. For example, versions of selfhood or human nature could include 'the person as unique collection of traits', 'the person as the bearer of original sin', or 'underneath the skin, people are basically all the same'. Such accounts of selfhood could be used, say, to justify competition, to advocate some form of social control, or to gain support for a multicultural initiative. Gergen implies that these different versions of selfhood have emerged as people throughout history have found it necessary to construct and elaborate them into an armoury with which to fight their own personal or group battles for 'voice'.

This view suggests that the prime motivation in social interaction is to gain voice, which of course will have a diversity of practical, social consequences. Those who are able to warrant voice are likely to enjoy greater power in society, may be given greater resources (money, jobs, education etc.) and will enjoy generally higher social standing. Gergen seems to see the individual's motivation to acquire 'voice' as the source of the variety of representations or discourses of selfhood that are currently available.

Some versions of events warrant voice more than others; they are heard more frequently and are more likely to receive the label of truth or common sense. This may be because those in relatively powerful positions have both the resources and the authority to make their versions of events 'stick'. For example, companies may spend huge amounts of money to fill the media with certain representations of their products, and those in positions of authority such as doctors warrant voice in the sense that they have the capacity to legitimate their own version of an event (the patient's symptoms) by making a diagnosis, possibly denying that of their patient who may have a different story to tell about what is happening to their body. Thus in these examples the ability to bring off an effective construction of events is tied to the power of money and medical authority. We can therefore say that, in Gergen's terms, those in relatively powerful positions warrant voice more easily than others.

However, in ordinary everyday life, we are all nevertheless engaged in this process with each other, and in this context, with our friends, family and workmates, 'voice' is determined by how skilful a person is at using the warranting conventions belonging to their particular society. So that an important part of warranting one's actions, of making them appear reasonable and justifiable, is having the ability to present oneself in different ways according to the demands of the moment. The person who successfully manages to warrant voice does so because they are particularly adept at using these warranting conventions. Therefore the person who is a skilled discourse user has at their disposal the means to bring off their desired identity construction for themselves, and to resist those offered by others. Billig's view of the person as rhetorician has similar qualities, focusing upon the ways that people use their capacity for argument, justification, criticism and so on to achieve particular social effects (Billig, 1987).

This gives us an insight into why different people or groups may employ different constructions of events, and why the same people may use different constructions of the same event on different occasions. Constructions arise not from people attempting to communicate supposed internal states but from their attempts to bring off a representation of themselves or the world that has a liberating, legitimating or otherwise positive effect for them. This would include the tendency for those in positions of power to legitimate and endorse constructions or discourses, which maintain and justify that position.

Subjectivity in discursive psychology

If our experience of ourselves is not derived from an essential nature, either biologically pre-programmed or acquired, how should we explain our apparent psychological nature? That we experience ourselves as the possessors of personalities, attitudes, motivations and so on requires some explanation if we are to regard these as fictions, or at least as entities that do not lie behind and cause our talk. Discursive psychologists do not regard this question of subjectivity as their central concern. Nevertheless, they have offered some indication of how we are to understand subjectivity, although this is not an issue that has been given attention in their more recent publications (however, see Harré, 1998 for a detailed discussion of the concepts of 'person' and 'self').

Potter and Wetherell (1987) suggest that the kinds of ways we have available for talking about ourselves gives rise to our experience of ourselves as human beings. By way of an illustrative example, they describe selfhood from the perspective of a culture very different from that of western industrialised societies, that of the Maori. Drawing upon Harré (1983) and Smith (1981) they describe what appears to constitute personhood for the Maori. For the Maori, the person is invested with a particular kind of power, called 'mana', which is given to the person, by the gods, in accordance with their family status and birth circumstances. This 'mana' is what enables the person to be effective, whether in battle or in their everyday dealings with each other. This power, however, is not a stable resource, but can be enhanced or diminished by the person's day-to-day conduct. For example, their power could be reduced if they forget one of the ritual observances or commit some misdemeanour. A person's social standing, their successes and failures and so on, are seen as dependent upon external forces, not internal states such as their personality or level of motivation. For the Maori, accounting for oneself in terms of external forces such as 'mana' means that all mental life and subjective experience will be read off from this framework. Potter and Wetherell suggest that a person living in such a culture, holding such beliefs, would necessarily experience themselves in quite a different way from that which we are used to:

> If one views the world in this kind of way, with the individual seen as the site of varied and variable external forces (and

mana is only one of these possible forces, which inhabit the individual), then different kinds of self-experience become possible. Specifically, individuals can cease to represent themselves as the centre and origin of their actions, a conception which has been taken to be vital to Western concepts of the self. The individual Maori does not own experiences such as the emotions of fear, anger, love, grief; rather they are visitations governed by the unseen world of powers and forces, just as an inanimate object, a stone or pebble, can be invested with magical taboo powers so that touching it places the offender in danger.

(Potter and Wetherell, 1987: 105)

They therefore suggest that the very experience of being a person, the kind of mental life one can experience, perhaps even how we experience sensory information, is dependent upon the particular representations of selfhood, the particular ways of accounting for ourselves, that are available to us in our culture. Harré expresses this point well: 'To be a self is not to be a certain kind of being, but to be in possession of a certain kind of theory' (1985: 262).

For Harré the form of subjectivity we live out and experience depends upon the particular theories or stories about the nature of humanity that are to be found embedded in our language. He suggests that our psychology is structured by these things and encourages us to look to our accounts of ourselves and each other for clues to the theories we are operating. The human subjects described here are beings who learn the socially acceptable ways of accounting for themselves and who learn to become adept at the practice of these, and uses them for their own purposes. The human subject is therefore trainable in linguistic practices, but is also liable to be misled by those practices into thinking that grammatical devices, such as the self, have ontological status, i.e. that they have some existence outside of language and texts. The experience of selfhood that we acquire as we develop language represents our structuring of experience. This structuring is made possible by the particular internal logic, underlying categories, metaphors and so on of the language we use. We should therefore expect people of all cultures and societies to organise their personal experience into a meaningful system which can be called the 'self', but we should not expect this selfhood to be similar cross-culturally, and the differences between two cultures' versions

of selfhood will be rooted in the underlying grammar or logic of
their languages.

The self in relationship

Some writers who align themselves with a social constructionist
theoretical framework have proposed relocating the crucible of
behaviour and experience in the interpersonal space between
people, within relationships and interactions.

The self in dialogue

John Shotter (1993a, 1993b, 1995a, 1995b) talks of 'joint action', a
term borrowed from the symbolic interactionist Herbert Blumer,
where the behaviours of each participant are not isolable and
cannot be said to cause each other. He was trying to get away from
the idea that what people do and say somehow emanates from
internal psychic structures such as personality. When people interact, it is rather like a dance in which they are constantly moving
together, subtly responding to each other's rhythm and posture.
The dance is constructed between them and cannot be seen as the
result of either person's prior intentions. Likewise, when we
interact our talk and behaviour is a joint effort, a dialogue, and not
the product of internal states or forces.

In Kenneth Gergen's more recent work (Gergen, 1997, 1999,
2000, 2001a) he too locates psychological events inside relationship
exchanges and has developed a concern to embed the psychological
person within a vast network of social and historical relationships.
He regards the current value that we place on being an individual
as destructive and dangerous. He sees this as at the root of both
interpersonal and international conflict, a lack of trust and
intimacy between people, a tendency toward self-interest, the idea
that personal relationships are somehow not natural for us, and the
view that relationships are about self-gratification rather than
commitment and support. He argues that individualism is at the
root of our instrumental, exploitative attitude towards others and
toward nature. It invites us into a 'posture of competition', and to
blame individuals rather than society for social ills. The ideology of
individualism can be seen, he says, in international relations, where
we routinely fail to see how our own interests are inevitably bound
up with those of other nations. He calls instead for a relational

view of the person. Like Shotter, he sees the person not as an isolable phenomenon but as a function of our relations with others. Here, the self is a complex product of all our past and present relations. Drawing on Bakhtin (the Russian linguist and philosopher), Gergen argues that our selves are negotiated and constructed in relationships, and each new relationship we make will in turn bear the mark of the other, earlier relationships we have formed. The person that we are, in this view, depends upon – rather than stands in isolation against – other people. He calls for us to reflect on our own use of language, leading to more emancipatory ways of constructing things. Such reflecting, he says, is a way of acknowledging and bringing together the community of voices in which we are immersed, leading to less conflict in the world through a 'greater knitting of human community' (1999: 63). He sees a move toward 'relational being' not as a way of ending conflict and difference but as a way of helping us manage it less damagingly. He wants to encourage dialogue between people in order to manage conflict in the world, to get away from people seeing themselves as individuals or groups with competing interests. He recommends using conversational practices that de-emphasise individuality, blame and rights, that demonstrate the complexity of our beliefs and that validate the other and reduce the distance between us. This concern that we should make opportunities to hear and encourage the multiplicity of voices (discourses, opinions, points of view, stories) that exist in the world is consistent with his relativism as discussed in Chapter 5.

The self in narrative

Social constructionism paints a picture of the person as multiple, fragmented and incoherent. We have a multiplicity of different selves, each called forth or conjured by our immersion in discourse and in the processes of social interaction. But our subjective experience is often the opposite; we still feel that there is coherence to the person we are, that it bears themes both historically and across the different areas of our lives that give us this sense of self, and this needs some explanation. One possibility is that our feelings of consistency and continuity in time are provided by our memory. Memory allows us to look back on our behaviours and experiences, to select those that seem to 'hang together' in some narrative framework, literally the story of our lives, and to look for patterns, repetitions and so on that provide us with the impression of continuity and coherence. The application of the concept of narrative in understanding the self has attracted much attention from psychologists and others in recent years, and has been attractive to some social constructionists because of the opportunity it offers to sketch a theory of the self that is not essentialist and that locates this self in the social domain. Indeed, narrative psychology itself has been influenced by social constructionist thinking.

One of the classic contributions to narrative psychology has been that of Sarbin (1986). Sarbin argues that human beings impose a structure on their experience, and that this structure is present both in our accounts of ourselves and our experience that we give to others, and in how we represent those things to ourselves. This structure is a narrative structure; we organise our experience in terms of stories. This is in no way to suggest that people are living in a fantasy world or that the stories that people produce are in some way whimsical. Just as Harré sees the structuring of our experience and our self-understandings to be given by the internal logic or grammar of our language, Sarbin suggests that this structuring takes a particular form, the narrative form, and that this is ubiquitous throughout human cultures. He sees it as fundamental to what it means to be human.

Sarbin sees narrative, as the organising principle of our psychology, to be present in many facets of daily life. It is present in our dreams and daydreams, in our rememberings, in our plans for the future or for the day ahead, and in our accounts that we tell to others. When we remember a dream, we do not recount a list of unconnected events and images, we see it and recount it as a story that has a beginning, a middle and an end. In some cases, we are aware of having to do a good deal of story construction with the dream material in order to give it a sense of narrative. Even quite abstract and, on the surface of it meaningless, perceptual events tend to be given narrative structure by people. Heider and Simmel (1944) and Michotte (1963) both report experimental studies in which observers were asked to report what they saw after watching a film of moving geometric shapes. Their reports typically took the form of stories, in which the shapes were cast as human actors engaged in some endeavour.

When we tell someone the story of our life so far, we do not recount, or even remember, the entire content of our experience to date. We are selective about what is included in our story and what is left out, and this is not simply about judging which facts a stranger may or may not know about us. We craft our tale according to a theme; has our life been an adventure story, a comedy or a tragedy? Who are the heroes and anti-heroes? Will it have a happy ending? The consistency of our narrative demands that we engage in much 'smoothing', choosing and moulding events to fit the theme of our life story. If the theme of a person's self-narrative is 'life has always dealt me an unfair hand' then events which might be seen as lucky or otherwise positive might be smoothed over in order to fit them to the theme, or left out altogether. This process should not be thought of as necessarily a conscious activity, though it sometimes is. We may not be in a position to readily articulate to ourselves the narrative that we have constructed about our life. It is useful to think of these narratives as the ways we live out our lives as well as the way we privately or publicly tell of them.

Sarbin sees the emergence of narrative structure in human thought as evidence of and dependent upon the perception of time. The fundamental defining feature of a narrative is that it joins events together in a beginning–middle–end sequence, which places those events in time as well as space. The concepts of time and space are therefore fundamental to human life, since narratives cannot be built without them. Although narrative structure is seen as fundamental to human life, it is not clear whether this is 'hard-wired' into the human psyche, or acquired by the kinds of processes described by Harré earlier. Sutton-Smith (1986) and Mancuso (1986) show that as children grow up they gradually begin to adopt traditional plot structures in their own story telling and to represent themselves and their actions by using narrative structures.

Gergen and Gergen (1986) have further developed the idea of narrative structure to include the following criteria: a stated goal or valued end-point of the story, narrative events which are represented as having causal connections between them and which relate to the end-point or goal, and movement through time. They go as far as suggesting that we use a limited number of basic narrative forms, such as the 'romance', the 'tragedy' or the 'comedy', each having a characteristic plot shape regarding the rise and fall of fortunes as the story develops. However, Gergen and Gergen do not only concern themselves with individual psychological functioning. They assert that narrative structure applies just as much to the accounts of science and social science as it does to personal accounts, and they suggest that we address ourselves to the task of understanding how theorists use narrative criteria to enable them to formulate powerful or compelling accounts of human functioning. Although they do not explicitly draw upon work in the poststructuralist tradition, this aspect of their writing bears a resemblance to those who question the facticity of scientific knowledge and seek to lay bare its political implications. They argue that psychology and social psychology have traditionally set out with the assumption that universal and timeless laws of human behaviour and experience can be discovered. Such an assumption, they say, dooms the project to failure since human life is characterised essentially by change, and we cannot hope to understand ourselves or our predicament if we do not recognise the historical, social and political contexts of both our own experience and our theories about human life. In common with other social constructionist writers, they ask not whether our theories of human nature are true or false, but whether they have 'generative potential'. Do they enable us to throw into question the traditional, accepted rules and moral values of our culture and offer fresh alternatives for action? What new narratives in psychology might be useful for people in changing their lives? (see McNamee and Gergen, 1992).

In our personal lives, too, our self-narratives have implications well beyond our own functioning. The narratives that we construct about ourselves are not simply a private matter. Crossley (2002) says: 'I cannot be a self on my own but only in relation to certain "interlocutors" who are crucial to my language of self-understanding' (p. 3). These interlocutors do not have to be physically present. Mary Gergen (2001) talks of 'social ghosts'; we hold private dialogues with absent or imagined others when reflecting on our experience and in constructing our narratives. Furthermore, we are heavily dependent upon the willingness of co-actors in the construction of our story. To the extent that we construct our identity through narrative accounts, then our stories must be compatible with those of other people who feature in our accounts. For example, a person may have constructed their life history as a tragedy in which their father has the role of thwarting their ambitions, resulting in their failure to establish a career. But if the father's life story is a 'progressive' one in which he is portrayed as struggling against all odds and eventually succeeding to raise a healthy family and turn his children into responsible adults, then we can see that the father and son will have great difficulty in playing a part in and supporting each other's self-narratives. We are dependent for our identity upon the willingness of others to support us in our version of events. Narratives are subject to social sanctioning and negotiation. Similarly, in furnishing accounts of and justifying our actions we are subject to the same limitations. In our attempts to represent ourselves in particular ways, we are dependent upon the willingness of others to allow us to paint a picture of their part in the action that suits our story. Our version of their behaviour must be compatible with their own self-narratives. This feature of narrative construction therefore has fundamental implications for identity; how can we bring off a publicly sanctioned version of ourselves, and what are the limitations imposed on our capacity to do this?

Crossley (2000, 2002), building on the earlier work of Sarbin and others, addresses the relationship between personal narratives and the social realm, as well as the apparent coherence of our lives as told in our stories. As inhabitants of a culture, we are immersed, from the time of our birth, in a rich variety of stories, myths, fairy tales and narratives of ordinary lives played out on TV and in film. We are thus inducted not only into narrative thinking but also into the form and content that our narratives may take. Livesey (2002) talks of 'tellable' narratives; what counts as a 'hearable' story is dependent on the form and content of other, similar stories circulating in our culture. For example, Livesey notes how personal accounts of childhood sexual abuse are pulled toward a narrative in which the victim needs therapeutic intervention in order to overcome an inability to move on in their relationships. Discourses circulating in our culture and constructing our identity also place limitations on what kind of stories we can tell about our experience. For example, Seymour-Smith (2002) notes how, in her study of men with testicular cancer, the men, who had made video diaries, used ironic humour in order to present their story of serious illness without transgressing dominant representations of masculinity.

Crossley challenges the view that narratives make a coherent, smooth story out of the incoherence of our selves and our lives; that lives, unlike narratives, do not have an 'implicit contract toward order' (Crossley, 2002: 9). Drawing on a number of earlier writers, she argues that not only do we *tell* stories about ourselves, that we *live* them also. We conduct our lives by living in the present and planning a future in a way that links us meaningfully with our understanding of our past. Furthermore, drawing on the ideas of Kierkegaard and the literary theorist Paul Ricouer, Crossley suggests that it is through the process of selecting and telling our self-narratives that we actually become ethical beings, taking responsibility for our lives. She argues that the reality of the storying of our lives is most dramatically and painfully made apparent in the case of traumatising experiences such as chronic and serious illness. In such circumstances we are typically not only physically but also psychologically disabled. Our most basic assumptions about the world, about ourselves and our life projects are thrown into question and thus revealed; our implicit life stories have become derailed. Narrative psychology can therefore be used to contradict the social constructionist vision of the person as decentred and as without coherence. However Kenneth Gergen (1994) argues against this degree of coherence and against the idea that our lives are conducted in narrative form to any great degree. He sees our use of narrative as a way of telling a multiplicity of stories about ourselves, and our self-narratives as primarily conversational resources used in our accounting processes during interaction. In this respect they appear similar to interpretative repertoires.

Agency

The individual is commonly seen as capable of making choices and acting accordingly; we see our behaviour as the result of an act of will rather than the outcome of forces beyond our control. To what extent is personal agency to be found in these social constructionist accounts of the person?

Discursive psychology generally does not explicitly address this question, although it seems obvious that this perspective demands an agentic person at least in some respects, in the person's ability to manipulate discourse and use it for their own ends. If people build accounts for purposes that are motivated by practical and moral considerations, then persons must to some degree be strategists able to choose courses of action and carry out intentions. Harré (1995a), although his primary aim is to propose that the self as agent is constructed in the kind of talk we use to defend and excuse our actions, recognises the implicit agent in his own account. He sees agency as constituted in the accounts that we give of our actions, the way we represent ourselves as responsible for, or not responsible for, our behaviour. Our responsibility is indexed through 'the grammar of the first person', the use of the word 'I'. Nevertheless, he points to a paradox in all this:

> Behind whatever is the presentation, whether of activity or passivity, there must be an active player, the person as strategist. Speaking and hearing, conversing, is something we do. It is not something that happens to us. In the very act of displaying oneself as a patient one demonstrates one's agency!
>
> (Harré, 1995a: 136)

Narrative and relational views of the person seem relatively easy to align with personal agency. Although our own narratives may be to some degree moulded by cultural narrative form and content, we are nevertheless the authors of our own stories. Even where the self and self-narratives are seen as jointly produced, we must at least have as much agency in their production as our co-authors.

Summary

Discursive psychology reframes what we normally think of as the content of the person and locates it in the public, social realm of interpersonal interaction. It casts these things as constructed in accounts for particular interactional purposes. The person is an actor in a moral universe, motivated to build credible and defensible accounts of their actions. The psychology of the person who uses discourse is not of primary interest, although there is some indication that the symbolic system we are born into will have profound implications for the nature of our subjectivity. Where the nature of the person has been more explicitly addressed, for example in Harré's work, it is suggested that our sense of self is a product of and structured around the particular linguistic conventions of our culture such as the grammar of the first person. Narrative psychology also focuses upon the way that experience is psychologically organised. Here, human beings are fundamentally storytellers who experience themselves and their lives in narrative terms. Perspectives that see the person in relational, dialogic or narrative terms see the person as a co-production, constructed during interaction or other symbolic dialogue. Within all of these views it is possible to regard personal agency as actual or as an effect of and constituted in language.

Chapter 8

Social constructionist research

If we take on board the social constructionist arguments concerning the nature of personhood, the role of language in identity, subjectivity and social life and the historical and cultural specificity of traditional psychology and social psychology, it becomes evident that the aims and practices of social enquiry must be radically transformed. We cannot investigate the psychological and social world using our old assumptions and practices, because their focus on internal psychic structures and processes such as attitudes and personality traits is inappropriate. We must also build into our new practices of scientific enquiry our understanding of how the knowledge produced within the traditional scientific paradigm is a function of a power imbalance between researchers and the objects of their study. And our new research practices must take a greater interest in language and other symbolic systems, since the uses and effects of these are of central importance to social constructionists. In this chapter I will overview some of the theoretical and methodological issues raised for research by social constructionism, before going on to describe and give examples of some of the forms of research associated with it.

Concern with the issues outlined above has led to new developments in research and a flurry of research activity, as well as a preference for qualitative methods of enquiry since these are often ideal for gathering linguistic and textual data and are viewed as less likely to decontextualise the experience and accounts of respondents. The data are then often analysed using approaches that are referred to as 'discourse analysis' (see Potter, 1996b, who challenges the idea that discourse analysis can simply be described as a 'method'). A social constructionist theoretical position does not necessarily mean that one must use a discourse analytic approach in one's research, or that to use a discourse analytic approach means that one must be a social constructionist. Social constructionism as a loose collection of theoretical perspectives and discourse analysis as an approach to doing social research do not coincide each other in a one-to-one fashion. Social constructionists may validly use other qualitative or even quantitative methods in their research. Gergen (1999, 2001a) argues that it is not empirical methods, such as experiments, that are incompatible with social constructionism but the universalistic truth claims that usually accompany them. And, as Burman and Parker (1993) point out, researchers who are not social constructionists may find that they have been doing discourse analysis without labelling it as such. Having said this, it seems to be the case that discourse analysis has been enthusiastically adopted by many social constructionists as an approach to research.

There are now a number of types of such research that, in one way or another, analyse language and texts. They vary not only in their conceptual and analytic tools but also in the aims of their research. Foucauldian discourse analysis is interested in how language is implicated in power relations, but is concerned more broadly with the ways in which discourses produce subjectivity, for example through positioning (see Chapter 6). Foucauldian discourse analysis may use either spoken or written texts of all kinds, or indeed any material with symbolic content, such as film, photographs, clothes or buildings. Discursive psychologists focus upon the analysis of talk in interaction. This can include both naturally occurring interactions, such as business meetings, case conferences and ordinary conversations, as well as specially designed research interviews. Discursive psychology aims to identify the forms of argument and rhetorical devices being used by the participants. For example, Gill (1993) looked at how male radio broadcasters built accounts which justified the lack of female radio presenters, and Auburn et al. (1999) studied police interviews in criminal investigations and showed how disbelief of a suspect's account was constructed and used persuasively by the police interviewer.

Those discursive psychologists who want to maintain a concern with issues of ideology and power tend to make use of the interpretative repertoire as an analytical tool. Others are more interested in exploring the skilful use of rhetorical devices that speakers display in constructing accounts and managing their position in the interaction on a moment-to-moment basis. Conversation analysis (CA) limits itself to the study of small-scale naturally occurring interactions, and is concerned to identify the regularities, patterns and sequences in language use, such as greetings and turn taking. It studies the performative capacity of speech, how talk makes things happen and achieves effects for interactants. CA is not especially informed by or concerned with social constructionist theory, although the analytic method it adopts has influenced others who do take a social constructionist approach and its method is often used by discourse psychologists (see Potter et al., 1990 for a brief overview of the different discourse analytic approaches and their origins, and also Wetherell et al., 2001a).

Theoretical and methodological issues

Before going on to look at these different kinds of research it is important to set the scene by first making explicit the way that social constructionism radically changes the rules of the game of social science. I will therefore outline some of the theoretical assumptions underlying the approach that are of particular relevance in a research context, and some of the major methodological issues that social constructionist research raises. It should be noted that these theoretical assumptions are not necessarily confined to social constructionism. In particular, those taking a feminist approach to research (for example Harding, 1991 and Wilkinson, 1996) have also been concerned with issues of objectivity, value-freedom and the position of those people who are the subjects of psychological research.

Objectivity and value-freedom

Within the traditional research paradigm of science, the researcher can claim truthfulness for their findings by recourse to the supposed objectivity of scientific method. The experimenter is able to stand back from their own humanity and reveal the objective nature of the phenomena under study without bias and without contaminating the results with leakage from their own personal involvement. However, within a social constructionist framework, the 'objectivity-talk' of scientists becomes just part of the discourse of science through which a particular version, and vision, of human life is constructed. Gilbert and Mulkay (1984) examined the way that scientists defend their work and criticise that of others. They identified two contrasting interpretative repertoires: the empiricist repertoire and the contingent repertoire. The empiricist repertoire included references to the objective and impersonal, data-driven nature of their research. The contingent repertoire made reference to researchers' possible motives and biases and other aspects of their work that could be regarded as bad science. When a researcher's own work was challenged by another's use of the 'contingent' repertoire, they sometimes resorted to a rhetorical device that Gilbert and Mulkay call 'The Truth Will Out'; here, scientists implied that their own position would eventually be seen to be the truthful one.

Furthermore, social constructionism would regard objectivity as an impossibility, since each of us, of necessity, must encounter the world from some perspective or other (from where we stand) and the questions we come to ask about that world, our theories and hypotheses, must also of necessity arise from the assumptions that are embedded in our perspective. No human being can step outside of their humanity and view the world from no position at all, which is what the idea of objectivity suggests, and this is just as true of scientists as of everyone else. The task of the researcher therefore becomes to acknowledge and even to work with their own intrinsic involvement in the research process and the part that this plays in the results that are produced. The researcher must view the research as necessarily a co-production between themselves and the people they are researching. For example, in an interview it can be readily seen how the researcher's own assumptions must inform what questions are asked and how, and that the interviewer as a human being cannot be seen as an inanimate writing pad or machine that records the interviewee's responses uncontaminated by human interaction.

In addition, facts themselves can never be impartial. They are always the product of someone asking a particular question, and questions always derive from, albeit often implicit, assumptions about the world. For example, the huge research literature on sex differences (see Maccoby and Jacklin, 1974) says less about the psychological differences between the sexes, which turn out to be relatively few, than it does about psychologists' assumptions that women and men must be different kinds of people. But the values underpinning psychological research may equally be very explicit. The values informing applications of social psychology in the manipulation of wartime morale, public attitudes and worker productivity are clear (see Howitt, 1991 for a discussion of values in psychology). Social constructionists argue that, since there can never be any objectively defined truth about people – something which remains true regardless of the time or culture in which they live – that all claims to have discovered such truths must be regarded as political acts. They are attempts to validate some representations of the world and to invalidate others, and therefore to validate some forms of human life and to invalidate others. The criticism of the discipline of psychology is therefore not that it is political, since all our knowledge claims must of necessity be so, but that it has achieved its political effects precisely through its claim to be value-free and therefore apolitical. This also obscures the ways that psychological research has been used, and continues to be used, to address the concerns of relatively powerful groups in society. Psychology may be used to address 'a problem', but problems, like facts, have no objective existence. They are always problems *for someone*. And, to adapt a popular saying, one person's problem is another's solution. For example, we often hear that the breakdown of the family is a contemporary problem. Certainly, the divorce rate and the consequent rise in the number of single-parent families poses financial, employment and housing problems for the government. But the 'flight from the family' can also be seen as the solution to the problem of oppressive marriages and abusive partners for many women. Also, as Willig (1999b) notes, using psychological knowledge to understand and to influence individual behaviour, as in the field of health education, can draw a veil over the importance of factors such as poverty and unemployment for morbidity and mortality.

Researcher and researched

Within a social constructionist framework traditional psychology, as a scientific enterprise, is seen as making powerful truth claims. The discourse and rhetoric of science constructs the findings of psychological research as 'knowledge' or 'truth', and puts the psychologist, the researcher, in a relatively powerful position with respect to those people whom they are researching, their 'subjects'. Psychology, in so far as it has adopted a scientific discourse, accords researchers and academics a greater claim to truth than the subjects of their study, i.e. lay people, the terms 'scientist' and 'lay person' representing readily available subject positions within a scientific discourse. The researcher's version of events has greater warrant and is given more 'voice' than that of the subject, whose experience is interpreted and given sometimes quite different meanings by the researcher. The researcher is the holder of knowledge, the one who tests theories and interprets results. The subject merely passively responds to the experimental conditions, and their voice is not present in the resultant research report. As Howitt (1991) points out, the use of the term 'subject' indicates a power differential between researcher and subject:

> There are two significant implications of the use of the term 'subjects' that probably reveal more about psychology than a mere word should. First, people become merely objects to which something is done, thereby losing many of the features of their humanity – including having choice of action and being active rather than passive. Second, psychology is the realm of psychologists not of their subjects. So rather than psychology being what people who take part in research give to other people conducting the research, it is separated from people and in the hands of those who *do* this sort of psychology to people. Very clearly this is a power relationship for the production of social knowledge.
> (Howitt, 1991: 51–2. Italics in original)

The preferred method of a psychology that models itself on the natural sciences is the experiment, and here not only do experimenter and subject become caught up in an undemocratic relationship but the reported experience of the subject becomes decontextualised. The control of variables supposedly extraneous to the concerns of the experiment effectively strips the subjects' behaviour of the context that gives it its meaning and rationale, replacing this with the experimenter's own interpretations. This is one of the concerns that fuelled the 'crisis' in social psychology of the 1970s (see Chapter 1).

Social constructionists therefore call for the democratisation of the research relationship. If the scientist's or researcher's account of a phenomenon is seen as 'fact' as a result of the warranting voice of science, we must then acknowledge that other accounts, for example the accounts of respondents in interviews, must be equally valid in principle. There no longer appears to be a good reason to privilege the account or reading of the researcher above that of anyone else, and this puts the researcher and the researched in a new relation to each other. The subject's own account of their experiences can no longer be given an alternative interpretation by the researcher who then offers their reading as truth. In the development of alternative research practices, the validity of the participants' accounts must be acknowledged (this is part of what is referred to as 'reflexivity' – see below). Gergen (1999, 2001a) advocates 'collaborative inquiry', where the research process is informed by the needs and aims of the participants; Orford (1992) recommends 'community psychology', which aims to empower service-users by involving them in identifying problems and finding solutions. These approaches can include 'action research', where the aim of the research is not just to study some existing state of affairs but to change them for the better, and where the values and political agenda motivating the research is therefore explicitly acknowledged. Such research is potentially empowering, since 'it is about finding participant-led ways of improving specific problematic social situations. The psychologist's role in this is to facilitate this process by making available to participants the use of data gathering and analysis skills' (Willig, 1999b: 7). Other researchers who are interested in power issues but are worried about some of the implications of action research prefer to use the approach as social critique, that is 'exposing the ways in which language conspires to legitimate and perpetuate unequal power relations' (Willig, 1999b: 10). For example, Mehan (1996/2001) analysed interactions between various professionals and lay persons with respect to a child who became classified as suffering from a learning disability. He noted how certain ways of talking, especially the technical vocabulary used by professionals, gave their representations of the problem greater weight and authority than those of the parents, whose accounts were more vernacular.

However, it would not be accurate to say that political concerns are central to all social constructionist research. Some social constructionists are more interested in investigating the workings of language and the construction of accounts for their own sake. Such an approach can be seen as valid, in terms of building up a new model of psychology and social psychology and identifying new ways of understanding social phenomena. But those with an explicitly political agenda may well feel uncomfortable with research which appears to deny or at least disregard the power issues embedded in discourse. It is probably fair to say that those working with critical discourse analysis, deconstruction or Foucauldian discourse analysis, and in the identification of interpretative repertoires all, to a greater or lesser degree, have a concern with issues of power and ideology. Those working in discursive psychology and CA are less likely to be explicitly concerned with these matters in their research.

Reflexivity

Reflexivity is a term which is widely used in social constructionist writing, and can often mean a number of different things. As well as referring to the way that the theory re-constitutes the role of respondents, their relationship to the researcher and the status of their accounts, the term is also used in at least two other ways.

Firstly, it is used to draw attention to the fact that, when someone gives an account of an event, that account is simultaneously a description of the event *and* part of the event because of the constitutive nature of talk. This open acknowledgement of the social construction of one's own account as a researcher undermines its potential claim to be the only possible truth, deriving from the greater knowledge and expertise of the researcher, and can thus provide a platform for the discussion of power and authority. For example, does a researcher ever have the right to speak about or for other groups, no matter how well intentioned their research might be? Parker and Burman (1993) are concerned that attempts to include participants more fully in the analysis may not in the end escape the problem of power relations between researcher and researched. They agree with Marks (1993) who, in her own research, found that despite efforts at reflexivity, the researcher's own reading was the one that appeared to carry weight. Thus reflexivity may only bring the illusion of democratisation of the research relationship, which is worse than what it strives to replace.

Reflexivity also refers to the equal status, within discourse analysis, of the researcher and their respondents, as well as of the accounts offered by each. This means that discourse analysts may wish to find a way of building into their research opportunities for participants to comment upon their own accounts and those of the researcher. Sherrard (1991) criticises discourse analysts for not always doing this in their research. Parker and Burman (1993) also are aware that the researcher is tempted to close the text to alternative readings other than their own, and this view is endorsed by Mills (1997). Using as an example the work by Wetherell and Potter (1992), in which they analysed the racist discourse of white New Zealanders, she identifies a:

> problematic eliding of the position of the speaker with that of the analyst . . . Thus, in this discussion of racism, the utterances of white New Zealanders are considered to be transparent in meaning; the opinions of Maoris or Polynesian migrants are not sought and nor are their interpretations of these utterances considered.
>
> (Mills, 1997: 146)

Secondly, reflexivity refers to the fact that social constructionism itself is not exempt from the critical stance it brings to bear on other theories. Social constructionism, as a body of theory and practice, therefore must recognise itself as just as much a social construction as other ways of accounting. Some writers are interested in analysing their own writing, reflexively discussing how their own accounts have been constructed (e.g. Ashmore, 1989; Mulkay, 1985), sometimes leading to an 'infinite interpretative regress, analysing their own analysis, and then analysing their own analysis of their own analysis to demonstrate the layers of construction' (Wetherell, 2001: 397). However, Sherrard (1991) claims that discourse analysts generally fail to address the part played by their own contribution to the discourse when they are taking part in the interaction as an interviewer. She points out that interviews, like conversations, are constructed by both participants, and yet discourse analysts typically fail to explicitly examine their role in the production of the discourse they are analysing. Figueroa and Lopez (1991) also note a general problem with discourse analysts' lack of attention to the methodological processes by which their data were gathered. In general, if one wants to say something insightful about the way an account is constructed or the discourses apparently in operation in a text, the production of the account/text itself, its context, history, intended audience and so on must surely be included in the analysis.

Thirdly, reflexivity refers to the issue of explicitly acknowledging the personal and political values and perspective informing the research. The purpose might be, say, to set the research within a

specific political agenda; or it might be so that the researcher and
reader can explore the ways in which the researcher's own history
and biography may have shaped the research. The experiences
and social location of the participants will also, of course, give
a particular context to their accounts, and this must also be
acknowledged.

The response of social constructionist researchers to the demand
for reflexivity placed on them by the theoretical base of their work
varies a good deal. Some, particularly those working in CA,
maintain some commitment to the value-neutrality of traditional
psychological research and therefore they argue that the issue of
reflexivity does not arise. Some researchers put reflexivity at the
heart of their research design and analysis, while for others it is
sufficient to simply include some commentary on their own
background and values.

Reliability and validity

These are terms familiar to social scientists operating within the
positivist, empiricist paradigm and are the cornerstones of legitimate research in that paradigm. Reliability is the requirement that
the research findings are repeatable, and therefore not simply a
product of fleeting, localised events and validity is the requirement
that the scientist's description of the world matches what is really
there, independent of our ideas and talk about it. But social constructionist research is not about identifying objective facts or
making truth claims. There can be no final description of the
world, and reality may be inaccessible or inseparable from our
discourse about it; all knowledge is provisional and contestable,
and accounts are local and historically/culturally specific. The
concepts of reliability and validity, as they are normally understood, are therefore inappropriate for judging the quality of social
constructionist work.

Social constructionist researchers have struggled with the problem of how to justify their analyses, and a variety of general and
more specific criteria and practices have been put forward. At
present there appear to be no criteria that are universally applied,
although most researchers do seem to recognise the need to
legitimate their analysis in some way. I will do no more than
provide a few examples here, since there are a number of good,
more detailed discussions to be found in other publications. Taylor

(2001) outlines a number of criteria that have been proposed as a way of enhancing the general coherence and rigour of research, that is showing that the analysis has been carried out systematically and that the interpretation has been soundly argued. Some discourse analytic techniques are compatible with quantitative methods of making such assurances, such as calculating indices of agreement between researchers in the coding of textual material. Providing in-depth information about the steps in the analytic procedure enables the reader to make a judgement about its adequacy, and 'member checking' can be used, whereby the researcher asks for feedback from the research participants themselves. 'Usefulness' and 'fruitfulness' are general criteria that could apply to any research, and refer to the power of the analysis to generate theory developments and novel explanations and to cast further light on previous research findings. Wood and Kroger (2000) discuss a number of criteria that contribute toward the overall 'trustworthiness' and 'soundness' of the analysis. In addition to some of those identified by Taylor (2001), they suggest using an audit trail, whereby the investigator provides documentation that allows the reader to track the analytic process from original text to final analysis, perhaps through specific examples. Soundness can also be demonstrated by explicitly showing the logic of the argument being advanced, explaining how it arose from the steps of the analysis and being careful to include revisions and exclusions. Wood and Kroger also attend to the issue raised by Mills (1997) above, regarding the assumption that the researcher's position is identical with that of the respondent. They suggest that a way of ensuring that the participant's orientation is reflected in the analysis is to pay close attention to the participant's use of language, noting what categories, identities and interactional problems appear to be salient for them in the interaction.

Approaches to research

In the rest of this chapter, I will provide illustrative examples of some of the different kinds of research used by social constructionists, and go into a little more detail about their theoretical and political orientations where necessary. I will discuss four approaches to research: conversation analysis, discursive psychology, interpretative repertoires and Foucauldian discourse analysis. While CA is perhaps only minimally social constructionist in theoretical flavour, its close relation to discursive psychology and its occasional use by researchers working within a constructionist or political framework provide a rationale for including it here. These do not exhaust the types of analysis that can be found under the rubric of 'discourse analysis' (for example, a form of discourse analysis is used in linguistics), nor do they describe the range of methods potentially compatible with social constructionism. Nevertheless they represent the kinds of new research developments that will be of particular interest to the social constructionist. My aim will be to show what is distinctive about each of these approaches, to say something about the ways in which they differ from each other, and to comment upon their stance with respect to some of the theoretical and methodological issues outlined above. However, it must be stressed that any one piece of research may bear characteristics of more than one type of analysis. What I am providing here is not a classificatory system but a way of trying to understand some of the differences in emphasis. It is important to understand that the differences between these approaches to research often lie more in the kinds of questions they are trying to answer and in the theoretical assumptions underlying these questions, than in the form that the data gathering and analysis takes in practice; and for this reason I have preferred to talk about 'approaches to research' rather than 'research methods'. So there is much overlap between them; for example, discursive psychologists may extensively use conversation analysis methods and conceptual tools to answer research questions that have not been the traditional focus of CA. I will not go into procedural details about how the analyses are performed; this is beyond my area of expertise and there are now numerous excellent texts that do just this (see Suggested further reading). In any case, such procedural conventions as have grown up in the field often exist more as guidelines aimed at steering what is in the end a subjective, interpretative analysis rather than providing recipe-type instructions.

Conversation analysis

CA may be described as the most 'micro' level approach to discourse analysis. It is concerned with the structure of naturally occurring speech, and studies the phenomena involved in managing social interactions such as turn taking, arguments and conversational repair. It originated in sociology, with the work of Harvey Sacks in the 1960s. Sacks was concerned about the tendency of sociology toward developing abstract, general theories of social life. He was interested in developing a form of sociology that was based on the systematic study of real, specific examples of human action. He saw interpersonal interaction as a potentially rich source of information about how people actually go about the business of social life. One of his first observations was that people use numerous conversational gambits for bringing about certain effects in an interaction. For example, in studying calls to a suicide help-line, he noted how a caller avoided giving his name by re-routing the interaction into an exchange about problems in hearing the other speaker, the member of staff taking the call. CA therefore stresses the active role of the person in interaction. Work in CA has led to the development of a number of key conceptual tools for the analysis of interactions, for example the 'adjacency pair'. This is where an utterance by one speaker places an expectation on the other speaker to respond in a particular way, such as a question and answer, or an invitation and acceptance or refusal. 'Membership categorisation devices' are ways that speakers either explicitly or implicitly place themselves or the other speaker into certain categories of person, for example 'friend' or 'victim', which then bring certain expectations and assumptions with them. CA has also developed a sophisticated and detailed system of transcription, so that researchers are able to record as accurately as possible all the different nuances of spoken language, such as pauses and emphasis.

The brief example in Box 1, taken from Silverman (2001), gives the flavour of the approach.

Box 1

Silverman recorded interviews between HIV counsellors and patients. One of the features of these interviews that interested him was how patients responded when they were asked why they had decided to have an HIV test. He provides this extract from one such interview:

1 **C** erm: what made you decide to come in then [softer]
2   to be tested?
3   (1.0)

continued . . .

```
 4  P   er: well I (1.2) actually I'd been thinking about
 5      doing it for some ti:me er:: (0.5) I had (.) I was
 6      in a relationship about er six or eight months ago
 7      (0.7) which lasted (1.0) well it ended six or eight
 8      months ago it lasted for about three years and er
 9      (1.0) er we had engaged in some unsafe sex
10      activities and er I later found that er my partner
11      had been having (.) sex with other people
```

Silverman notes that the patient does not immediately offer the information that he had engaged in unsafe sex. He begins hesitantly with 'er: well I' followed by a pause, but then 'repairs' this shaky start by talking about having thought about it for some time, effectively delaying the revelation of his unsafe sexual practices. This, says Silverman, puts the patient in a favourable light, making available to him the category 'responsible person'. Later, the patient sets up a 'good news/bad news' sequence. Already cast as a 'responsible person', he consolidates this by reference to a long-term relationship with a partner before delivering the 'bad news' of his unsafe sexual practices. The hesitations and pauses in his account of his unsafe practices and later discovery about those of his partner also help to make these events hearable as dispreferred; that is, they are normatively understood as undesirable.

It is important to be clear that CA, and for that matter other forms of social constructionist research, takes no stance with respect to the factual correctness of people's accounts; its interest is entirely in the strategies and techniques that people employ in building accounts and managing interactions. For example, Silverman was not interested in whether the patient was telling the truth about his reasons for seeking a test, but in how the interaction was managed and what effects, opportunities and limitations this produced for the interactants.

Although it is concerned with how people bring about effects with their talk, CA draws back from making interpretations about the power relations that might be implicated in the interaction. Conversation analysts maintain that the researcher is in no position to make assumptions, based upon the interaction, about possible power relations and inequalities that may provide the key to what the interaction was about. This would just be a return to the traditional view of the researcher as holding privileged, expert knowledge and possibly also blinds the researcher to any phenomena that do not fit their own preconceptions. For conversation analysts, only the interactants themselves can know what the interaction is about, even if they are unable to articulate its meaning, because they themselves are building it from moment to moment. CA therefore distrusts any attempt to 'go beyond the text', and focuses upon identifying more or less objectively present features of interaction. In this respect CA is more akin to the traditional paradigm of social science, showing a concern for objectivity, reliability and validity. It is also least likely to be concerned about issues of reflexivity for the same reason. However, although CA does not bring with it a political agenda this does not mean that it cannot be used to explore power relations by those researchers with a more political orientation. For example, Kitzinger and Frith (1999), working with a feminist perspective on rape, used CA to study the difficulties involved for women in 'just saying no' to sex.

Discursive psychology

With its origins in the concerns of social psychologists, the work of discursive psychology is centred on questions about identity and subjectivity. Its primary concern is about how people construct versions of themselves, how they build defensible identities, how they present versions of themselves and events as factual and how they legitimate their actions. Like CA, discursive psychology looks to the micro-processes of interaction for answers to these questions. And, also like CA, it has developed some key conceptual tools for aiding analysis. For example 'category entitlement' refers to the way that speakers can justify the way they feel or have behaved due to the category they have placed themselves in, such as 'patient' or 'jilted lover'. 'Stake' and 'interest' refer to the way that speakers, in their accounts, orient themselves to the possible spin put on events by those with something to gain or lose by the account. Another important feature of the way that discursive psychology understands discourse is its rhetorical organisation. That is, accounts are constructed so as to undermine other potential alternatives; they are constructed as implicit defences against

the objections that might be raised to them. Discursive psychologists sometimes take a CA approach, but in order to grasp the
nature of an interaction at the level of larger meaning units such as
'accounts' and 'arguments' their analysis is often not confined to
the kinds of micro conversational structures typical of CA. In
addition, they are less likely to confine themselves to naturalistic
interactions and to perform their analyses on interviews specially
carried out for the purpose.

In the example in Box 2, Throsby (2002) reports on her interviews with women who had undergone or applied for IVF treatment. While not describing her approach as discursive psychology
she shows how the women constructed accounts of themselves that
defended their decision to apply for IVF. Throsby shows how they
legitimated their claim on resources by, for example, presenting
themselves as more responsible and morally worthy than others.

Box 2

One of Throsby's respondents, Alice, was 47 and menopau-
sal. She tells the researcher that she had tried to increase her
chances of conception by living a healthy lifestyle. Alice
clearly recognised that she may be seen as less deserving than
younger women and in her account of her decision to apply
for IVF she constructs her claim as legitimate by contrasting
herself with someone whom she constructs as less-deserving:
a pregnant woman she had seen in the street, who had two
small children with her, and who was smoking:

> *Alice:* [. . .] it would be nice to think that women that
> tried to look after themselves were perhaps given a bit
> better treatment . . . well, not better treatment, but given
> more of a chance, and I mean, for all I know, that
> woman could get married again. There she is with three
> kids by three men, but couldn't have one with the next
> one, probably smoked all her life, and gets funding just
> because she happens to be 33 or whatever.

Throsby argues that physical and moral health have become
merged in Alice's account. By presenting herself as a woman
who was trying to do everything possible to keep healthy in
order to maximise treatment success she demonstrates her

status as a good candidate for treatment. Her presentation of herself as responsible and committed also casts her as a potentially good mother.

Another respondent, Stephanie, had been refused funding for IVF and used similar rhetorical devices in order to legitimate her claim:

> *Stephanie:* I think I've paid into the NHS since I was 17. I very rarely have had to use doctors, hospital – why shouldn't I be able to? You know, neighbours of mine are probably up the doctors every day with nothing wrong with them, so I think there should have been something for me.

Stephanie refers to her good health and the fact that she has made few demands on the NHS (the National Health Service in the UK). She uses this in her account to present herself as more morally deserving of resources than other, more demanding users.

Although discursive psychology, like CA, is not explicitly political in its primary aims, analysts often do locate their work within a relevant context of ideology or power relations, thus making a connection between the more micro level of the analysis itself and macro structures in society. For example, Wetherell (1996) uses an extract from an interview reported by Cashmore (1987), part of which is reproduced here. The speaker is a white, middle-class man, and he is talking about immigration policies:

> I would have allowed in people who'd shown educational ability, the people who want to become doctors, civil servants and so on, given them three or five years training and then sent them back. It's hindsight, I know, but even in those early days, we at the Rotary Club were saying, 'These people have got to stop coming in', and people turned their backs on it. The people who were coming over here were straight from the cane fields.
> We've always said, 'Anybody who's a member of our colonies is free to come into this country.' Undoubtedly there's a lot who come in just to draw the dole. I personally think we'd be much better off if nobody could draw national assistance

until they'd been in a job for six months. They come here and, within a month, they're living off the state, whether they're black, yellow or any other colour. I think that's wrong. I've got two Indian friends. One's a doctor and the other's a business associate, and they're always amazed at the number of Indians and West Indians floating around. Where do they all come from? Whereas they came in with nothing, they're now starting to climb the business ladder and very shortly, if we don't watch it, they'll be getting ahead of us.

(Cashmore, 1987: 166–7. Cited in Wetherell, 1996: 220)

Consistent with a discursive psychological approach, Wetherell sees this talk not as expressing an attitude but of actively constructing categories of person and mobilising these in a way that legitimates or excuses racist practices. The speaker constructs an image of people who are 'straight from the cane field' and contrasts these with 'educated people'. At other times he constructs more general oppositional categories of 'us' and 'them'. The speaker also orients his account toward possible counter-arguments and accusations that he is racist. In his mention of his Indian friends he is using a disclaimer, a rhetorical device that allows him to put forward what may be seen as racist views while representing himself as not racist. Sometimes disclaimers are quite explicit, such as 'I'm not a racist, but . . .'. Wetherell sees such accounts as ideological in nature. They actively construct persons as problematic, and such constructions become shared and circulated within a society's culture, and taken up as ways of legitimating societal inequalities. Billig (1997b) sees language as inevitably ideological. If we think of ideology as a society's 'common sense', the beliefs and assumptions that just seem obviously unquestionable to people, then it is clear that this ideology must get imparted and reproduced through language, through people talking to each other, and become part of our psychology by our own use of them in our talk. He therefore sees discursive psychology as entirely appropriate for the study of ideology.

Interpretative repertoires

The identification of interpretative repertoires is really part of the analytical approach that has emerged from discursive psychology. However, I have treated it as a separate section here since the aims of this kind of analysis have to do with identifying the culturally available linguistic resources that speakers use in building their accounts rather than the specific rhetorical moves that they make in an interaction. Of course, any single piece of research may have both of these aims. I have already gone into some detail, in Chapter 3, concerning what is meant by interpretative repertoires. I will briefly recapitulate on some of that earlier material here in order to demonstrate the rationale for the analytic approach. Interpretative repertoires are seen as linguistic resources or tool kits available to speakers in the construction of their accounts. They are analogous to the repertoire of moves of a ballet dancer: finite in number and available to all ballet dancers for the design of different dances suitable for a variety of different occasions. If you went to enough ballet performances, you would eventually begin to recognise the repertoire of moves that the dancers have available to them. The idea of a repertoire therefore also involves the idea of flexibility of use; the moves can be put together in different ways to suit the occasion. Researchers look for the metaphors, grammatical constructions, figures of speech and so on that people use in constructing their accounts. By examining the talk of different people about a topic, it is possible to see patterns in the way that some figures of speech, metaphors and so on recur. By collating such usage across different speakers, the researcher identifies them as belonging to a particular repertoire. Therefore both variability and repetition are features which such analysts are looking for in their material. Variability can be expected within a single interview, because respondents can be expected to make use of different repertoires to suit their current purposes. Repetition across different interviews can be expected because the same repertoires will be used by different people. Transcripts of interviews or natural conversations are often used, although other kinds of material are occasionally analysed, such as newspaper reports and television programmes.

Potter and Reicher (1987) (Box 3) analysed the way that the terms 'community' and 'community relations' were used in different accounts of the St Paul's riot of 1980.

Box 3

The St Paul's riot was a period of some hours when fighting took place between police and youths in the St Paul's area of

continued . . .

Bristol, UK. Potter and Reicher subsequently analysed a number of accounts from local and national newspapers, television reports and records of parliamentary proceedings as well as transcripts of interviews with some of those involved in the incident. The researchers initially extracted from the accounts all instances of use of the word 'community' and its synonyms. These instances were then analysed by looking at the words describing 'community' in each case. Potter and Reicher found that some descriptions were repeatedly used across different accounts. They then grouped these into four further categories, examples of which are shown below:

Friendly
Warm
Happy
Harmonious

Close-knit
Integrated
Tight

Grows
Evolves
Matures
Acts
Feels
Knows

These groups of terms represent the community as embodying a particular cohesive style of social relationship (e.g. 'harmonious'), as having an organic nature (it 'grows' and 'evolves') and has agency (it 'acts' and 'knows'). Furthermore, it was universally used to carry a positive meaning and value; 'community' was seen as a good thing.

This community repertoire was used by different people, who were giving quite different accounts of the riot, and achieving quite different accounting ends with their use of this repertoire. For example, in some instances the riot was characterised as a problem of 'community relations'. Within these accounts, the police were represented as forming a part of a wider community which was suffering from difficulties in interpersonal relations and trust. Other accounts, by contrast, used the community repertoire to characterise the event as an open conflict between the 'black community' on the one hand and the police on the other. By using the repertoire in these contrasting ways, those giving the accounts could fashion and claim different versions of the event, motivations could be ascribed to participants and blame apportioned, as well as solutions to the problem put forward.

Potter and Collie (1989) suggest that the community repertoire is brought into use in a quite different context, that of 'community care' for the mentally handicapped. The use of the community repertoire in this context, they suggest, can be used to represent the closure of mental hospitals as somehow a cosy and neighbourly solution to a financial problem. It can be seen as a collection of metaphors and linguistic devices, which could be drawn upon by virtually anyone in order to bring about a particular desired representation of an event.

The concept of the interpretative repertoire is similar in some ways to that of the Foucauldian notion of discourse. It points to how our ways of speaking about the world are inseparable from our ways of understanding it. As we become adept as speakers in our native language, we inevitably become enculturated into our society's ways of seeing. This is what Billig (see above) means when he says that language is ideological. But the difference between interpretative repertoires and discourses is one of scale and of personal agency. Interpretative repertoires are conceptualised as existing on a smaller scale and are *resources* for speakers rather than structures that impose a certain kind of subjectivity upon them.

Foucauldian discourse analysis

The Foucauldian concept of discourse was outlined in Chapter 4. Within this view, discourses are ways of speaking about or otherwise representing the world which actually constitute us as persons. We are the subjects of various discourses and our subjectivity, our selfhood, is understood in terms of the positions within these discourses that are available to us. Although Foucauldian discourse analysis, like discursive psychology, is interested in instances of language use, it is also int ... d in two further questions. These are about the practices t. ...   licated in particular discourses, and about the material conditions and social structures that form the context for these. So, for example, prevailing discourses of the family involve representations and talk which construct parents as ideally loving and protective toward their children and responsible for their welfare. These representations go hand-in-hand with practices such as taking care of their daily needs for food, clothing and shelter and accompanying them on their journeys to school etc. These discourses are also tied to particular patterns of material circumstances and arrangements, for example houses built to accommodate four or more people, 'family size' packs of food, laws holding parents responsible for their children's welfare and school attendance, and benefits that acknowledge the financial cost for parents of giving their children adequate care. Discourses bring with them different possibilities for what a person is able to do, what they may do to others or what they are expected to do for them. Discourses therefore bring power relations with them. For example, discourses of family, childhood and adulthood make it possible for parents to limit their children's freedom by forbidding them to do certain things or go to certain places. Foucauldian discourse analysis aims to identify the discourses operating in a particular area of life and to examine the implications for sub- jectivity, practice and power relations that these have.

The kinds of materials that may be used in a Foucauldian discourse analysis are virtually limitless; any text or artefact that carries meaning may be analysed. So, to the extent that such things as family photographs, choices of interior décor, hairstyles, road signs and written instructions on bottles of medicine carry mean- ings that may be read by people, they may be analysed. Typically, however, it is written texts, including transcripts of conversations or interviews that are used. For the purposes of this book, I include under the rubric of Foucauldian discourse analysis the range of approaches referred to as critical discourse analysis (CDA). As I am not providing a separate section on this I will briefly say something about it here. The central concern of CDA is with the relationship between language and power, and with the use of discourse analysis to expose power inequalities and ideology. Two of the most prominent representatives of CDA are Teun Van Dijk and Norman Fairclough. Drawing closely on the work of Foucault, Fairclough (1992, 1995) sees discourse as both bearing the marks of social structures and relationships and also helping to construct and constitute these. Fairclough's work includes the analysis of both spoken and written texts. He analyses both the structure of the text itself, sometimes at the micro level more typically found in conversation analysis, for example single utterances or turn-taking, as well as how interactants produce and interpret texts, for example their use of commonly available discourses and narratives. At whatever level the analysis is being performed, Fairclough's aim is to identify the ideologies and power relations that are embedded in and being reproduced through discourse. He is also keen to show how discourses are struggled against and resisted in interactions.

Like in other forms of discourse analysis, the procedure for Foucauldian discourse analysis is a subjective, interpretative one. There aren't really any conceptual tools to guide the analysis as there are in discursive psychology and CA (for example turns, sequences, references to stake and so on). However, Willig (2001) provides guidelines for analysis consisting of six stages: identifying discursive constructions (looking for all the different ways in which the object is referred to in a text); locating discourses (deciding what kind of picture of the object is being painted by the different discursive constructions); action orientation (what is being done or achieved by these constructions, what effects they have for speakers or readers); positionings (identifying the subject positions made available by the discourses); practice (identifying the possibilities for action made available by subject positions); and subjectivity (what kinds of experience, thoughts and feelings these subject positions bring with them). She illustrates these stages with a worked example. A further, detailed account of this kind of discourse analysis is provided by Carabine (2001), using her research data on illegitimacy as an illustrative example. Following Foucault, she refers to this as a genealogical analysis. Although it in no way pretends to be a recipe for how to analyse discourses, Chapter 1 in Parker's (1992) book gives a number of theoretically grounded helpful hints about what to look for.

I will give a flavour of the approach here by using Willig's (1999b) discourse analysis of sex education (Box 4).

Box 4

The materials used for the analysis were interviews with heterosexual men and women about sexual activity, in the

continued . . .

context of HIV/AIDS. Willig argues that, by understanding how men and women are positioned within discourses of sexuality and sexual activity, we can better understand what practices it is possible for them to adopt. Willig identified several discursive constructions, including sexual safety, condom use, and trust. Furthermore, these were all understandable within a broader framework of a 'marital' discourse, where being married is not only about trusting your partner but also communicating and signalling that trust by one's sexual practices. In the words of one respondent:

> It's a matter of trust and I think if I were to start wearing a condom it would be a signal that I don't trust her and it would be a very hurtful thing to do.
>
> (p. 116)

In addition to the discursive construction of trust, Willig describes three ways in which sexual activity was constructed by her participants: sex as temptation, as romance and as a male preserve. She illustrates these with appropriate quotes from her interviews. For example, 'sex as temptation', with its potential hazards, is seen in the comment of a participant who says:

> Everybody is open to temptation in some form or other and you only need one slip and you've got it really haven't you?
>
> (p. 116)

Within this construction, individuals are not really in control of their sexual behaviour; if they drop their guard for a moment they may 'slip' and find they have given in to temptation. 'Sex as romance' constructs sex as a rather fragile and uncertain process that can easily be spoiled by saying or doing the wrong thing. It just isn't romantic to introduce the topic of sexual safety:

> It's a bit awkward when you have to go up to somebody and, say, excuse me, are you HIV positive, when you're in the middle of a romance. Kills the atmosphere a bit.
>
> (p. 116)

Sex-as-male-preserve constructed women as monogamous and sexually naïve, with men as promiscuous and sexually experienced. Within this construction, women were positioned as potentially passive victims of men's promiscuity:

> Probably one of the most catastrophic things about this is that innocent people can get so hurt, that if you've got an innocent little wife sitting at home with an apparently faithful husband for x number of years and for some reason he gets infected because he does have sexual relations outside the marriage that the wife's unaware of . . .
>
> (p. 117)

Willig argues that these constructions, and the positions available within them, are disempowering for people with regard to practising safer sex. The marital discourse positions spouses as automatically safe, and makes questioning this safety problematic. Constructions of sex-as-temptation position people as in some degree at the mercy of unpredictable sexual desires, sex-as-romance demands risky sexual behaviour to ensure a smooth path, at least in the early stages of a relationship, and sex-as-male-preserve support notions of women's passivity and lack of agency in sexual matters. In addition to pointing out the ways that these discursive constructions have implications for practice, Willig also comments on how material arrangements work to support these discourses and positions. Our society's understanding of what marriage and family life is about has given rise to forms of accommodation that are designed and built for single families rather than larger communities and which not only makes it difficult to create opportunities for open, collective discussions about sex but also reinforces the notion of sexuality as private. Willig concludes by making some recommendations for changes in sex education that acknowledge the power of discursive constructions to constrain behaviour. For example, condoms could be constructed and marketed as personal hygiene items by emphasising their role in preventing cervical cancer, and encouraging autoerotic practices for women could increase their sense of personal agency in their sexuality.

It is worth noting that a Foucauldian discourse analysis may look very similar to the analysis of a traditional qualitative interview approach. Research reports often take the form of presenting a brief summary of each discourse identified, followed by a few examples of the text to illustrate and support the analysis. The crucial difference is in the theoretical assumptions that are driving the analysis. As can be seen from Willig's example, what her participants had to say is taken as constituting much more than simply an account of their personal opinions or beliefs.

Criticisms of discourse analytic research

A number of criticisms have been directed at discourse analytic research, but the problems that have been identified are different for micro and macro forms of constructionism.

The major criticism aimed at discursive psychology comes from its practice of limiting its analysis to texts alone (interviews, conversations etc.). Discursive psychologists maintain that meaning is produced by the interactants within the interaction itself and that the text is therefore all that is needed in order to study that meaning. We do not need to look beyond the text, say to the status and power relationship between the interactants, or the wider social meaning of the words and concepts they are using, to understand what is going on. The problem with this is that our talk often draws its effectiveness from, and can help to reproduce, social and material power structures. Those working within a Foucauldian tradition argue that the meaning of a conversation cannot be fully grasped if we do not locate it within this wider social and material context.

The reciprocal criticism is made of Foucauldian discourse analysis. By turning discourses into objects, which have an existence independent of the people who use them and the contexts in which they are used, this approach neglects what the speaker is doing with their talk. The constructive process in which the speaker is engaged, and of course the talk itself, will vary according to the social context in which it takes place. It may be a mistake to treat spoken or written texts as if they were nothing more than manifestations of discourses.

The ultimate aim of CDA and Foucauldian analysis is to take a political stance to the truth claims made by discourses which help maintain oppressive power relations, and to increase the voice of marginalised discourses. However, the problematic status of reality and truth within social constructionism creates a difficulty in justifying one's perspective. If there is no truth, only competing discourses, if all readings are equally valid, in what sense is one justified in saying 'Yes, but some people are (really/in truth) oppressed'? How can one justify privileging one discourse over another? This is a very difficult issue for politically minded discourse analysts to deal with (e.g. see Burman and Parker, 1993; Burman, 1990, 1991). Abrams and Hogg (1990) put forward a particular criticism of the political intentions of those in the discourse field. They question the implicit assumption that discourse analysts are especially well qualified to identify and help marginalised groups. They point out that this would presumably mean that we should try to give voice to groups such as the National Front just as much as to blacks, women and gays, and question the right of academics to make decisions about just which groups ought to be empowered.

A further problem with Foucauldian discourse analysis, and to some extent this is also true of interpretative repertoires, is that the identification of discourses has a tendency to become little more than the labelling of everyday common-sense categories of events as discourses. Parker (1990) says that in order to see a set of statements as somehow coherent and representing the same discourse, one has recourse to culturally available ideas as to what we think of as a topic. Thus already existing ideas, objects, institutions etc., such as the family, science, medicine, the individual and so on each spawn an associated discourse. So we end up with 'familial discourse', 'science discourse' and so on, and we are therefore in danger of discovering a discourse for every common-sense category we operate. This leaves researchers in a weak position if they want to question culturally available common-sense categories or hold them in abeyance until validated by analysis, because those categories are at the outset implicitly taken to be a valid part of identifying and describing the discourses that one wishes to study. Without some guidelines which lie outside of common sense, it is hard to see how we could avoid the proliferation of discourses until there were as many as words in a dictionary.

However, it may be counter-productive to see discursive psychology (and CA) and Foucauldian analysis as competing approaches. Wetherell (1998) argues that they are not in principle incompatible and that the discourse analyst could and should attend to both situated language use and the wider social context within which these are produced.

Summary

Social constructionist theory brings with it a reformulation of what it means to do social science research. The concepts that are the cornerstones of traditional psychology, such as objectivity, value-freedom, reliability and validity take on new meaning or are radically questioned and the position of the researcher vis-à-vis the research participants is thrown into sharp relief. Within the body of research that can be called social constructionist there exist a variety of approaches to research that engage with these various issues in different ways and with different emphases. They also vary in the kinds of materials they typically analyse and the conceptual tools they use to perform their analysis. An important difference, leading to criticisms on both sides of the micro/macro divide, is the extent to which they are concerned with the workings of language beyond the confines of the text under analysis. Despite these differences, what they share is an understanding of language as performative and constructive, and this is what differentiates them from mainstream psychology.

There is still, as far as I am aware, no single source giving worked examples or detailed, practical instruction about how to carry out the various kinds of analysis outlined above. However, those who would like more detail of the approaches to the analysis of texts should consult one or more of the following sources:

Potter, J. & Wetherell, M. (1987). *Discourse and Social Psychology: Beyond attitudes and behaviour*. London: Sage. This, now classic, book includes a final chapter in which they identify ten stages in the analysis of discourse.

Wetherell, M., Taylor, S. & Yates, S.J. (Eds.) (2001a). *Discourse as Data: A guide for analysis*. London: Sage (in association with the Open University). This excellent book contains a chapter on each of six forms of analysis. The focus is upon the process of analysis itself and includes exercises designed to give the reader an appreciation of the relevant methodological issues.

Wetherell, M., Taylor, S. & Yates, S.J. (Eds.) (2001b). *Discourse Theory and Practice: A reader*. London: Sage (in association with the Open University). This is the companion text to *Discourse as Data* and consists of 26 readings, many of them previously published papers, illustrating the range of analytic methods and forms of data used by discourse analysts. It includes lots of research examples and clearly demonstrates how the process of data analysis is tied to theoretical concepts.

Willig, C. (Ed.) (1999). *Applied Discourse Analysis: Social and psychological interventions*. Buckingham: Open University Press. Each chapter of this book takes a social issue or practice and asks how a discourse analysis of relevant material might inform psychological or social interventions. The emphasis is therefore upon potential action, and the analyses, although ranging from Foucauldian discourse analysis to discursive psychology, are concerned with the implications of discourse for how people can live their lives. Issues of power are therefore central for several of the contributors.

Willig, C. (2001). *Introducing Qualitative Research in Psychology: Adventures in theory and method*. Buckingham: Open University Press. Includes two excellent chapters, one on discursive psychology and the other on Foucauldian analysis. Each chapter uses an example of data from existing research, gives guidelines for analysis and discusses key methodological issues.

Wood, L.A. & Kroger, R.O. (2000). *Doing Discourse Analysis: Methods for studying action in talk and text*. London: Sage. This book focuses upon the kinds of analysis preferred by discursive psychologists, including CA. It includes many examples, linking analysis to theoretical concepts, and includes helpful chapters on data collection, preparation for analysis and writing the research report.

Useful chapters can also be found in:

Burman, E. & Parker, I. (Eds.) (1993). *Discourse Analytic Research: Repertoires and readings of texts in action*. London: Routledge.

Smith, J.A., Harré, R. & Van Langenhove, L. (Eds.) (1995). *Rethinking Methods in Psychology*. London: Sage.

Chapter 9

Critiquing social constructionism

Although in previous chapters of this book I have pointed to some of the weaknesses in social constructionisms of various kinds, I have held back from a thorough discussion of these issues because this is what I want to achieve in this final chapter. The primary aim of the book has been to provide the reader with enough understanding of social constructionism to enable them to tackle more difficult sources, and I have tried to do this in a fairly even-handed, disinterested way while maintaining a basically sympathetic stance to this perspective. But to achieve my aim I must also include an understanding of the areas that are problematic for social constructionism, and here I am going to be less impartial. So, in addition to spelling out these problems I will also offer my own views, some of which I have expressed elsewhere (Burr, 1998, 1999, 2002; Burr and Butt, 2000). I should add that this critique focuses upon the questions that exercise me, and therefore does not necessarily address issues that other social constructionists might regard as of prime importance.

As I have pointed out more than once, social constructionism throws the whole project of mainstream psychology into question. Psychology's agenda over the last century, in which it has attempted to apply scientific method to the study of the individual's mind and behaviour, loses credibility. So, it would seem, we need a different way of doing psychology, and the research approaches that I outlined in Chapter 8 represent some of the ways that social constructionists have taken up this challenge. But social constructionism threatens to dispense with the need for psychology as a study of the experience and subjectivity of persons. Macro social constructionism tends toward the 'death of the subject', where the constitutive force of prevailing discourses produce all the features of being a person with which we are familiar. There is no need of a psychology here. No processes operating at the level of the individual have any explanatory power; once we have understood the workings of discourse at the level of society, we need look no further for an understanding of ourselves. Micro social constructionism loses the person in a different way. Discursive psychology brackets off the person who is the user of discursive devices, preferring to study only the latter and the accounts that are constructed with them. While there is no intention to claim that the person must necessarily be empty of content, questions about the possible nature of this content are never asked. Although some micro constructionists have proposed more relational or dialogic versions of the person (e.g. Gergen, 1994, 1999; Shotter, 1993a, 1995a, 1995b), I will argue that these fall short of a psychology.

My concern with the absence of a psychology in social constructionist accounts stems from a number of unanswered questions, and they seem to me undeniably psychological questions, that no version of social constructionism has adequately answered. Willig (2001) echoes some of my own concerns. With respect to Foucauldian discourse analysis and positioning theory she asks how we can account for the emotional investments that people make in particular discursive positions, how we can explain individual differences in the subject positions that people habitually adopt, and why people sometimes position themselves in ways that are disadvantageous for them. With regard to discursive psychology, she notes the absence of a concern with subjectivity, our self-awareness, thought, intentions and sense of life history. She asks why particular individuals work hard to claim or resist certain attributions in their accounts, why sometimes people seem to use discursive devices that do not work in their favour, and why they sometimes find it impossible to say things such as 'I love you' or 'I'm sorry' when this would be, strategically, very effective for them.

In broad terms, these unanswered questions are there because of the gaping hole left in social constructionist psychology by the absence of the 'self', the humanistic concept that provided mainstream psychology with the content of the person, in terms of personality characteristics, attitudes and motivations and so on as well as the personal agency to realise these in behaviour. Social constructionists seem agreed that this self just cannot be reconciled with social constructionism. It has become an effect of language, fragmented and distributed across discourses and interactions. But the humanistic self has not been replaced with something that performs its explanatory function. As Parker (1999) cautions, we need to build agency and subjectivity back into our theories without seeing these as unproblematically originating from or residing within the individual. I shall be recommending that the concept of the self can be reclaimed for social constructionist psychologists without compromising the latter's theoretical assumptions.

A further problem that social constructionist accounts run into is how to explain the desires, wants, hopes and fantasies of a person and their role in the choices that person makes in their lives. To say that people are negotiators of positions, or that their subjectivity is formed by discourses says nothing about how these processes are supposed to operate. In addition, it fails to properly explain such phenomena, which are after all very real experiences for us, and relegates them to a kind of side effect of discourse. But most importantly, it fails to explain why, even in the face of an understanding of the implications of discourse for our identity and the power relations in which we are thereby embedded, we do not feel free to choose an alternative way of life. For example, a woman may believe that discourses of motherhood constrain and control women, or that sexual relations with men are at the heart of women's oppression. Yet she may still desperately wish for a child, or be unable to quell her desire for a sexual relationship with a man. In order to address these problems, some social constructionist writers, such as Parker, Hollway and Walkerdine, have sometimes built psychoanalytic concepts into their accounts of subjectivity. Whether psychoanalytic ideas can be legitimately combined with social constructionism is questionable. It is quite easy for psychoanalysis to promote a slide back into essentialism, as it traditionally deals in terms of pre-existing motives, purposes and needs residing inside the individual and therefore may be legitimately seen as fundamentally incompatible with social constructionism. However, the use of psychoanalysis does represent an attempt to come to grips with some important issues which are left largely unresolved by social constructionism, and it is therefore appropriate to say something here about the kinds of ideas that readers may meet in the social constructionist literature.

The experience of conflicting desires, of knowing that something is bad for you but wanting it anyway, is of course entirely compatible with psychoanalytic thinking. Psychoanalysis is one of the few psychologies which does not assume at its centre the single, unified and coherent human subject. Psychoanalysis is fundamentally based upon the idea that humans are split, conflicted and therefore non-unitary beings. The conscious mind is dissociated from the unconscious, which nevertheless asserts itself through our behaviour and our dreams. One form of psychoanalysis which has been taken up with enthusiasm by some feminist and social constructionist writers is that of the French analyst Lacan. Lacan has devoted himself to a re-reading of Freud which is very much in the French intellectual tradition that also fostered Saussure's structuralism and the writing of poststructuralists such as Foucault and Derrida. Lacan's emphasis, as a psychoanalyst, upon the role of language and culture in psychosexual development is certainly idiosyncratic, but one that is sympathetic with many of the concerns of social constructionism. Lacan provides a useful account of subjectivity, which attempts to explain how cultural forces come to operate at the deepest levels of a person's experience. Writers such as Hollway (1984) and Walkerdine (1987) have produced some interesting analyses based on a combination of Lacan's ideas and discourse. For example, Walkerdine (1987) shows how the stories in girls' comics key into fundamental psychological issues and conflicts for girls and help to form and produce female desire along traditional, heterosexual lines, in preparation for their developing sexuality in adolescence. Lacan's writing is notoriously difficult and impenetrable, but a very accessible account of some of his ideas can be found in Frosh (1987).

A criticism that has been levelled at social constructionism from a variety of directions, particularly feminist writers, has been its lack of attention to embodiment. Social constructionism give us the model of the person-as-text, and the possible psychological and social consequences of inhabiting a human body are addressed only insofar as the body becomes another text that can be read for the operation of discourses. Harré alone gives embodiment an important place in understanding what it means to be a person (see Chapter 6). So, in addition to the problem of the self, I will say something about what I see as the proper place of the body in social constructionism.

The self and agency

Micro and macro forms of social constructionism run into problems because they have not adequately theorised the relationship between the individual and society. The person is reconfigured as constructed in the social realm, but the implications of this for personal and social change are not clear. Does the individual have the power to reconstruct themselves, to build new identities and change their life story? Do they have the capacity to change the society they live in? Or are these possibilities illusions? Are our lives determined by social structures that are beyond our control? With regard to such questions of change, the individual/society dualism becomes an issue of the familiar agency/structure debate within sociology.

The agency/structure debate

The problem of how to understand the relationship between the individual and society has revolved around the issue of the direction of influence; do individuals determine society (i.e. bottom up), or does society determine individuals (top down)? If individuals logically pre-exist society, that is if society arises from and is based upon the nature of the individual, then the notion of human agency is preserved. Society becomes the product of all the individual choices and decisions that people have made. What we call 'society' amounts to little more than the sum total of all the individuals living in it, and this is referred to as 'methodological individualism'. But it is hard to explain why the nature of human beings appears to change according to the kind of society in which they live, and to account for the orderliness of society. Why should millions of individuals independently choose to get married, have children, decorate their houses in similar ways or wear similar kinds of clothes? If society is seen as determining individuals, this problem is answered but in the process we lose human agency; it can be no more than an illusion or misconception. Individuals become the products of the kind of society they are born into, and their choices and decisions are explicable in terms of societal norms and values.

In fact, both top-down and bottom-up conceptions of the relationship between the individual and society are problematic for social constructionism. The top-down view leaves discourse as a side effect of social structure, and it therefore cannot be the focus for social change. The bottom-up view, worse still, cannot accommodate any kind of social constructionism, since the individual is taken to be logically prior to the social. The individual is a 'given' from which society arises, and therefore cannot be said to be constructed by that society. This methodological individualist view has all the attributes fiercely contested by social constructionists. It is humanistic and essentialist, claiming for the human being an essential nature, a coherent, unified self, and the capacity to make self-originated choices and decisions.

Macro social constructionism ultimately becomes socially deterministic (the 'structure' end of the debate), rendering the person a puppet of discursive structures, and micro social constructionism, while showing the constructive force of language, privileges the agency of the person as discourse-user. If the person is understood as a product of discourse, the individual and self are seen as illusions or at best constructions over which we have little control. Although some writers (e.g. Davies and Harré, 1990; Harré, 1998) have tried to argue that the person is as much constructing as constructed, the processes by which this two-way exchange is supposed to occur are not spelled out. Given the power that is accorded to language in macro social constructionist approaches to the person, there is therefore a tendency for these formulations, by default, to emphasise the formative power of the discourses we inhabit. They are therefore in danger of reproducing the same individual vs society dualism upon which mainstream social psychology is founded, but this time privileging the social rather than the individual side of the dichotomy. Worse, in its most extreme form it makes a nonsense of our arguments and debates, our attempts to persuade each other to see our point of view and to consider the benefits of different forms of conduct and social arrangements since the power to reconstruct the world is not in our hands. Also, as Craib (1997) rightly points out, there is an implicit hypocrisy in a social constructionism that must assume some agentic subject – the academic – who is capable of standing outside of discourse and commentating upon it for the benefit of lay people, who are simply subject to discourse. If we are not to allow our theorising to lead us into this blind alley, we must think carefully about what form human agency might take within a social constructionist framework.

By contrast, discursive psychology appears to privilege the individual person as the active constructor of events. However, it has not addressed the nature of the person as user of discursive devices and interpretative repertoires. It attempts to bracket off the person's psychological life with respect to our understanding of

language use. Although discursive psychology implicitly characterises the person as motivated to build socially credible and
defensible accounts it does not explicitly address the psychological
status of this. While discursive psychology does not deny the
possible existence of structures such as motivations, beliefs and
attitudes, it claims, as does behaviourism, that these are not
available for our inspection. Just what kind of 'person' we need to
create in our psychology in order to understand what it means to
be a discourse-user remains a mystery to us. I would agree with
Willig (2001) that '. . . Discursive Psychology brackets, and yet
relies upon, a notion of motivation or desire, which it is incapable
of theorizing' (p. 102). The view of the person as discourse user
does hold out the possibility of personal agency, but it could be
seen as paying insufficient attention to the fact that we do not all
have equal access to repertoires or discursive devices. Our class,
age, gender, ethnic origin and so on all impose restrictions upon
the kind of person we can claim to be and this is surely not best
understood as individual differences in discursive skills. The
question of the extent to which our use of discourse is constrained
or influenced by wider social and material circumstances is not
really addressed. Nevertheless, it does draw attention to the performative aspects of language, that is the way in which language is
used to do things, to bring about effects in the world. It has
practical advantages here, in that it offers some kind of implicit
recommendation as to what a person might actually do to claim
legitimation for a particular representation of themselves or of
others.

Both micro and macro forms of social constructionism are
ultimately unable to tell us to what extent we are able, either
individually or collectively, to reconstruct ourselves and our
society. Social constructionism therefore needs to reconceptualise
the relationship between individual and society, and in fact there
has been some attempt to do this. The problem seems to lie in the
way that the individual and society are seen as the two components
of a dichotomy. In the real world, we never actually see 'society' on
the one hand and 'individuals' on the other. One solution to the
individual/society problem is therefore to suggest that this is a false
dichotomy, a division that is an artefact of intellectual analysis by
human minds and not a division that represents discrete phenomena. In other words, the individual/society dichotomy can be
thought of as a construction, one way of thinking about the world,

but not necessarily a way we have to be committed to. In fact the sociologist Giddens (1984) has provided an alternative to this dichotomy in his 'structuration' concept, where he uses the metaphor of individual and society as like two sides of the same coin.

The social construction of reality

As Butt (2003) has pointed out, earlier work in symbolic interactionism is often cited as foundational to contemporary social constructionist psychology but this earlier work avoided the individual/society dualism more successfully. In their book *The Social Construction of Reality* (1966) sociologists Peter Berger and Thomas Luckmann argued that the seemingly objective social world is constructed by human action and interaction: '. . . despite the objectivity that marks the social world in human experience, it does not thereby acquire an ontological status apart from the human activity that produced it' (Berger and Luckmann, 1966: 78). In addition, humans are thoroughly social animals:

> Solitary human being is being on the animal level (which, of course, man [*sic*] shares with other animals). As soon as one observes phenomena that are specifically human, one enters the realm of the social. Man's specific humanity and his sociality are inextricably intertwined. *Homo sapiens* is always, and in the same measure, *homo socius*
> (Berger and Luckmann, 1966: 69. Italics in original)

Berger and Luckmann saw the relation between individual and society as operating in both directions: human beings continually construct the social world, which then becomes a reality to which they must respond. So that although human beings construct the social world they cannot construct it in any way they choose. At birth they enter a world already constructed by their predecessors and this world assumes the status of an objective reality for them and for later generations.

Berger and Luckmann identified three aspects of this circular process: externalisation, objectivation and internalisation. Basic to this cycle is human beings' ability to create symbols, things that can carry meaning beyond the 'here and now'. They give the example of a knife, which can be used to symbolise an aggressive act. The symbol of the knife can represent violence on occasions and at times remote from situations when actual knives were used for actual violent acts. Furthermore, language is a system of symbols that allows us to represent events. Through language we can make available or accessible (externalise) to other people our personal experience.

Externalisation is possible because we attach meaning to objects and turn them into signs. The knife (an object) becomes an objectification of aggression and may then become used by others as a 'sign' of violence on other occasions. Objectivations are therefore detachable from the here and now, from the original expression of human subjectivity that gave rise to them. But words and gestures are objectivations too because they express and externalise meaning in the same way, and can also be used in many places and at different times. Ultimately, our shared use of this symbolic system constructs huge social structures, structures that appear to have an existence and an origin outside of our own human activity but which are inevitable human constructions:

> Language now constructs immense edifices of symbolic representations that appear to tower over the reality of everyday life like gigantic presences from another world. Religion, philosophy, art, and science are the historically most important symbol systems of this kind. To name these is already to say that, despite the maximal detachment from everyday experience that the construction of these systems requires, they can be of very great importance indeed for the reality of everyday life.
>
> (Berger and Luckmann, 1966: 55)

Internalisation completes the cycle. As children acquire language and are socialised into the ideas and ways of their culture, meanings are passed on to future generations. Socialisation entails our coming to understand objectivated events, artefacts, words and signs in terms of the meanings previously conferred upon them by our society and so we become able to participate in meaningful interaction with other people.

This way of thinking about the relationship between individual and society, as a dialectical process rather than as a conflict between two pre-existing entities, allows us to think of the person as being both agentic, always actively constructing the social world, and constrained by society (to the extent that we must inevitably live our lives within the institutions and frameworks of meaning handed down to us by previous generations).

Individual/society as an ecosystem

Another possible model for understanding the relationship between the individual and society comes from Sampson (1989). Drawing on Bateson (1972) he argues that the appropriate unit of analysis is neither the individual nor society. In fact there can be no such unit, only a *system*, which Bateson calls the 'ecosystem'. This system comprises both the organism and its environment, both the individual and its society. Sampson therefore invites us to view the relationship between the individual and society as an ecosystem. The study of animals, the effects of one species upon another and the effects of environment upon species has not been well served by conceptualising each species as discrete from others, and the environment as some extraneous set of factors which has an effect upon a species. Such ways of thinking encouraged the use of chemicals in agriculture to control pests and diseases without any understanding of the ways that the existence of different species were closely interwoven with each other and with their habitat. Each species forms part of the environment for the other, each producing habitats by the subtle action and interaction of their behaviours. Thus it makes little sense to separate out 'species' from 'environment'; they must be considered as a single system. Sampson recommends that we view the individual and society as such an ecosystem. This system would not be divisible into its constituent parts and the question of the relationship between individual and society would cease to be relevant, since the concept 'relationship' is only needed in order to explain how one discrete entity affects another.

I am not going to debate the strengths and weaknesses of Giddens' or Sampson's model. The point I want to make is that I believe we must welcome such attempts to transcend the dichotomies that are entrenched in our thinking and that stand in the way of a coherent social constructionist model of the person. If we take up the suggestion that the individual and society, rather than existing as separate but related entities, are a single system, then the problems of human agency and the status of discourse are somewhat ameliorated. The individual, the social practices in which they engage, the social structure within which they live and the discourses which frame their thought and experience become aspects of a single phenomenon. This means that discourses are not simply a product of either social structure or individuals, but both. Such a conceptualisation allows us to retain some notion of personal agency and to see discourse as a valid focus for forces of social and personal change.

Agency in positioning

If we can conceive of personal agency in some form, what might this look like? Discursive psychology, although it abhors the intra-psychic self of liberal humanism with its cognitions, attitudes and values, nevertheless appears to accord the person a similar kind of agency. The agency of the person to use discursive devices and interpretative repertoires seems no different from the kind that traditionally allows us to use other tools, such as hammers and chisels, to carry out our intentions and projects in the world. Harré (1995a), arguing that the self as agent is constructed in the kind of talk we use to defend and excuse our actions, at least recognises the paradox of the implicit agent in his own account (see Chapter 7).

The concept of 'positioning' (see Chapter 6) is one that has possibilities here, since it is used by both macro and micro social constructionists. It allows us a conception of agency that acknowledges both the constructive force of discourse at a societal level as well as the capacity of the person to take up positions for their own purposes. Davies and Harré (1990) claim this duality for positioning. They see the person as simultaneously produced by discourse and manipulators of it. Discourses provide the possibilities and the limitations on what we may or may not do and claim for ourselves within a particular discourse. We may ourselves adopt a position by drawing upon a particular discourse, or we may assign positions to other speakers through the part that we give them in our account. Drewery (2001) explores the concept of agency that this view of positioning affords. She attends to the material consequences of the 'position calls' that are issued to others in our talk, the implicit invitations to them to take up certain subject positions. She points out that 'what will happen next is not necessarily the prerogative of the person doing the inviting.' Invitations may be accepted or rejected. However, she is particularly concerned about the kind of position calls that leave the other no way of responding as a full participant in the conversation. She calls these 'exclusionary position calls', and gives an example from her own experience:

> This kind of exclusion occurs frequently in everyday speech. For example 'Will you boys please put the dishes away after the dishwasher has finished? It would be really good if somebody did something round here besides me.' It no longer seems surprising to me that my boys seldom responded to this position call in the way I would have preferred because this is not an invitation to the boys to participate in a conversation about who does or does not do the dishes. In fact it quite specifically excludes them from a speaking position. It could be argued that I am taking up a position of martyr and requiring them to save me from it. It functions somewhat ambivalently as a statement of my own martyrdom and a kind of command, coming as it does from the powerful position of mother in the household. I suspect than none of these positions is the kind of invitation a self-respecting boy could easily accept.

She suggests that such exclusionary position calls, which require people to speak in terms provided by others, is a form of colonising and may be commonplace between adults and children, a function of their unequal power relationship. The issue is:

> one of how the invitation to engage is offered, whether the other is invited to speak in their own terms, or whether the interrogator is controlling the terms of the conversation/ narrative . . . Such forms of speech reproduce unequal power relations by reproducing the kinds of relationships where one party to a conversation is called into a non-agentive position in respect of the conversation.

She takes up Davies and Harré's (1990) claim that positions are also internalised by us, becoming part of our psychology, and then goes on to apply this to the concern in New Zealand that Maori children suffer from low self-esteem, poor motivation, lack of initiative and the apparent inability to alter their own situation. She argues that if people are repeatedly colonised, given exclusionary position calls, they may come to habitually adopt ways of speaking about, and therefore thinking about, themselves that are not agentic. She argues that this 'lack' may be better understood as the outcome of being repeatedly discursively positioned as passive participants in public life, and calls for a 'collaborative conversation' between Paheka and Maoris where both are given voice. Drewery points out that agency thus conceptualised is not the agency of liberal humanism, since the person cannot be agentic on their own. Agency is only possible in relation with others.

I particularly like Drewery's use of positioning because it retains a notion of agency while reformulating it in a way that is compatible with social constructionism – as something that exists between people rather than within the individual. At the same time she is careful to build into her account the way that talk can both manifest and reproduce material power relations, while also taking a little further our understanding of how positions can become part of our psychology, our subjectivity.

The relational self

It seems to me that a theoretically coherent social constructionism must transcend the dualisms that have informed traditional social science. I have talked about individual/society and agency/structure above, but a further dualism that is at the heart of mainstream psychology and which may be challenged by social constructionism is self/other. As should be clear by now, in developing an understanding of the way in which the person may be seen as socially produced, social constructionist approaches have often called upon some view of the person as a function of their relationships with others. Positioning, discussed above, provides a model of the person as at least partly fashioned within interpersonal interactions over which no single interactant has control. The concept of 'joint action' also gives us a way of understanding interaction in a way that does not see one person as simply responding to the interactional moves of the other. Narrative psychology sees each of us as negotiating a life story that is to some degree constrained by the life stories of others in which we must play a part, and our relations with others plays a central role in Kenneth Gergen's account. I shall comment on what these have to offer, before going on to explain why I think that symbolic interactionism, the area of micro-sociology that grew from the work of George Mead (1934), should be given greater attention by social constructionists.

As I indicated above, I like the concept of positioning for a number of reasons. It works at both the individual and the structural level, offering a way of acknowledging both the power of societal discourses to construct persons and the capacity of persons to construct themselves and others. It allows a version of personal agency that I feel is compatible with social constructionism and also gives us some purchase on subjectivity. Narrative psychology, too, although its implicit conception of agency is perhaps too near to that of humanism, can give us a way of collapsing the self/other dichotomy as well as offering a way of understanding the relationship between personal narratives and societal discourses. 'Tellable' narratives are those that present the narrator's experience as a version of a currently widely circulated account, for example being a victim of child abuse or recovering from a trauma. Burr and Butt (2000) argue that the increasing numbers of people who are diagnosed or self-label as, say, dyslexic, suffering from premenstrual syndrome or post-traumatic stress disorder, as well as the explosion in the actual number and diversity of syndromes that are being identified, can be understood in part as an effect of the wide circulation, both in professional and lay circles, of particular ways of understanding and narrating our experience.

Kenneth Gergen takes his concept of the 'relational self' beyond the interpersonal realm and into global politics. In this respect he appears to take a similar line to Sampson (1990), who focused upon the increasing globalisation of the modern social world and argued that the future welfare of human beings is more likely if we take up a view of the individual as 'embedded' in social relationships:

> To be an individual by virtue of one's connections and interconnections, introduces a constitutive view of the person that I believe can more adequately include the possibility of human welfare than the current self-contained formulation allows. The embedded or constitutive kind of individuality does not build upon firm boundaries that mark territories separating self and other, nor does it abandon the connectedness that constitutes the person in the first place.
>
> (Sampson, 1990: 124)

Gergen's recent work heavily criticises the 'cult of the individual' and calls for a new way of thinking which recognises and acknowledges the interdependency of people, at both an individual and a global level. His argument, which at times seems to me rather idealistic, suggests that once we realise that the self is relational and allow ourselves to really listen to the many voices in the community that forms us, we will see that there is no need to be self-seeking or to treat others instrumentally.

Like other micro social constructionists, Gergen (1997) locates psychological events like emotion inside relationship exchanges. But he argues for what he calls a 'de-psychologised account of human action', and this is where I disagree. His view seems to arise from the fear that 'psychology' means mental states that cause behaviour. I think this assumption is quite unnecessary. It is important to emphasise here that the psychological need not be equated with essentialist mental states, nor be causative in any way. The dimensions of private vs public, psychological vs social and determined vs constructed do not map onto each other or reduce to each other. Social and even relational realms can be used in just as deterministic a fashion as the psychological, and the psychological and private can be just as contingent as social phenomena. So that claiming back a personal, private and psychological space as the proper realm of our enquiries as psychologists and social psychologists in no way automatically returns us to essentialism, determinism or possessive individualism (Sampson, 1993). I prefer to think of psychology as the study of the processes by which the mental and behavioural *emerge* from the social. As Dodds et al. (1997) put it 'It becomes important to describe how the social becomes personal without denying the activity and contribution of either social or personal domains'.

What I like about relocating conduct within relationships is that it attempts to get rid of causality, the idea that mental states cause behaviour, and emphasises the social embeddedness of conduct, apparently without inverting the problem and creating a reductionistic social determinism. But what is missing here is any understanding of how or why interactions take the particular course that they do. They seem to emerge magically. The psychological realm appears to have no role to play in producing them. I see the silence of psychologists and social psychologists on this issue as a problem, and so I want to go on now to draw on some older work in social psychology that I feel can help us out here.

The case for an interactionist concept of self

The term symbolic interactionism was introduced by Blumer (1962), who built on and extended the earlier work of George

Mead (1934). Mead's contribution lies in transcending the dualism of self/other, and in providing an account of the individual that is thoroughly social. His conception of mind and of consciousness, and of the relationship between these and society was based upon the interdependency of self and other. Furthermore, language and social interaction were for Mead crucial to the development of the mind, consciousness and the self. For Mead, the self does not pre-exist society, but emerges from it.

Mead turns on its head mainstream psychology's question of how individual persons, who are conscious and have minds, come to interact with other individuals, affect and be affected by them, so producing something that is called society. Instead, he sees consciousness and mind, our ability to reflect upon our actions and those of others, as the outcomes of social interaction. Mead's individual does not exist independently of society but is instead made possible *by* social interaction between people. And the key to the development of mind is something distinctly human; our ability to use symbols to represent things and events, especially our use of language. It is language, says Mead, that allows us to internalise social interaction, to represent it to ourselves and to think about and reflect upon it.

According to symbolic interactionism both society and individuals arise from interaction and communication between people. This interaction takes place through the use of symbols, which have meaning for people. Consciousness, our ability to reflect on our experience, and the self are seen as emerging from these interactions. Fundamental features of being a person are therefore seen as socially contingent, dependent upon social interaction for their development. Mind, that is our ability to reflect upon our experience, is not possible until we can use language to represent events to ourselves. And language acquisition depends on social interaction. Babies are capable of rudimentary interaction, readily engaging in turn-taking and imitation games. The baby's part in this 'conversation' acquires meaning through others' responses. People respond to a baby as if its actions were already meaningful, so both baby and others come to an 'agreed' meaning of the baby's behaviour. Mead (1934) called this a 'conversation of gestures'. As its cognitive abilities become more sophisticated the child can replace gestures with words and, through continued social inter-action, the child is eventually able to participate in its society's system of shared symbols and their meanings, that is, language.

Language can therefore be seen as a kind of a conversation of gestures carried out privately through the use of symbols. The child is now able to reflect upon its own actions and its experience of the world and to represent these things to itself and to others. It has acquired both mind and a sense of self.

Social relationships and human interaction and communication are key to the development of the person for symbolic interactionists. But successful interaction also requires that we have some understanding of what our behaviour means to others. We can imagine the likely effects of our actions on others and act accordingly, and this is because of our system of shared meanings. When we interact through a conversation of gestures and later through language, we know that a gesture or word has the same meaning for others as it has for us. This give us access to the minds of others; we can imagine the meaning that our actions have for others because of the meaning they have for us. And this gives us choice. We can imagine what would happen *if* we were to act in a certain way and can therefore consider alternative actions, which is a way of describing agency. Mead saw this capacity as what separates the meaningful interaction of humans from the meaningful interaction of other animals.

So the person is a thoroughly social and socially contingent phenomenon. Harré once referred to the person as a 'fenced-off' section of the prairie-land that is the social realm. He was reflecting on the way in which what counts as 'me' extends well beyond the physical boundary of my being. I agree with Harré on this point. But the person is not *only* this. There *is* a difference between private and public, though not one that is so sharply drawn as in mainstream psychology, and what happens in my private realm has consequences for joint action. But we do not need to resort to causality to acknowledge a role for mental processes. Reflectiveness and memory are processes that inform my future conduct and make choices possible. And it is here that I think the idea of self can be of value.

The idea of a self does not dictate any particular content to that concept. The fact that our western concept of self contains such things as personality, individuality and agency can be accounted for, in social constructionist terms, by prevailing discourses. But the fact that we have a concept of self at all cannot. I am happy to dispense with personality, attitudes and such like as pre-existing or environmentally produced mental states that cause behaviour, but the self is different in kind from these. It is socially contingent rather than pre-existent; it is not fixed and does not have to be seen as causing anything.

So while our particular concept of self is not trans-cultural, I believe that human beings always have and always will be conscious of selfhood. The only thing this is contingent upon is social interaction. Human beings become persons when they become engaged in social encounters, and this makes some form of selfhood possible and even inevitable. My self-concept arises out of reflection and is present during all social interactions, in effect constituting a third 'other' that exerts the same pull on my conduct as real interactants. We can therefore see the self as a positive asset, grounding moral choices and agency. It gives me something against which to assess current interactions and check possible future conduct, through monitoring myself during social encounters. Without it, it is hard to see how we can avoid regarding all actors as interchangeable. Where do moral choices come from? We surely do not want to claim that people's experience of wrestling with moral dilemmas and choices is illusionary, that in fact our moral behaviour is simply determined by pre-existent psychological processes, by social rules that we have internalised or by force of social structures, which would be to slide back into the dichotomies that social constructionism is trying to escape. So we have to explain how it is that we have such choice and how it is that we can have some form of collective conception, at some level, of what is good; that is, basic values. It is possible to find a route to these through Mead's concept of the 'generalised other'; the other is so much a part of my make-up that my experience is not differentiated from that of the other. It is much more than simply imagining what others would feel like if I treated them in a certain way; we intuitively feel the consequences of our actions upon others because we are not differentiated from the other. This is the 'care' that Gergen speaks of and wants, but he can only reach it through the recognition that all outcomes are jointly produced, that we all depend on each other. It is too utilitarian and reduces to moral expediency.

Gergen regards analyses that see psychological events as *existing* in the social realm as superior to those that see them as *derived from* the social realm. I disagree with this, for the reasons I gave above about misunderstanding the relationship between various dichotomies. In any case, just what it might mean for phenomena to 'exist' in the social realm is not clear. Gergen (1997) calls his paper 'the place of the psyche in a constructed world' but seems to find *no* place for it. He leaves it lying between people, but neither of them knows how it got there or has access to it.

Embodiment

Ironically, social constructionism potentially gets into the same difficulties as other forms of psychology because of its almost exclusive attention to language and discourse. It has reframed as 'social' those psychological phenomena that were previously seen as cognitive and intra-psychic, but has generally left intact the mind–body dualism of mainstream psychology. With the exception of Harré (see Chapter 7) micro social constructionism has generally not concerned itself with the body or embodiment. While Harré stresses the role of language in the construction of the self – both what we mean by a 'self' and the content of individual selves – he does not agree with Gergen's 'radical relativism' (Harré, 1995c). He reserves a place for the body as that which guarantees some foundation, however basic, to human personhood and I would agree with him here. Within macro social constructionism, the status of the body has been rewritten as an effect of discourse. This is little more than a translation into social constructionist terms of the relationship between mind and body of mainstream psychology. Whereas our bodily experience was often formerly explained as the effect of the mind, for example, attitudes towards pain affect how much pain we experience, now it is the effect of our subject positions in discourse.

Macro social constructionists have often found the work of Foucault helpful in understanding the body as a site of power relations. Through the concept of disciplinary power (see Chapter 4) Foucault showed how those bodily processes that so deeply concern us, especially those of a sexual nature, are implicated in a wider process of social control. Foucault's ideas have been enthusiastically taken up by those who have been interested in understanding power relations in areas where the body is highly salient, like sexuality and gender, and have therefore been of particular interest to feminist writers. For example, Gavey (1997) analysed women's experiences of sexual coercion, showing how these experiences may be seen as produced through dominant discourses of heterosexuality; and Sawicki (1991) sees reproductive technologies and the discourses surrounding these as producing and shaping not only certain identities for women but also their desires for motherhood.

However, as I have argued elsewhere (Burr, 1999), although some (like Sawicki, above) have been keen to show the possibilities for resisting the effects of such discourses, many writers taking a Foucauldian approach have privileged the power of discourse to produce bodily experience and to give it meaning. Even where the intention appears to be to reclaim the 'material body' and to validate the accounts of those speaking about their embodied experiences (Ussher, 1997), it appears very difficult to escape the conclusion that bodily experience is contingent upon prevailing discourses. But, as with other kinds of subjectivity, this approach gives us no purchase on the different ways that individuals engage with such discourses. As Grosz (1994) points out: '. . . in feminist terms at least, it is problematic to see the body as a blank, passive page, a neutral "medium" or signifier for the inscription of a text . . . one and the same message, inscribed on a female or male body, does not always or even usually mean the same thing or result in the same text' (p. 156).

I would go further than Grosz and argue, following Radley (1995), that the meaningfulness of the body is not confined to its social construction through discourse. Radley draws on phenomenology to provide a way of understanding how the body can express meaning without resorting to cognitive structures in the head or rendering the body merely subject to discourse. Phenomenology is useful here because it takes experience, including bodily experience, as foundational. It is the raw material out of which meaning is constructed. A variety of human experiences involve the body as a way of knowing the world in a non-cognitive, non-representational way, and of expressing that knowledge. Many forms of art may be included here, most obviously those where the body and its movement are directly involved such as dance and music. In addition, the capacity of the body to know and to be expressive is at the centre of our sexual experience; the way in which one body 'knows' another is not captured by language. In fact it is characteristic of such embodied knowledge that it is *difficult* to translate into thought and language. For this reason, I have argued (Burr, 1999) that we should regard such forms of experience and expression as 'extra-discursive', that is, existing in a realm outside of language and discourse.

The expressivity of the body and of the forms of art that it can create also open up possibilities for resisting discursive power, as Radley (1995) points out: the body 'eludes discourse, not because of its physicality per se, but because it signifies in ways that discourse cannot adequately embrace' (p. 12). We can 'speak' of experiences and of the conditions under which we live and these expressions cannot be silenced or reframed by discourse. The expressivity of the body can therefore be subversive. Further, Radley argues that we can only really appreciate the experience of others whose lives are very different from our own if we stop regarding accounts of experience as the only valid form of communication:

> However, the serious charge against the move towards narrative as the privileged medium of enlightenment is that it attempts to render experience legitimate only when it is spoken. This cuts away the content of experience from the form (the body-subject) in which its meaning originated, and to which it must continue to be referred if others are to understand what it means to be sick or oppressed.
>
> (Radley, 1995: 19)

In order to truly grasp the experience of another it may be that we must, literally, walk a mile in their shoes.

Conclusion

I have called this final section of the chapter, and of the book, 'conclusion' rather than 'summary' because what I am presenting here is not so much a thumbnail sketch of the issues I have addressed in this chapter but more a final statement of my own concerns about social constructionism. As a relatively new body of critical theory and practice that has taken shape out of the concerns of psychologists and social psychologists, social constructionism has perturbed psychology's complacency. It has insisted upon a radical rethinking of not only what psychology as a discipline should be, but of what it means to do social science and what kinds of research questions can and should be asked.

But I am interested in a social constructionism that does more than function as a critic. The foundational assumptions of the discipline of psychology, as it has been practised over the last century, may have been radically questioned but I do not think that this signals the end of psychology. I am in agreement with Ryan (1999) who foresees, through the social constructionist turn, a radical shift in the aim and constitution of the behavioural sciences, but not their elimination. Psychology will need to find new concepts and new questions. What I want to see is a social constructionist psychology, and by this I mean a body of theory and research that can give us some purchase upon the experience of being a person without sliding back into essentialism and without re-invoking the troublesome dualisms of mind/body, self/other, individual/society and agency/structure. A social constructionism that fails to address individual differences in and subjective experience of such things as desires, choices, embodiment, sense of self and personal change is, for me, inadequate as a psychology.

This is a tall order, but I believe that there are a number of fruitful lines of thought, both older and more recent, that hold potentially rich resources for the social constructionist psychologist. I welcome the various formulations that attempt to transcend the individual/society and agency/structure dualisms, such as the 'relational self' and viewing the individual/society as an ecosystem. But the older work of the symbolic interactionists seems to me to be of great value because of the additional possibilities it holds for understanding the emergence and maintenance of a socially contingent self. Theoretical constructs that are capable of bridging the gap between individual experience and societal structure with respect to language and discourse are likewise attractive. Narrative psychology is promising here, since stories operate at both the level of myth and the level of individual life histories. But the concept of 'positioning' is even richer because it also gives us some purchase on the notion of personal agency. A psychology that does not theorise embodied experience, or does so in a deterministic or reductionistic way, is also inadequate. Phenomenology shares with social constructionism a rejection of essentialism while taking embodied experience seriously, and may provide a possible resource here.

Social constructionism has perhaps had the most visible impact upon psychological research. When I began to write *An Introduction to Social Constructionism* almost ten years ago, discourse analysis was uncommon and its practice veiled in vague and unspecified procedures. Today there are numerous detailed accounts of discourse analytic research and several fine publications explaining its theoretical and methodological features. But the social constructionist psychology that I would like to see would need to turn its attention to questions that may not be addressed by analysing discourse. Questions such as 'by what processes do people co-construct themselves and each other?' and 'what role does our self-concept play in this constructive process?' may demand a further creativity in our approach to research.

A research programme aimed at answering these questions would capitalise on our capacity for reflexive self-consciousness. Elsewhere (Butt et al., 1997) I have described how, for example, personal construct methods have been used to investigate how our sense of self is fragmented across relationships and is dependent upon them, and how our feelings of authenticity are dependent upon the self-monitoring processes during interaction described by Mead. Such an approach lies broadly within a phenomenological framework, and I would additionally see phenomenological methods of enquiry as potentially able to inform us about the psychological processes taking place during joint actions of all kinds, from conversations to playing a game of tennis.

Social constructionism is in a state of flux. It is a field of enquiry which is changing and expanding very rapidly, and it is therefore quite difficult to gain a stable perspective on the issues. This book is a snapshot of what the social constructionist world looks like to me at present, and, like any snapshot it is a likeness that is recognisable without passing itself off as the only true image. I hope that you have found it useful.

Glossary

Agency The capacity to make choices and to act upon them. Often contrasted with **determinism**.

Behaviourism School of psychological theory which holds that the observation and description of overt behaviour are all that is needed to understand human beings.

Cognitivism In this context, the assumption that psychological processes such as thinking, perception and reasoning are expressed in individual and interpersonal behaviour.

Constructivism Forms of psychology that see the person as having an active role in the creation of their experience; each person perceives the world differently and creates their own meanings from events.

Conversation analysis (CA) Method of analysis of (usually naturalistic) interaction used by some discursive psychologists. It involves identifying often quite small units of speech and analysing their function and effects within accounts.

Critical psychology Looks at how people are affected by their position in society, for example by virtue of their gender or ethnicity, and by power relations, and at how psychology itself may contribute to inequalities.

Critical realism See **realism**.

Dark social constructionism Term used by Danziger (1997) to refer to forms of social constructionism that emphasise the operation power relations though discourse. See also **light social constructionism**.

Deconstruction The analysis of a piece of text to reveal the discourses and systems of oppositions operating within it.

Determinism Theoretical position which sees human behaviour as brought about by factors beyond the control, and often awareness, of the individual. Such factors may be societal, such as social norms, or they may be psychological, such as personality traits.

Discourse   This term is used primarily in two senses: (1) to refer to a systematic, coherent set of images, metaphors and so on that construct an object in a particular way, and (2) to refer to the actual spoken interchanges between people.

Discourse analysis   The analysis of a piece of text in order to reveal either the discourses operating within it or the linguistic and rhetorical devices that are used in its construction.

Discursive psychology   Approach to research and theory which focuses on the situated use of language. It is action-oriented, asking how speakers manage to build accounts that have particular effects within an interaction, as well as constructing and legitimating particular identities for themselves.

Empiricism   The view that the only valid knowledge is that which is derived from observation and experiment.

Epistemology   The philosophy of knowledge. The study of the nature of knowledge and the methods of obtaining it.

Essentialism   The view that objects (including people) have an essential, inherent nature which can be discovered.

Ethnomethodology   Research methodology arising from microsociology. It is concerned with observing and describing the everyday practices by which ordinary people construct their social worlds. It focuses on the way people give their behaviour meaning through the accounts they produce.

Externalisation   Externalisation, objectivation and internalisation are the three points in a cycle of the social construction of reality suggested by Berger and Luckmann (1966). Potentially shared ways of thinking about the world ('knowledge') become externalised when they take the form of social practices or artefacts. These then become 'objects' (objectivation) for a social group, and acquire a sense of pre-givenness. They then become part of the thinking of individual members of the social group (internalisation), and of new members as they are born into it.

Foucauldian discourse analysis   See also **deconstruction**. Named after Michel Foucault, the analysis of texts of all kinds to reveal the discourses operating within them. This often entails an attention to implicit **subject positions** and power relations.

Genealogy The term used by Foucault to refer to his method, based on that of Nietzsche, of tracing the history of concepts and ideas. Rather than showing how the past has inevitably led to the present, Foucault was concerned to show the irregularities and discontinuities in history, to reveal subjugated knowledges and to disrupt the tendency of historians to create 'grand narratives' which smooth out these inconsistencies.

Humanism Often used in the narrow sense of referring to the view of human beings as individual agents who are the originators of their own thoughts and actions.

Idealism An ontological theory which states that only minds and their ideas exist. Material objects exist only as objects of perception. This is opposed to **realism**.

Internalisation See **externalisation**.

Interpretative repertoire Term introduced by Potter and Wetherell (1987) to refer to a stock of culturally available linguistic devices from which people may construct accounts.

Joint action The idea that interaction and its outcomes are co-produced by interactants and are indeterminate. This is in contrast to the idea that interaction consists of each person responding in turn to the other's behaviour and that the outcome of interaction is the result of interactants' plans.

Light social constructionism Term used by Danziger (1997) to refer to forms of social constructionism that focus on and celebrate the multiplicity of constructions produced by people. See also **dark social constructionism**.

Macro social constructionism Term used in this book to refer to forms of social constructionism that focus on the constructive force of culturally available discourses, and the power relations embedded within these.

Micro social constructionism Term used in this book to refer to forms of social constructionism that focus on the construction of accounts and personal identities within interpersonal interactions.

Narrative psychology The study of the storied nature of human experience and human accounts.

Objectivation See **externalisation**.

Ontology The study of being and existence. The attempt to discover the fundamental categories of what exists.

Perspectivism See **relativism**.

Positioning   In interaction, practice of locating oneself or others as particular kinds of people through one's talk.

Positivism   The belief that we can only know what we can immediately apprehend. That which exists is what we perceive to exist.

Postmodernism   The rejection of 'grand narratives' in theory and the replacement of a search for truth with a celebration of the multiplicity of (equally valid) perspectives.

Poststructuralism   The rejection of structuralism's search for explanatory structures underlying social phenomena. In linguistics, also the view that the meanings of signs (e.g. words) is not fixed, but shifting and contestable.

Pragmatism   A predominantly North American school of philosophy. Pragmatists believe that knowledge is relative; it is 'true' to the extent that it serves our current needs and goals.

Realism   An ontological theory which states that the external world exists independently of being thought of or perceived. This is opposed to **idealism**. **Critical realism** is the view that, although we cannot be directly aware of the material objects in the world, nevertheless our perceptions do give us some kind of knowledge of them.

Reflexivity   Term used by social constructionists to refer to the application of the theory back onto itself and its practices. Used particularly in the context of research, where the researcher reflects upon their own position in the research process.

Relativism   The view that there can be no ultimate truth, and that therefore all perspectives are equally valid.

Speech act theory   Developed by Austin (1962), speech act theory is concerned with how utterances can have 'illocutionary force'; utterances do not just describe the world but in some circumstances bring about material consequences for speakers and listeners.

Structuralism   The belief in and search for explanatory structures which are held to give rise to the 'surface' phenomena of, for example, society or human thought and behaviour.

Subjectivity   The term used by social constructionists to refer to the state of personhood or selfhood. It replaces traditional psychological terms such as 'personality' and 'individual'.

Subject position   Implied position within a particular discourse which may be occupied or taken up by a person, providing a basis for their identity and experience.

Symbolic interactionism Body of theory and research originating with the work of George Mead and later developed by Herbert Blumer. Symbolic interactionism emphasises the construction of the social world and meaning through the human use of symbols in communication, most importantly language.

Text Anything which can be 'read' for meaning. As well as written material, this potentially includes pictorial images, clothes, buildings, food, consumer goods and so on.

Suggested further reading

I have provided two lists of sources that I would like to recommend. The first consists of a relatively small number of books, some of which are edited collections of chapters focusing in depth on a particular range of social constructionist theories and research. Others are written about specific aspects of social constructionism in a particularly accessible way:

Burman, E. & Parker, I. (Eds.) (1993). *Discourse Analytic Research: Repertoires and readings of texts in action*. London: Routledge.

Harré, R. & Stearns, P. (Eds.) (1995). *Discursive Psychology in Practice*. London: Sage.

Mills, S. (1997). *Discourse*. London: Routledge.

Palmer, D.D. (1997). *Structuralism and Poststructuralism for Beginners*. New York: Writers and Readers Publishing.

Parker, I. & the Bolton Discourse Network (1999). *Critical Textwork: An introduction to varieties of discourse and analysis*. Buckingham: Open University Press.

Potter, J. & Wetherell, M. (1987). *Discourse and Social Psychology: Beyond attitudes and behaviour*. London: Sage.

Sarup, M. (1993). *An Introductory Guide to Post-Structuralism and Postmodernism*. Hemel Hempstead: Harvester Wheatsheaf.

Smith, J.A., Harré, R. & Van Langenhove, L. (Eds.) (1995). *Rethinking Methods in Psychology*. London: Sage.

Smith, J.A., Harré, R. & Van Langenhove, L. (Eds.) (1995). *Rethinking Psychology*. London: Sage.

Wetherell, M., Taylor, S. & Yates, S.J. (Eds.) (2001a). *Discourse as Data: A guide for analysis*. London: Sage.

Wetherell, M., Taylor, S. & Yates, S.J. (Eds.) (2001b). *Discourse Theory and Practice: A reader*. London: Sage.

Willig, C. (Ed.) (1999). *Applied Discourse Analysis: Social and psychological interventions*. Buckingham: Open University Press.

Willig, C. (2001). *Introducing Qualitative Research in Psychology: Adventures in theory and method.* Buckingham: Open University Press.

The second list of further texts and articles will be of interest to the reader who wants to extend their understanding of the historical development of social constructionism or to pursue specialist areas or avenues of academic debate within it:

Craib, I. (1997). Social constructionism as a social psychosis. *Sociology*, 31(1), 1–15.
Davies, B. & Harré, R. (1990). Positioning: The discursive production of selves. *Journal for the Theory of Social Behaviour*, 20(1), 43–63. Reproduced in Wetherell, M., Taylor, S. & Yates, S.J. (Eds.) (2001). *Discourse Theory and Practice: A reader*. London: Sage.
Danziger, K. (1997). The varieties of social construction. *Theory and Psychology*, 7(3), 399–416.
Edwards, D. (1997). *Discourse and Cognition*. London: Sage.
Edwards, D. & Potter, J. (1992). *Discursive Psychology*. London: Sage.
Edwards, D., Ashmore, M. & Potter, J. (1995). Death and furniture: The rhetoric, politics and theology of bottom line arguments against relativism. *History of the Human Sciences*, 8, 25–49.
Fairclough, N. (1995). *Critical Discourse Analysis: The critical study of language*. London: Longman.
Fee, D. (Ed.) (2000). *Pathology and the Postmodern*. London: Sage.
Gergen, K.J. (1973). Social psychology as history. *Journal of Personality and Social Psychology*, 26, 309–320.
Gergen, K.J. (1985). The social constructionist movement in modern psychology. *American Psychologist*, 40, 266–275.
Harré, R. & van Langenhove, L. (Eds.) (1999). *Positioning Theory*. Oxford: Blackwell.
Henriques, J., Hollway, W., Urwin, C., Venn, C. & Walkerdine, V. (1984). *Changing the Subject: Psychology, social regulation and subjectivity*. London: Methuen.
Nightingale, D.J. & Cromby, J. (Eds.) (1999). *Social Constructionist Psychology: A critical analysis of theory and practice*. Buckingham: Open University Press.
Parker, I. (Ed.) (1997). *Social Constructionism, Discourse and Realism*. London: Sage.
Parker, I., Georgaca, E., Harper, D., McLaughlin, T. & Stowell-Smith, M. (1995). *Deconstructing Psychopathology*. London: Sage.
Potter, J. (1996). *Representing Reality: Discourse, rhetoric and social construction*. London: Sage.
Rabinow, P. (1984). *A Foucault Reader*. New York: Pantheon.

Rose, N. (1989). *Governing the Soul: The shaping of the private self.* London and New York: Routledge.

Sawicki, J. (1991). *Disciplining Foucault: Feminism, power and the body.* London: Routledge.

Weedon, C. (1987). *Feminist Practice and Poststructuralist Theory.* Oxford: Blackwell.

Wood, L.A. & Kroger, R.O. (2000). *Doing Discourse Analysis: Methods for studying action in talk and texts.* London: Sage.

The following journals frequently publish social constructionist articles:

Discourse and Society
Discourse Studies
Theory and Psychology
DAOL (Discourse Analysis On-Line – www.shu.ac.uk/daol/)

Bibliography

Abrams, D. & Hogg, M.A. (1990). The context of discourse: Let's not throw the baby out with the bathwater. *Philosophical Psychology*, 3(2), 219–225.

Aries, P. (1962). *Centuries of Childhood: A social history of family life*. New York: Vintage.

Armistead, N. (1974). *Reconstructing Social Psychology*. Harmondsworth: Penguin.

Ashmore, M. (1989). *The Reflexive Thesis*. Chicago: Chicago University Press.

Auburn, T., Lea, S. & Drake, S. (1999). It's your opportunity to be truthful: Disbelief, mundane reasoning and the investigation of crime. In C. Willig (Ed.), *Applied Discourse Analysis: Social and psychological interventions*. Buckingham: Open University Press.

Austin, J.L. (1962). *How to Do Things with Words*. London: Oxford University Press.

Averill, J. (1985). The social construction of emotion: With special reference to love. In K.J. Gergen & K.E. Davis (Eds.), *The Social Construction of the Person*. New York: Springer.

Bateson, G. (1972). *Steps to an Ecology of Mind*. New York: Chandler.

Berger, P. & Luckmann, T. (1966). *The Social Construction of Reality: A treatise in the sociology of knowledge*. New York: Doubleday.

Billig, M. (1987). *Arguing and Thinking: A rhetorical approach to social psychology*. Cambridge: Cambridge University Press.

Billig, M. (1990). Rhetoric of social psychology. In I. Parker & J. Shotter (Eds.), *Deconstructing Social Psychology*. London: Routledge.

Billig, M. (1995). *Banal Nationalism*. London: Sage.

Billig, M. (1997a). Rhetorical and discursive analysis: How families talk about the royal family. In N. Hayes (Ed.), *Doing Qualitative Analysis in Psychology*. Hove: Psychology Press.

Billig, M. (1997b). Discursive, rhetorical and ideological messages. In C.

McGarty & A. Haslam (Eds.), *The Message of Social Psychology*. Oxford: Blackwell.

Billig, M., Condor, S., Edwards, D., Gane, M., Middleton, D. & Radley, A. (1988). *Ideological Dilemmas: A social psychology of everyday thinking*. London: Sage.

Blaxter, M. & Paterson, E. (1982). *Mothers and Daughters: A three generational study of health attitudes and behaviour*. London: Heinemann.

Blumer, H. (1962). Society as a symbolic interaction. In A.M. Rose (Ed.), *Human Behaviour and Social Processes: An interactionist approach*. London: Routledge.

Botella, L. (1995). Personal construct psychology, constructivism, and postmodern thought. In R.A. Neimeyer & G.J. Neimeyer (Eds.), *Advances in Personal Construct Psychology* (Vol. 3, 3–36). Greenwich, CT: JAI Press.

Brown, P. (1973). *Radical Psychology*. London: Tavistock.

Burkitt, I. (1999). Between the dark and the light: Power and the material contexts of social relations. In D.J. Nightingale & J. Cromby (Eds.), *Social Constructionist Psychology: A critical analysis of theory and practice*. Buckingham: Open University Press.

Burman, E. (1990). Differing with deconstruction: A feminist critique. In I. Parker & J. Shotter (Eds.), *Deconstructing Social Psychology*. London: Routledge.

Burman, E. (1991). What discourse is not. *Philosophical Psychology*, 4(3), 325–342.

Burman, E. (1999). Whose constructionism? Points from a feminist perspective. In D.J. Nightingale & J. Cromby (Eds.), *Social Constructionist Psychology: A critical analysis of theory and practice*. Buckingham: Open University Press.

Burman, E. & Parker, I. (Eds.) (1993). *Discourse Analytic Research: Repertoires and readings of texts in action*. London: Routledge.

Burr, V. (1998). Realism, relativism, social constructionism and discourse. In I. Parker (Ed.), *Social Constructionism, Discourse and Realism*. London: Sage.

Burr, V. (1999). The extra-discursive in social constructionism. In D.J. Nightingale & J. Cromby (Eds.), *Social Constructionist Psychology: A critical analysis of theory and practice*. Buckingham: Open University Press.

Burr, V. (2002). *The Person in Social Psychology*. Hove: Psychology Press.

Burr, V. & Butt, T.W. (2000). Psychological distress and postmodern thought. In D. Fee (Ed.), *Pathology and the Postmodern*. London: Sage.

Bury, M.R. (1986). Social constructionism and the development of medical sociology. *Sociology of Health and Illness*, 8(2), 137–169.

Butt, T.W. (2003). *Understanding People*. Basingstoke: Palgrave.

Butt, T.W., Burr, V. & Bell, R. (1997). Fragmentation and the sense of self. *Constructivism in the Human Sciences*, 2, 12–29.

Carabine, J. (2001). Unmarried motherhood 1830–1900: A genealogical analysis. In M. Wetherell, S. Taylor & S.J. Yates, *Discourse as Data: A guide for analysis*. London: Sage.

Cashmore, E. (1987). *The Logic of Racism*. London: Allen and Unwin.

Clegg, S.R. (1989). *Frameworks of Power*. London: Sage.

Collier, A. (1998). Language, practice and realism. In I. Parker (Ed.), *Social Constructionism, Discourse and Realism*. London: Sage.

Craib, I. (1984). *Modern Social Theory: From Parsons to Habermas*. Brighton: Harvester Press.

Craib, I. (1997). Social constructionism as a social psychosis. *Sociology*, 31(1), 1–15.

Cromby, J. & Nightingale, D.J. (1999). Reconstructing social constructionism. In D.J. Nightingale & J. Cromby (Eds.), *Social Constructionist Psychology: A critical analysis of theory and practice*. Buckingham: Open University Press.

Crossley, M.L. (2000). *Introducing Narrative Psychology: Self, trauma and the construction of meaning*. Buckingham: Open University Press.

Crossley, M.L. (2002). Introducing narrative psychology. In C. Horrocks, K. Milnes, B. Roberts & D. Robinson (Eds.), *Narrative, Memory and Life Transitions*. Huddersfield: University of Huddersfield Press.

Danziger, K. (1997). The varieties of social construction. *Theory and Psychology*, 7(3), 399–416.

Davies, B. (1998). Psychology's subject: A commentary on the realism/relativism debate. In I. Parker (Ed.), *Social Constructionism, Discourse and Realism*. London: Sage.

Davies, B. & Harré, R. (1990). Positioning: The discursive production of selves. *Journal for the Theory of Social Behaviour*, 20(1), 43–63. Reproduced in Wetherell, M., Taylor, S. & Yates, S.J. (Eds.) (2001), *Discourse Theory and Practice: A reader*. London: Sage.

Davies, B. & Harré, R. (1999). Positioning and personhood. In R. Harré & L. Van Langenhove (Eds.), *Positioning Theory*. Oxford: Blackwell.

Davis, F. (1961). Deviance disavowal: The management of strained interaction by the visibly handicapped. *Social Problems*, 9, 120–132.

Denzin, N. (1995). Symbolic interactionism. In J.A. Smith, R. Harré & L. Van Langenhove (Eds.), *Rethinking Psychology*. London: Sage.

Derrida, J. (1976). *On Grammatology*. Baltimore, MD: Johns Hopkins University Press.

Dodds, A., Lawrence, J.A. & Valsiner, J. (1997). The Personal and the Social: Mead's theory of the 'Generalised Other'. *Theory and Psychology*, 7(4), 483–503.

Drewery, W. (2001). Everyday speech and the production of colonised selves, unpublished paper, University of Waikato, New Zealand.

Edley, N. (2001). Unravelling social constructionism. *Theory and Psychology*, 11(3), 433–441.

Edley, N. & Wetherell, M. (1995). *Men in Perspective*. Hemel Hempstead: Harvester Wheatsheaf.

Edwards, D. (1997). *Discourse and Cognition*. London: Sage.

Edwards, D., Ashmore, M. & Potter, J. (1995). Death and furniture: The rhetoric, politics and theology of bottom line arguments against relativism. *History of the Human Sciences*, 8, 25–49.

Edwards, D. & Potter, J. (1992). *Discursive Psychology*. London: Sage.

Edwards, D. & Potter, J. (1993). Language and causation: A discursive action model of description and attribution. *Psychological Review*, 100(1), 23–41.

Edwards, D. & Potter, J. (1995). Remembering. In R. Harré & P. Stearns (Eds.), *Discursive Psychology in Practice*. London: Sage.

Ehrlich, S. (1998). The discursive reconstruction of sexual consent. *Discourse and Society*, 9(2), 149–171.

Fairclough, N. (1992). *Discourse and Social Change*. Cambridge: Polity Press.

Fairclough, N. (1995). *Critical Discourse Analysis: The critical study of language*. London: Longman.

Figlio, K. (1982). How does illness mediate social relations? Workmen's compensation and medico-legal practices 1890–1940. In P. Wright & A. Teacher (Eds.), *The Problem of Medical Knowledge*. Edinburgh: Edinburgh University Press.

Figueroa, H. & Lopez, M. (1991). Commentary on discourse analysis workshop/conference. Paper for Second Discourse Analysis Workshop/Conference, Manchester Polytechnic, July.

Foucault, M. (1972). *The Archaeology of Knowledge*. London: Tavistock.

Foucault, M. (1973). *The Birth of the Clinic: An archaeology of medical perception*. London: Tavistock.

Foucault, M. (1976). *The History of Sexuality: An introduction*. Harmondsworth: Penguin.

Foucault, M. (1979). *Discipline and Punish*. Harmondsworth: Penguin.

Fox, D. & Prilleltensky, I. (Eds.) (1997). *Critical Psychology: An introduction*. London: Sage.

Friedman, M. & Rosenman, R.H. (1974). *Type A Behaviour and Your Heart*. London: Wildwood House.

Fromm, E. (1942/1960). *The Fear of Freedom*. London: Routledge and Kegan Paul.

Fromm, E. (1955). *The Sane Society*. New York: Rinehart.

Frosh, S. (1987). *The Politics of Psychoanalysis: An introduction to Freudian and post-Freudian theory*. London: Macmillan.

Gavey, N. (1997). Feminist poststructuralism and discourse analysis. In

M.M. Gergen & S.N. Davis (Eds.), *Toward a New Psychology of Gender: A reader*. London: Routledge.

Gergen, K.J. (1973). Social psychology as history. *Journal of Personality and Social Psychology*, 26, 309–320.

Gergen, K.J. (1985). The social constructionist movement in modern psychology. *American Psychologist*, 40, 266–275.

Gergen, K.J. (1989). Warranting voice and the elaboration of the self. In J. Shotter & K.J. Gergen (Eds.), *Texts of Identity*. London: Sage.

Gergen, K.J. (1994). *Realities and Relationships: Soundings in social construction*. Cambridge, MA: Harvard University Press.

Gergen, K.J. (1997). The place of the psyche in a constructed world. *Theory and Psychology*, 7(6), 723–746.

Gergen, K.J. (1998). Constructionism and realism: How are we to go on? In I. Parker (Ed.), *Social Constructionism, Discourse and Realism*. London: Sage.

Gergen, K.J. (1999). *An Invitation to Social Construction*. London: Sage.

Gergen, K.J. (2000). The self: Transfiguration by technology. In D. Fee (Ed.), *Pathology and the Postmodern*. London: Sage.

Gergen, K.J. (2001a). *Social Construction in Context*. London: Sage.

Gergen, K.J. (2001b). Construction in contention: Toward consequential resolutions. *Theory and Psychology*, 11(3), 433–441.

Gergen, K.J. & Gergen, M.M. (1984). The social construction of narrative accounts. In K.J. Gergen & M.M. Gergen (Eds.), *Historical Social Psychology*. Hillsdale, NJ: Lawrence Erlbaum Associates.

Gergen, K.J. & Gergen, M.M. (1986). Narrative form and the construction of psychological science. In T.R. Sarbin (Ed.), *Narrative Psychology: The storied nature of human conduct*. New York: Praeger.

Gergen, M. (2001). *Feminist Reconstructions in Psychology: Narrative, gender and performance*. London: Sage.

Giddens, A. (1984). *The Constitution of Society: An outline of the theory of structuralism*. Cambridge: Polity Press.

Gilbert, G.N. & Mulkay, M. (1984). *Opening Pandora's Box: A sociological analysis of scientists' discourse*. Cambridge: Cambridge University Press.

Gill, R. (1993). Justifying injustice: Broadcasters' accounts of inequality in radio. In E. Burman & I. Parker (Eds.), *Discourse Analytic Research: Repertoires and readings of texts in action*. London: Routledge.

Gillies, V. (1999). An analysis of the discursive positions of women smokers: Implications for practical interventions. In C. Willig (Ed.), *Applied Discourse Analysis: Social and psychological interventions*. Buckingham: Open University Press.

Gough, B. & McFadden, M. (2001). *Critical Social Psychology: An introduction*. Basingstoke: Palgrave.

Grosz, E. (1994). *Volatile Bodies: Toward a corporeal feminism*. Bloomington and Indianapolis, IN: Indiana University Press.

Hall, S. (2001). Foucault: Power, knowledge and discourse. In M. Wetherell, S. Taylor & S.J. Yates (Eds.), *Discourse Theory and Practice: A reader*. London: Sage.

Hardey, M. (1998). *The Social Context of Health*. Buckingham: Open University Press.

Harding, S. (1991). *Whose Science? Whose Knowledge? Thinking from women's lives*. Buckingham: Open University Press.

Harré, R. (1983). *Personal Being: A theory for individual psychology*. Oxford: Basil Blackwell.

Harré, R. (1985). The language game of self-ascription: A note. In K.J. Gergen & K.E. Davis (Eds.), *The Social Construction of the Person*. New York: Springer.

Harré, R. (1989). Language games and the texts of identity. In J. Shotter & K.J. Gergen (Eds.), *Texts of Identity*. London: Sage.

Harré, R. (1993). *Social Being* (2nd edn). Oxford: Blackwell.

Harré, R. (1995a). Agentive discourse. In P. Harré & P. Stearns (Eds.), *Discursive Psychology in Practice*. London: Sage.

Harré, R. (1995b). Discursive psychology. In J.A. Smith, R. Harré & L. Van Langenhove (Eds.), *Rethinking Psychology*. London: Sage.

Harré, R. (1995c). The necessity of personhood as embodied being. *Theory and Psychology*, 5(3), 369–373.

Harré, R. (1998). *The Singular Self: An introduction to the psychology of personhood*. London: Sage.

Harré, R. (1999). Discourse and the embodied person. In D.J. Nightingale & J. Cromby (Eds.), *Social Constructionist Psychology: A critical analysis of theory and practice*. Buckingham: Open University Press.

Harré, R. & Gillett, G. (1994). *The Discursive Mind*. London: Sage.

Harré, R. & Secord, P.F. (1972). *The Explanation of Social Behaviour*. Oxford: Basil Blackwell.

Harré, R. & Stearns, P. (Eds.) (1995). *Discursive Psychology in Practice*. London: Sage.

Harré, R. & Van Langenhove, L. (Eds.) (1999). *Positioning Theory*. Oxford: Blackwell.

Heider, F. & Simmel, E. (1944). A study of apparent behavior. *American Journal of Psychology*, 57, 243–259.

Henriques, J., Hollway, W., Urwin, C., Venn, C. & Walkerdine, V. (Eds.) (1984). *Changing the Subject: Psychology, social regulation and subjectivity*. London: Methuen.

Hollinger, R. (1994). *Postmodernism and the Social Sciences: A thematic approach*. Thousand Oaks, CA: Sage.

Hollway, W. (1981). 'I just wanted to kill a woman.' Why? The Ripper and male sexuality. *Feminist Review*, 9, 33–40.

Hollway, W. (1984). Gender difference and the production of subjectivity. In J. Henriques, W. Hollway, C. Urwin, C. Venn & V. Walkerdine

(Eds.), *Changing the Subject: Psychology, social regulation and subjectivity*. London: Methuen.

Hollway, W. (1989). *Subjectivity and Method in Psychology: Gender, meaning and science*. London: Sage.

Howitt, D. (1991). *Concerning Psychology*. Buckingham: Open University Press.

Hruby, G.G. (2001). Sociological, postmodern and new realism perspectives in social constructionism: Implications for literacy research. *Reading Research Quarterly*, 36(1), 48–62.

Ibáñez, T. & Iñiguez, L. (Eds.) (1997). *Critical Social Psychology*. London: Sage.

Ingleby, D. (1985). Professionals as socialisers: The psy-complex. *Research in Law, Deviance and Social Control*, 7, 79–109.

Jackson, J.M. (1998). *Social Psychology: An integrative orientation*. Hillsdale, NJ: Erlbaum.

Kelly, G. (1955). *The Psychology of Personal Constructs*. New York and London: W.W. Norton.

Kitzinger, C. (1987). *The Social Construction of Lesbianism*. London: Sage.

Kitzinger, C. (1989). The regulation of lesbian identities: Liberal humanism as an ideology of social control. In J. Shotter & K.J. Gergen (Eds.), *Texts of Identity*. London: Sage.

Kitzinger, C. (1990). The rhetoric of pseudoscience. In I. Parker & J. Shotter (Eds.), *Deconstructing Social Psychology*. London and New York: Routledge.

Kitzinger, C. & Frith, H. (1999). Just say no? The use of conversation analysis in developing a feminist perspective on sexual refusal. *Discourse and Society*, 10, 293–317.

Laclau, E. (1983). The impossibility of society. *Canadian Journal of Political and Social Theory*, 7, 21–24.

Laclau, E. & Mouffe, C. (1985). *Hegemony and Socialist Strategy: Towards a radical democratic politics* (trans. Moore, W. & Cammack, P.). London: Verso.

Liebrucks, A. (2001). The concept of social construction. *Theory and Psychology*, 11(3), 363–391.

Livesey, L. (2002). Telling it like it is: Understanding adult women's life long disclosures of childhood sexual abuse. In C. Horrocks, K. Milnes, B. Roberts & D. Robinson (Eds.), *Narrative Memory and Life Transitions*. Huddersfield: University of Huddersfield Press.

Lutz, C. (1982). The domain of emotion words on Ifaluk. *American Ethnologist*, 9, 113–128.

Lutz, C. (1990). Morality, domination and understanding of 'justifiable anger' among the Ifaluk. In G.R. Semin & K.J. Gergen (Eds.), *Everyday Understanding*. London: Sage.

Maccoby, E.E. & Jacklin, C.N. (1974). *The Psychology of Sex Differences.* Stanford, CA: Stanford University Press.

McNamee, S. & Gergen, K.J. (Eds.) (1992). *Therapy as Social Construction.* London: Sage.

Makin, T. (1995). The social model of disability. *Counselling,* 6(4), 274.

Mancuso, J.C. (1986). The acquisition and use of narrative grammar structure. In T.R. Sarbin (Ed.), *Narrative Psychology: The storied nature of human conduct.* New York: Praeger.

Marks, D. (1993). Case-conference analysis and action research. In E. Burman & I. Parker (Eds.), *Discourse Analytic Research: Repertoires and readings of texts in action.* London: Routledge.

Mead, G.H. (1934). *Mind, Self and Society.* Chicago, IL: University of Chicago Press.

Mehan, H. (1996). The construction of an LD student: A case study in the politics of representation. In M. Silverstein & G. Urban (Eds.), *Natural Histories of Discourses.* Chicago, IL: University of Chicago Press. Reproduced in M. Wetherell, S. Taylor & S.J. Yates (Eds.) (2001). *Discourse Theory and Practice: A reader.* London: Sage.

Michael, M. (1999). A paradigm shift? Connections with other critiques of social constructionism. In D.J. Nightingale & J. Cromby (Eds.), *Social Constructionist Psychology: A critical analysis of theory and practice.* Buckingham: Open University Press.

Michotte, A.E. (1963). *The Perception of Causality.* London: Methuen.

Mills, S. (1997). *Discourse.* London: Routledge.

Mulkay, M. (1985). *The Word and the World: Explorations in the form of sociological analysis.* London: Allen and Unwin.

Neisser, U. (1981). John Dean's memory: A case study. *Cognition,* 9, 1–22.

Nightingale, D.J. (1999). Bodies: Reading the body. In I. Parker & the Bolton Discourse Network, *Critical Textwork: An introduction to varieties of discourse and analysis.* Buckingham: Open University Press.

Nightingale, D.J. & Cromby, J. (2002). Social constructionism as ontology: Exposition and example. *Theory and Psychology,* 12(5), 701–713.

Orford, J. (1992). *Community Psychology: Theory and practice.* Chichester: Wiley.

Palmer, D.D. (1997). *Structuralism and Poststructuralism for Beginners.* New York: Writers and Readers Publishing.

Parker, I. (1990). Discourse: Definitions and contradictions. *Philosophical Psychology,* 3(2), 189–204.

Parker, I. (1992). *Discourse Dynamics: Critical analysis for social and individual psychology.* London: Routledge.

Parker, I. (1998a). Realism, relativism and critique in psychology. In I. Parker (Ed.), *Social Constructionism, Discourse and Realism.* London: Sage.

Parker, I. (1998b). Constructing and deconstructing psychotherapeutic discourse. *European Journal of Psychotherapy, Counselling and Health*, 1(1) April, 65–78.

Parker, I. (1999). Critical reflexive humanism and critical constructionist psychology. In D.J. Nightingale & J. Cromby (Eds.), *Social Constructionist Psychology: A critical analysis of theory and practice.* Buckingham: Open University Press.

Parker, I. & the Bolton Discourse Network (1999). *Critical Textwork: An introduction to varieties of discourse and analysis.* Buckingham: Open University Press.

Parker, I. & Burman, E. (1993). Against discursive imperialism, empiricism and construction: Thirty-two problems with discourse analysis. In E. Burman & I. Parker (Eds.), *Discourse Analytic Research: Repertoires and readings of texts in action.* London: Routledge.

Parker, I., Georgaca, E., Harper, D., McLaughlin, T. & Stowell-Smith, M. (1995). *Deconstructing Psychopathology.* London: Sage.

Potter, J. (1996a). *Representing Reality: Discourse, rhetoric and social construction.* London: Sage.

Potter, J. (1996b). Discourse analysis and constructionist approaches: Theoretical background. In J.T.E. Richardson (Ed.), *Handbook of Qualitative Research Methods for Psychology and the Social Sciences.* Leicester: BPS Books.

Potter, J. (1998). Fragments in the realization of relativism. In I. Parker (Ed.), *Social Constructionism, Discourse and Realism.* London: Sage.

Potter, J. & Collie, F. (1989). 'Community care' as persuasive rhetoric: A study of discourse. *Disability, Handicap and Society*, 4(1), 57–64.

Potter, J. & Reicher, S. (1987). Discourses of community and conflict: The organisation of social categories in accounts of a 'riot'. *British Journal of Social Psychology*, 26, 25–40.

Potter, J. & Wetherell, M. (1987). *Discourse and Social Psychology: Beyond attitudes and behaviour.* London: Sage.

Potter, J. & Wetherell, M. (1995). Discourse analysis. In J.A. Smith, R. Harré & L. Van Langenhove (Eds.), *Rethinking Methods in Psychology.* London: Sage.

Potter, J., Wetherell, M., Gill, R. & Edwards, D. (1990). Discourse: Noun, verb or social practice? *Philosophical Psychology*, 3(2), 205–217.

Rabinow, P. (1984). *A Foucault Reader.* New York: Pantheon.

Radley, A. (1994). *Making Sense of Illness.* London: Sage.

Radley, A. (1995). The elusory body and social constructionist theory. *Body and Society*, 1(2), 3–23.

Rose, H. (1993). Rhetoric, feminism and scientific knowledge: Or from either/or to both/and. In R.H. Roberts & J.M.M. Good (Eds.), *The Recovery of Rhetoric.* Charlottesville, VA: University Press of Virginia.

Rose, N. (1985). *The Psychological Complex: Psychology, politics and society in England 1869–1939.* London: Routledge.

Rose, N. (1989). *Governing the Soul: The shaping of the private self.* London and New York: Routledge.

Rose, N. (1990). Psychology as a 'social' science. In I. Parker & J. Shotter (Eds.), *Deconstructing Social Psychology.* London and New York: Routledge.

Ryan, B.A. (1999). Does postmodernism mean the end of science in the behavioural sciences, and does it matter anyway? *Theory and Psychology*, 9(4), 483–502.

Sampson, E.E. (1989). The deconstruction of the self. In J. Shotter & K.J. Gergen (Eds.), *Texts of Identity.* London: Sage.

Sampson, E.E. (1990). Social psychology and social control. In I. Parker & J. Shotter (Eds.), *Deconstructing Social Psychology.* London: Routledge.

Sampson, E.E. (1993). *Celebrating the Other.* Hemel Hempstead: Harvester Wheatsheaf.

Sarbin, T.R. (1986). The narrative as root metaphor for psychology. In T.R. Sarbin (Ed.), *Narrative Psychology: The storied nature of human conduct.* New York: Praeger.

Sarup, M. (1993). *An Introductory Guide to Post-structuralism and Postmodernism.* Hemel Hempstead: Harvester Wheatsheaf.

Saussure, F. de (1974). *Course in General Linguistics.* London: Fontana.

Sawicki, J. (1991). *Disciplining Foucault: Feminism, power and the body.* London: Routledge.

Seymour-Smith, S. (2002). Illness as an occasion for story telling: Social influences in narrating the masculine self to an unseen audience. In C. Horrocks, K. Milnes, B. Roberts & D. Robinson (Eds.), *Narrative, Memory and Life Transitions.* Huddersfield: University of Huddersfield Press.

Sherrard, C. (1991). Developing discourse analysis. *Journal of General Psychology*, 118(2), 171–179.

Shotter, J. (1993a). *Conversational Realities.* London: Sage.

Shotter, J. (1993b). *Cultural Politics of Everyday Life.* Buckingham: Open University Press.

Shotter, J. (1995a). In conversation: Joint action, shared intentionality and ethics. *Theory and Psychology*, 5(1), 49–73.

Shotter, J. (1995b). Dialogical psychology. In J.A. Smith, R. Harré & L. Van Langenhove (Eds.), *Rethinking Psychology.* London: Sage.

Silverman, D. (2001). The construction of 'delicate' objects in counselling. In M. Wetherell, S. Taylor & S.J. Yates, *Discourse Theory and Practice: A reader.* London: Sage. Reproduced from Silverman, D. (1997). *Discourses of Counselling: HIV counselling as social interaction.* London: Sage.

Sloan, T. (Ed.) (2000). *Critical Psychology: Voices for change.* New York: St Martin's Press.

Smith, J. (1981). Self and experience in Maori culture. In P. Heelas & A. Lock (Eds.), *Indigenous Psychologies.* London: Academic Press.

Stainton-Rogers, R., Stenner, P., Gleeson, K. & Stainton-Rogers, W. (1995). *Social Psychology: A critical agenda*. Cambridge: Polity.

Stainton-Rogers, W. & Stainton-Rogers, R. (2001). *The Psychology of Gender and Sexuality*. Buckingham: Open University Press.

Stearns, P. (1995). Emotion. In R. Harré & P. Stearns (Eds.), *Discursive Psychology in Practice*. London: Sage.

Stenner, P. (1993). Discoursing jealousy. In E. Burman & I. Parker (Eds.), *Discourse Analytic Research: Repertoires and readings of texts in action*. London: Routledge.

Sutton-Smith, B. (1986). Children's fiction-making. In T.R. Sarbin (Ed.), *Narrative Psychology: The storied nature of human conduct*. New York: Praeger.

Taylor, S. (2001). Evaluating and applying discourse analytic research. In M. Wetherell, S. Taylor & S.J. Yates, *Discourse as Data: A guide for analysis*. London: Sage.

Thompson, J.B. (1990). *Ideology and Modern Culture*. Cambridge: Polity Press.

Throsby, K. (2002). *Discourse of Health and Illness in Accounts of IVF Failure*. Paper presented at Narrative and Memory Conference, University of Huddersfield, 20th April.

Ussher, J. (Ed.) (1997). *Body Talk: The material and discursive regulation of sexuality, madness and reproduction*. London: Routledge.

Ussher, J. (2000). Women's madness. In D. Fee (Ed.), *Pathology and the Postmodern*. London: Sage.

Van Langenhove, L. & Harré, R. (1994). Cultural stereotypes and positioning theory. *Journal for the Theory of Social Behaviour*, 24(4), 358–372.

von Glasersfeld, E. (1981). *An Introduction to Radical Constructivism*. Originally published in P. Watzlawick (Ed.) (1981), *Die Erfundene Wirklichkeit*. Munich: Piper. Author's translation in P. Watzlawick (Ed.) (1984), *The Invented Reality*. New York: Norton.

Walkerdine, V. (1981). Sex, power and pedagogy. *Screen Education*, 38, 14–23. Reprinted in M. Arnot & G. Weiner (Eds.) (1987). *Gender and the Politics of Schooling*. London: Hutchinson.

Walkerdine, V. (1987). No laughing matter: Girls' comics and the preparation for adolescent sexuality. In J.M. Broughton (Ed.), *Critical Theories of Psychological Development*. New York: Plenum Press.

Weedon, C. (1987). *Feminist Practice and Poststructuralist Theory*. Oxford: Blackwell.

Wetherell, M. (1996). Group conflict and the social psychology of racism. In M. Wetherell (Ed.), *Identities, Groups and Social Issues*. London: Sage.

Wetherell, M. (1998). Positioning and interpretative repertoires: Conversation analysis and post-structuralism in dialogue. *Discourse and Society*, 9(3), 387–413.

Wetherell, M. (2001). Debates in discourse research. In M. Wetherell, S. Taylor & S.J. Yates (Eds.), *Discourse Theory and Practice: A reader*. London: Sage.

Wetherell, M. & Edley, N. (1999). Negotiating hegemonic masculinity: Imaginary positions and psycho-discursive practices. *Feminism and Psychology*, 9, 335–56.

Wetherell, M. & Potter, J. (1988). Discourse analysis and the identification of interpretative repertoires. In C. Antaki, *Analysing Everyday Explanation: A casebook of methods*. London: Sage.

Wetherell, M. & Potter, J. (1992). *Mapping the Language of Racism: Discourse and the legitimation of exploitation*. Hemel Hempstead: Harvester Wheatsheaf.

Wetherell, M. & Still, A. (1998). Realism and relativism. In R. Sapsford, A. Still, M. Wetherell, D. Miell & R. Stevens (Eds.), *Theory and Social Psychology*. London: Sage in association with the Open University.

Wetherell, M., Taylor, S. & Yates, S.J. (Eds.) (2001a). *Discourse as Data: A guide for analysis*. London: Sage.

Wetherell, M., Taylor, S. & Yates, S.J. (Eds.) (2001b). *Discourse Theory and Practice: A reader*. London: Sage.

Whorf, B. (1941). The relation of habitual thought and behaviour to language. In L. Spier (Ed.), *Language, Culture and Personality: Essays in memory of Edward Sapir*. Salt Lake City, UT: University of Utah Press.

Wilkinson, S. (Ed.) (1996). *Feminist Social Psychologies: International perspectives*. Milton Keynes: Open University Press.

Williams, R. (1989). *The Trusting Heart*. New York: The Free Press.

Willig, C. (1997). Social constructionism and revolutionary socialism: A contradiction in terms? In I. Parker (Ed.), *Social Constructionism, Discourse and Realism*. London: Sage.

Willig, C. (1999a). Beyond appearances: A critical realist approach to social constructionist work. In D.J. Nightingale & J. Cromby (Eds.), *Social Constructionist Psychology: A critical analysis of theory and practice*. Buckingham: Open University Press.

Willig, C. (1999b). Discourse analysis and sex education. In C. Willig (Ed.), *Applied Discourse Analysis: Social and psychological interventions*. Buckingham: Open University Press.

Willig, C. (2001). *Introducing Qualitative Research in Psychology: Adventures in theory and method*. Buckingham: Open University Press.

Wodak, R. (1996). *Disorders of Discourse*. Harlow: Addison Wesley Longman.

Wood, L.A. & Kroger, R.O. (2000). *Doing Discourse Analysis: Methods for studying action in talk and text*. London: Sage.

Young, A. (1976). Internalising and externalising medical belief systems: An Ethiopian example. *Social Science and Medicine*, 10, 147–156.

Author index

Subject index